Charles Meek was a distinguished colonial administrator. He served in Tanganyika – now Tanzania – for 20 years. He was latterly Permanent Secretary to Julius Nyerere and the first post-colonial Head of Tanganyika's Civil Service.

Innes Meek, who is Charles Meek's son, has worked in industry, banking and public service, including a spell in the British High Commission in Nigeria in the 1980s, and for many years with the Commonwealth Development Corporation. He continues to work on investment in Africa.

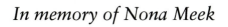

In memory of Nona Meek

Brief Authority

A Memoir of Colonial Administration in Tanganyika

Charles Meek

Edited by Innes Meek

The Radcliffe Press
LONDON • NEW YORK

First published and reprinted in 2011 by Radcliffe Press
An imprint of I.B.Tauris & Co. Ltd
6 Salem Road, London W2 4BU
175 Fifth Avenue, New York NY 10010
www.ibtauris.com

Distributed in the United States and Canada Exclusively by Palgrave Macmillan,
175 Fifth Avenue, New York NY 10010

ISBN 978 1 84885 833 6

A full CIP record for this book is available from the British Library
A full CIP record for this book is available from the Library of Congress
Library of Congress catalog card: available

Typeset in Sabon by Dexter Haven Associates Ltd, London
Printed and bound by CPI Group (UK) Ltd, Croydon, CR0 4YY

CONTENTS

List of Plates		ix
Acknowledgements		xi
Maps		xiii
Introduction: Cheap, Efficient and Just		1
1	Prologue	29
2	Lindi	33
3	Shinyanga	51
4	Maswa	69
5	Elephant	78
6	Arusha	88
7	Monduli	111
8	Mbulu	120
9	Domestic Matters	143
10	Mbulu and the Road Out	153
11	Postscript	163
Appendices		173
Notes		237
Bibliography		245
Glossary		247
Index		251

LIST OF PLATES

1. Mount Kilimanjaro in the early 1950s.

2. Hunting for elephant in Masailand, 1949.

3. CIM relaxing after a day prospecting for elephant in Masailand.

4. Setting out on safari, 1949.

5. Washing in a collapsible canvas basin on safari, c.1955.

6. The box-body Bedford.

7. Meeting with the Masai in the Ngorongoro Crater.

8. A Barabaig *baraza*.

9. CIM sitting with the Barabaig and the Wanyaturu

10. CIM and Sir Edward Twining at a *baraza* with the Barabaig, 1954.

11. The Boma at Mbulu.

12. Sir Edward Twining investing Herman, the son of Chief Elias of the Iraqw, with a medal, 1954.

13. Nade Bea, 1956.

14. The road down the Rift to Magara, 1956.

15. CIM and Nona Meek outside the Hunter's log-built house in Oldeani in 1961.

16. Julius Nyerere's Cabinet in 1961.

ACKNOWLEDGEMENTS

Thanks to my brother, Kip, for his unstinting support in helping me to introduce our father's memoir to a wider audience. My sister, Sheena, has helped with material and recollection. Like many others, I am indebted to Michael Holman for his motivational powers. Tony Lee, my father's colleague in Mbulu and now well into his ninth decade, has been most helpful with his comments and memories. The photographs are from the family album, but some of the best, including the view of Kilimanjaro and that of the Barabaig *baraza*, are, I believe, by Matthis Möller. Hugh Macnair was enthusiastic and diligent in compiling the excellent maps. Lester Crook at the Radcliffe Press has been a patient and gentlemanly supervisor. Gretchen Ladish and Robert Hastings have been careful and intelligent editors.

My wife and children have been patient and kind as I have done my homework. The unsung heroine, though, is my mother, my father's stay for over fifty years, without whose love and encouragement the memoir would not have been written and preserved.

TANGANYIKA

Tanganyika in the 1940s and 50s

Province — Town
★ District Offices where the author was stationed

Road —— Railway ········· River

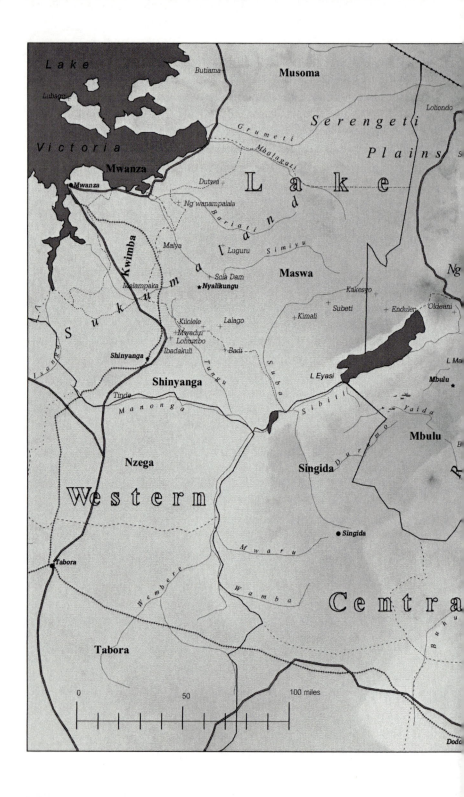

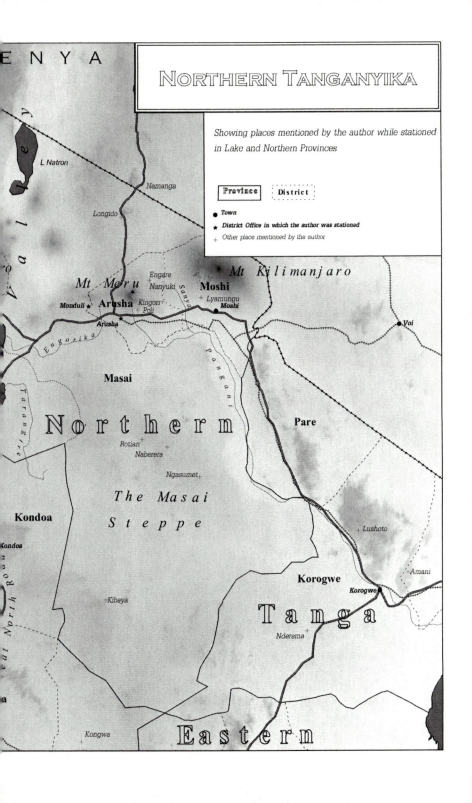

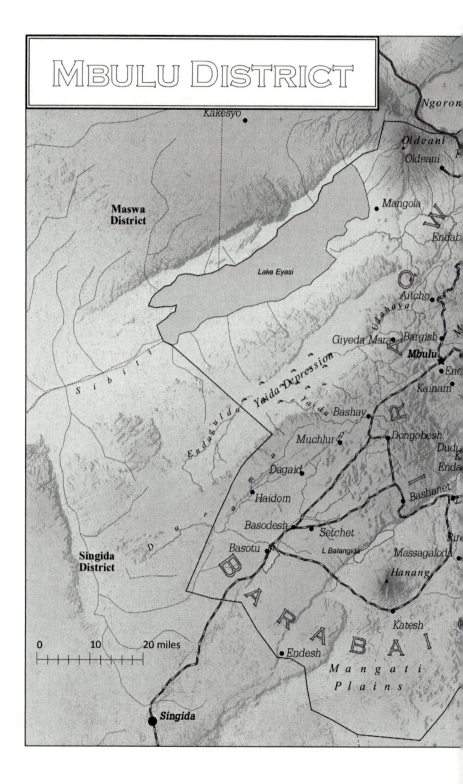

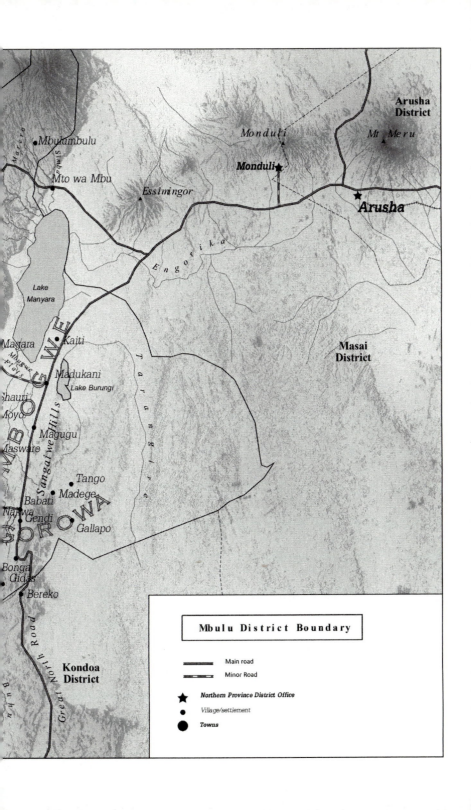

I recollect an instance in which one morning, in full paint of blue uniform, I was addressing a vast concourse of people at one of the Sukuma headquarters – Kwimba, I think. I had been expatiating on the fact that the railway from Tabora to Mwanza had now been constructed as I had promised at an earlier meeting, and that we had also provided good feeder roads, as I had further promised, so that motor lorries might bring the produce into the railway from interior markets and thus save the producers the long and wasteful journey carrying their goods on their heads.

We have done all this, I pointed out, given you the railway and the roads, and more time to cultivate your fields instead of walking long distances to a market. Now, as I warned you before, we want a response from you; I want you to grow more cotton, more groundnuts, more sim-sim, so that the construction of the railway and the roads may be justified. As I said this I noticed in the crowd an old man had raised his hand as if he wished to say something, and he at once proceeded to express his views. He appeared to be an ordinary typical peasant of some age and he spoke forcibly. I stopped the proceedings and inquired what the man had said (he was speaking in Ki-Sukuma). He said:

'We know all that, we realise it; what we want from you is rain in due season.'

Sir Donald Cameron, *My Tanganyika Service and Some Nigeria*

INTRODUCTION
Cheap, Efficient and Just

British control of Tanganyika in East Africa lasted 42 years, and my father, Charles Meek, served in its Administration for roughly half that brief span. When he died in 1999, he left behind a memoir of his experiences in various posts, mainly in the bush, during the 1940s and '50s. He had been working on the memoir for some time, but it is clear that there was more he would have said if he had not been overtaken by illness and death, particularly about the politics in Dar es Salaam in the build up to independence in December 1961. Even as it is, however, the document has interest for the tale it tells of an exotic career and for the light it casts on the administration of a remote part of the British Empire at the time when the sun was about to set on it with tropical suddenness.

At this distance, Tanganyika needs a little introduction. First, the name. Tanganyika became Tanzania after the union with Zanzibar in 1964, an unlovely amalgam of the names of the two countries. We should not jib too much, though, because the choice of the name Tanganyika for the mainland part of the country had been just as haphazard. When Britain took control of the former German East Africa in 1919, the Colonial Secretary of the day, Lord Milner, had wanted a name which had local connotations. He settled on Tanganyika, which was the name given by Richard Burton in 1858 to the large and deep lake in the west of the country. Other options considered were Kilimanjaro and Eburnea, the latter from the Latin word for ivory.

The arbitrary nature of the naming process is not surprising, for Tanganyika was a factitious country of disparate peoples, artificial borders and no coherent history. Such history as it had was in the main unwritten. The indigenous languages were not transcribed, and reliable primary sources were few. In the absence of documentary

1

evidence, European historians in the colonial era assumed that there was no story, or at least that there was no story of any significance. It was only with the advent of colonial rule that written sources began to accumulate, and these of course gave a European rather than an African perspective. In the 1960s a school of historians emerged in the University of Dar es Salaam determined to set this right by putting the African back at the centre of his own history. Its leading practitioners were European and North American academics attracted to Tanzania by the hope and energy of Julius Nyerere's[1] African socialism, and their history reflected their left-wing views and a sense of post-imperial guilt.

It is possible to be aggrieved by this, but not surprised. In the wake of the collapse of European rule in Africa, there were few historians willing to write sympathetically of the imperial project. This bias has continued, and there is to this day a lack of balance in what has been written about the brief colonial interlude in Africa, particularly in Tanzania. Malign intent or incompetence on the part of the colonial power and its agents is the usual starting place. The achievements of the departed colonial governments were either ignored or disparaged. This approach is both unjust and intellectually dishonest. The efforts of the colonial regime deserve a more even-handed assessment than they have generally received.

The standard work of the Dar es Salaam school, John Iliffe's *Modern History of Tanganyika*,[2] pulls together the scattered threads of the country's past. A British academic himself, Iliffe sees the British Administration in class terms, characterising its officials as coming mostly from upper-middle-class families with traditions of authority and service, adding that they 'romanticised their work, especially in retrospect'.[3] In a footnote, he cites, as a good example of this tendency, E.K. Lumley's book *Forgotten Mandate*.[4] To my eye, coming from a colonial family myself, this short book gives an intelligent, dispassionate and drily humorous account of what it was like to be an administrator in the field. Like another colonial civil servant, John Beames, whose nineteenth-century *Memoirs of a Bengal Civilian*[5] is a colonial classic, Lumley (we never learn his first name) does not seem to have got on with the hierarchy and was frequently passed over for promotion; at one point, after 18 months in a lonely post on the border with Rwanda and suffering from overwork and malaria, he has a breakdown. So one would not expect him to be too romantic about his time as a District Commissioner (DC) in Africa. But it was an extraordinary kind of life, and it is not possible to remove the romance from the telling of it. This is also true of my father's memoir, though it is more personal and more concerned with pleasure, friends and family than Lumley's. Its main theme, like Lumley's, is his interaction with the Africans in his districts. Once again it is a story about Africa and Africans as seen through European eyes.

My father was born in 1920, shortly after the end of the First World War. He was christened Charles Innes Meek, but was always known in his time in Tanganyika as Kim. His career in Africa started in 1941 and was cut short 20 years later when, immediately after independence in December 1961, Nyerere decided to take a sabbatical and resigned as Prime Minister. He was succeeded by a young trade unionist, Rashidi Kawawa, who summoned my father, then Secretary to the Cabinet and Head of the Civil Service, to State House in Dar es Salaam and told him: 'Thank you for all you have done to set up our African government, but we need an African to take the top job.' So that was that. My father was 41 at the time. His memoir was written in the long years that followed, which were not without their successes and pleasures, but which he could not help but see as an anticlimax after his 20 years in Africa: 16 in the bush, followed by four years of intense involvement in the policy and politics leading up to Tanganyika's independence, a process in which he played a significant and influential part, alongside Nyerere and the Governor, Sir Richard Turnbull.[6]

He joined the Colonial Service by accident, as a result of the exigencies of war. Well, not entirely by accident, for his own father, C.K. Meek, was in the Nigerian Administration from 1912 to 1933. I have always wondered what prompted my grandfather, the son of a Presbyterian minister in Rothesay on the west coast of Scotland, to take the hazardous step of going to Nigeria in 1912. My father simply said that he needed a job, which may have been correct, but seems an unsatisfactory explanation for making the journey to the Bight of Benin, whence in those days few came out, though many went in.[7] In any event, that was what he did and, though he did not rise high in the Administration, he distinguished himself by observing and recording the belief systems and customs of the peoples among whom he worked. His subsequent publications give a good account of indigenous societies in Nigeria just before they felt the full impact of European culture. His books eventually brought him a living as a don at Oxford and as one of the founding fathers of anthropology. Indeed I remember in my own brief career in Africa as a junior diplomat in Lagos being asked by the head of Shell in Nigeria, Peter Holmes, later Sir Peter, whether I was related to the great Meek and denying the connection on the grounds that no one in my family had earned the epithet, erroneously as it turned out. Holmes, who made a study of all the countries where he was posted, was profoundly acquainted with my grandfather's books. My father, on the other hand, never read any of them, partly out of filial reaction and partly because he never considered West Africa to be proper Africa. In any event, the colonial-service ethos rubbed off.

His prejudice against West Africa was not based on direct experience. It was not considered safe in the 1920s for European children to live on that coast, and he never went there. In due course it was decided that it was not healthy for my grandmother either, and she returned to England, to the detriment of her marriage. But for the first five years of my father's life she mainly accompanied her husband in Nigeria, and in consequence her son was brought up during this period by her parents. Her father, Charles Innes Hopkins, was a redoubtable figure who during the course of a long life fought in the Zulu War at the battle of Ulundi and served in the army in India for 19 years. After leaving the army he enjoyed a colourful business career. He helped to raise a regiment, the Scottish Tyneside, to fight in the First World War and commanded one of its battalions on the Western Front. Two of his three sons were killed in action and his daughter, my grandmother, served as a nurse in that war. He is famous in family lore for having given away an estate in Yorkshire to the Canadian Red Cross during the course of a drunken party. My father used to recount with veneration that he got through a bottle of whisky and a cigar a day until the end of his life. The addictions to whisky and tobacco were both passed on to his grandson, as well as a taste for expensive shoes and occasional extravagance.

My father's school career was brilliant and hard to match, as I found to my mortification when I was compelled to follow in his footsteps. He was sent to a preparatory school in Surrey, owned by a great uncle, with the Trollopian name of Orley Farm, from where he won scholarships to King's School, Canterbury. King's had a strong colonial tradition, and one of my father's scholarships was endowed by Lord Milner. He continued to prosper academically. The school was under the tutelage of an ambitious and ruthless headmaster, Canon John Shirley, who was determined to improve its status by coaching star pupils to win scholarships to Oxford and Cambridge. When my father won a scholarship to read history at Magdalen College, Oxford in the winter of 1938, the school was given a day's holiday in celebration. But he was not an all-rounder: except for boxing, where his slim build and long reach gave him a natural advantage, his sporting record was undistinguished. Despite this lack of prowess, he was an avid follower of rugby and cricket throughout his life and an admirer of sporting achievement among his peers.

He went up to Oxford in the fateful autumn of 1939. He was tutored by two famous historians, K.B. McFarlane and A.J.P. Taylor, but in the *fin du monde* atmosphere of the time he did not take his studies seriously and only did enough work to gain his War Degree prior to joining the Argyll and Sutherland Highland regiment in 1940, which is the point at which the memoir starts.

So his upbringing was completely consistent with Iliffe's characterisation – professional family with a history of colonial and military service, public school and Oxford education. Displaced by war, he was very young when he was thrown into his first job, and the impact of his schooling on his subsequent career was disproportionately marked. As with many others, his background and education gave him a taste for authority, an attachment to fair play and the confidence of his caste. All three of these traits had a strong bearing on his subsequent career, and it is worth expanding on how they came about and how they influenced his career.

First, authority. He refers in his memoir to his own 'authoritarian methods', though he immediately qualifies this by adding that they were tempered by 'a proper respect for the individual and by fair play'. This is as you would expect from someone with a successful public-school career behind him. Malcolm Muggeridge tartly describes colonial administrators as 'permanently adolescent prefects in grown-up dress, who would put up with discomfort and sometimes danger from a sense of duty, finding their reward in the social eminence accorded them and in the ribbons and stars which they were permitted to pin on their persons'.[8] The observation is apt, except for the reference to grown-up dress, since, as the photographs show,

DCs mostly wore shorts. But the prefect's cast of mind stayed with many of them, including my father. A prefect's authority depended on asserting status, and 'stars and ribbons' were an important part of this. At King's, prefects were entitled to wear purple gowns over their Edwardian school uniforms, and the gowns were an effective means of projecting authority. Similarly, in the colonies ceremonies and symbols were used to reinforce imperial mystique. The first time my father caught sight of Sir Edward Twining in 1949, just after his appointment as Governor, he was marching down the main street in Arusha at the head of a pipe band in full dress uniform, including feathered hat. In a largely peasant society, symbols exerted a beguiling power: the defendants in the Meru court case described in the memoir refused to believe the evidence of one of the witnesses without seeing 'a paper with the King's crown on it and on one side a horse and on the other a lion', a graphic if slightly inaccurate reference to the royal coat of arms.

This ornamentalism needed to be backed by the threat of sanction. In other parts of the Empire in earlier times the threat was real.[9] In the Punjab in the 1840s, the Lawrence brothers were prepared to resort to prompt punishment in order to render unnecessary more severe punishment later on. In Tanganyika the suppression by the Germans of the Maji-Maji rebellion in 1905 had demonstrated the costs to local people of resistance to European weaponry, and was sufficiently savage to stamp out the notion of armed resistance for a couple of generations. As it happened, by the 1940s in Tanganyika, with the only armed presence being a regiment of the King's African Rifles, overwhelmingly indigenous in composition, the threat was mainly bluff. Fortunately, the bluff was not called: serious force never had to be used in Tanganyika while it was a British colony.

Next, fair play. British public schools of the nineteenth and early twentieth centuries have been called factories for gentlemen, and their code of behaviour simplified to the point of caricature: 'teamwork, exaggerated masculinity, cold showers and stiff upper lips'.[10] The code was supported by a belief system which was Christian and rules-based. The ethos of the public school had been Christian since the time of Dr Arnold at Rugby in the mid-nineteenth century; it was particularly so at King's, whose premises lie in the shadow of the great cathedral and where the headmaster was an ordained though worldly priest, famous for his trenchant sermons of a Sunday. 'Do to others what you would have them do to you'[11] was the critical precept: the schoolboy hierarchy was ordered by age, but seniors were constrained to behave towards their juniors in ways that they themselves would have found acceptable when they had been juniors themselves. The view that social life in the public schools existed not far from a Hobbesian state of nature misses the mark: the concept of fair play was central to their ethos.

Fair play, that is a respect for the rules and an inclination to protect the weak against the strong, carried over into the Colonial Service and acted as a brake on a potentially oppressive system. An anecdote may illustrate this. In 1971, ten years after independence, Nyerere invited a group of former colonial administrators back to see what had been achieved in the intervening period. My father was among them, and so was Sir Richard Turnbull. Overall, they were greatly impressed. But when they got to Zanzibar, they were driven at speed round the narrow roads of the island in a motorcade. In the process, the car in which Turnbull and my father were travelling knocked an old man off his bicycle. The motorcade did not stop. Turnbull, who had a fierce temper, told the driver that in colonial days such behaviour would not have been sanctioned. And he was right. Within the constraints of a colonial regime, the British in Tanganyika aimed at an administration that respected the individual and was even-handed. The law was designed to protect the humble against the great. Tax was progressive, with wealthy regions paying more than poor ones and rich men more than peasants.

Finally, the confidence of his caste. For some, this was the whole point of a public-school education. Confidence is an effective tool of leadership, and the public schoolboy was trained to demonstrate it. 'Looking back now, after all these years, what strikes me most is the colossal cheek of it all,' says A.C.G. Hastings, recalling how in Nigeria in the early 1900s he and six African soldiers had persuaded a hostile body of some three hundred men from the pagan Awok tribe to surrender their weapons. 'I called for tea and drank it in the open, a book upon my knee,' he says, and in due course, to his relief, spears, bows and arrows were delivered up for burning.[12] My father was not called upon in the same way, and indeed he had none of the bluff, soldierly self-confidence of Hastings. On the other hand, he never doubted that he and his colleagues were the right people to be in authority and to be administering the rules in Tanganyika.

But self-confidence was not just a matter of public-school training. There were other contributory factors: race, Britishness and class. The Colonial Service was never crudely racist, but Europeans in Africa in general considered themselves to be representatives of a superior culture. In technological terms, they were indeed superior: as well as the Maxim gun, they had introduced the car, the train and the aeroplane to Africa. One of my father's proud boasts was that he had been able to arrange for Nade Bea, the very old ritual leader of the Iraqw people in Mbulu, who had grown up in a society where the wheel had not been invented, to travel by aeroplane down to Dar es Salaam. Many Europeans, though, went on to make the much less defensible assumption, often reflexively and thoughtlessly, that their society was also socially and politically more advanced. Africans were like children and not ready to carry out certain tasks, such as flying an aeroplane or indeed governing themselves. As a result, in a colony like Tanganyika, the process by which Africans were assimilated into government was painfully slow. Sir Donald Cameron, 'the great Governor' in my father's words, whose tenure lasted from 1925 to 1931, set out an admirably liberal credo in 1925: 'We are here on behalf of the League of Nations to teach Africans to stand by themselves. When they can do that, we must get out. It will take a long time, yet everything we do must be based on this principle.'[13] But when he said a long time, he meant it. The 13-man Legislative Council, which he set up in an advisory role in 1926, contained no Africans, on the grounds that none had mastered English to the requisite level. By 1939, there was one Indian on the Council, but still no Africans. When the size of the Council was expanded to 29 in 1945, seven of the 14 'unofficial' nominees were whites, three were Asians and only four were Africans. (The term 'unofficial' was used to refer to anyone who was not part of the official colonial Administration.) Three of the Africans were Chiefs and the fourth a schoolmaster. Ten years later, in 1955, the Council was further expanded by Sir Edward Twining to 58, of which 30 were unofficial, representation being split evenly between the races, white, Asian and black. Since the official nominees were all white, this meant in effect that 38 of the 58 members of the Legislative Council were white and only ten black. Whites represented less than 0.1 per cent of the population.

To be European was good, to be British was better. My mother used to tell me that British superiority was a function of the bracing effect of the British climate, a theory which always puzzled me. Nevertheless, as a 13-year-old boy walking round the beautiful and tranquil harbour of Dar es Salaam, I thought how lucky I was to have been born British – the Africans were poor and the Asians, though some were clearly very wealthy, were merely shopkeepers. Great efforts were made to plant and nurture the manners and domestic ceremonies of the metropolitan culture. 'Home' was usually England, sometimes Scotland, Wales or Northern Ireland, but never Africa. 'Made in England' in those far off days still signified quality, whether we were talking about cars, laws or government. When Tanganyika became independent, there was no question but that it should adopt the Westminster model of government.

The final brick on the pyramid was class. My father and his colleagues in the Administration were not simply European and British in an overwhelmingly African country, they were of the officer class in their own country. There was some variety, in that some of members the Colonial Service had been through the South African public-school system, but that system was very similar to the English one, and in any event most of them had gone on to Oxford or Cambridge, generally the former. They tended to be rugby-playing rather than football-playing, and at least two of them played at international level. If they did not consider themselves to be quite the 'Heaven-born', as the elite members of the Indian Civil Service did, they nevertheless thought of themselves as a cut above anyone else in their immediate society, particularly those engaged in commerce. My teenage disdain for shopkeepers reflected the prejudices of my parents' caste. The Colonial Service was not well paid by the standards of other professions, and at the time when boarding-school fees kicked in my parents had to make uncomfortable economies to make ends meet. But in the social pecking order, the administrators and what they stood for – the rule of law, firm government and trusteeship of the country's future – had status and respect. They were the people to bring the Africans to the point where they could stand by themselves. It was only proper that the administrators should be the ones who garnered the 'ribbons and stars' – for those in business, money was its own grubby reward.

So my father came to Dar es Salaam in June 1941 with a background, education and cast of mind which was typical. I do not, however, wish to present him as a caricature. I have drawn out those features of his background which have a bearing on his subsequent career, but he was never simply an identikit colonial administrator, if there was such a thing. He was more cerebral and less rugged than most of his peers. Although he subjected himself to walking many miles in rough bush, he was not physically tough and never thought of himself as such. As is often the way with men who are successful early, he was keenly ambitious: in later years my mother would remind him of how he fretted during his seven long years in the idyllic district of Mbulu in northern Tanzania, worrying that he was stuck in a backwater, would not be noticed and would never get on. He had normal human weaknesses, including penchants for the social vices of drinking, smoking and gambling. As a young man he was shy and he was into his twenties before he had his first affair. Later on in his bachelor life, he says in a note he left behind, he had a beautiful African mistress, news which came as a surprise to me and will, sadly, always remain a mystery. As a father, he was occasionally fierce, but fair and fundamentally kind-hearted. He had a wry sense of humour and his children loved him, as did others, for the twinkle in his eye. My siblings and I had a happy childhood, though I have always thought that my early despatch to boarding school in England at the age of eight was brutal. But, as my father says, that was the way of his forbears for generations, and he was not one to buck a tradition.

The profession that he had chosen was not an easy one. The postings that lay ahead of him were in remote and unhealthy places. His medical record shows that between 1941 and 1949 he was ill with typhoid, paratyphoid, pneumonia and pleurisy and five times with malaria. Although the Administration styled itself a service, the human resources function was rudimentary: there is a note on his file from a personnel officer in response to his request towards the end of his six-year tour in 1947 for some information as to where his next posting might be when he returned from leave, if only so as to know where he might best deposit his baggage. The note says that there is no information of any value on this point, save that it would almost certainly be in some other province. His bags should be left where they were. No cuddles there. And it was not well paid. His starting salary in 1941 was £350. Ironically, this turned out to be adequate during the war years when there was nothing to spend his earnings on anyway, apart from beer and cigarettes and paying off his university debts. His salary rose, but slowly: £525 in 1947, £1005 in 1952 and £1863 in 1957. In 1955 he took out a loan of £550, about a third of his salary, to buy a Ford Anglia, now something of a cult design, but in its time never more than a car of modest pretensions. When he left Tanganyika in 1962 he owned no house, shares or other property. It was not until his final year of service and after a series of rapid promotions that he was to be free of financial worries.

The Tanganyika that he found in 1941 had a population of some seven million, most of whom were desperately poor. It was made up of over 120 different tribal groupings, with no tribe being large enough to dominate. The Sukuma were the largest with 12 per cent of the total population in 1948, no other tribe constituting more than 5 per cent. Two thirds of the country was virtually uninhabited and people tended to settle on land where simple hand agriculture was possible. The population was overwhelmingly rural and engaged in subsistence agriculture, which accounted for over 30 per cent of gross domestic product throughout the period from the end of the Second World War up to independence. Sisal was the main export crop, with a heavy concentration of foreign-owned estates near the coast around Tanga, followed by coffee which was grown by African peasants on the slopes of Meru and Kilimanjaro.

In the 1940s the view gained hold in the metropolis that government should have an active role in promoting economic and social development. With the single disastrous exception of the Groundnut Scheme[14] in the late 1940s and early 1950s, which was mainly driven from London, this thinking was never reflected in Dar es Salaam. Resources were limited, but the Government did little to boost them or to stimulate the growth of a market economy. Investment had been stunted by the depression in the 1930s and war in the 1940s. Spending on education and infrastructure was completely inadequate to the country's needs. Outside the main towns, there were no tarred roads anywhere in the country in 1945. Though growth between 1948 and 1958 was estimated by the World Bank to be 5 per cent, this was from a low base and Tanganyika remained desperately poor when my father left in 1962. It still is.[15]

By 1941, Tanganyika had been under British administration for just over twenty years. The colony had been declared a protectorate, somewhat reluctantly, by the German Government in 1885, partly as a result of the interplay of European politics and partly in consequence of the machinations of the brutal and half-mad adventurer Dr Carl

Peters. Despite these unpromising beginnings, the Germans had sought to develop German East Africa as an overseas estate, encouraging white settlement, introducing major cash crops such as sisal and coffee, and building railways from Tanga to Arusha and Dar es Salaam to Kigoma on Lake Tanganyika. The style of government was direct and authoritarian, with German officials operating through a Swahili bureaucracy headed by officials with the Arab titles 'liwali' in the towns and 'akida' in the districts. In 1905 resistance to the compulsory growing of cotton in the Southern Province erupted into the Maji-Maji rebellion, so-called because of the belief that ritual water ('maji' in Swahili) could provide protection against European bullets. The rebellion was put down with such savagery that some two hundred thousand people died and large swathes of the country were depopulated, the consequences of which could still be felt when my father arrived in the province 36 years later.

During the First World War, the British fought a long, expensive and moderately incompetent campaign against a diminutive German force to ensure that the country's ports could not be used to threaten shipping routes to India. By 1918, the greater part of German East Africa was in British hands, with the Belgians camped in the north-west corner, in what was later to become Rwanda and Burundi. Despite the expenditure of men and matériel, the British Government was ambivalent about incorporating the captured territory into the Empire. It harboured none of the illusions about great untapped resources which had animated the original partition of Africa and, having gone to war to thwart territorial aggression, did not want to put itself in a position where it could be painted as having fought a war of imperial expansion. These negative sentiments were reinforced in the negotiations leading up to the Treaty of Versailles by Woodrow Wilson's deep intellectual antipathy to any imperial project. On the other hand, the abiding British preoccupation with security argued for a solution which as far as possible prevented the territory from falling back into German hands. The compromise eventually negotiated was the mandate system, under which the victorious powers received mandates from the League of Nations to govern the conquered German colonies on its behalf, the mandate for German East Africa being awarded to Britain. The mandate required Britain to 'promote to the utmost the material and moral well-being and social progress of Tanganyika's inhabitants'. This was in tune with the concept of trusteeship which was at the time the guiding principle of British colonial policy.[16]

Although Sir Donald Cameron claimed that the terms of the mandate did not trouble or preoccupy him in any way, since they were entirely consistent with the recognised principles of British administration, the source and form of the Government's authority was to have a significant impact on the political development of Tanganyika. First, it articulated formally the transitional nature of the British 'guardianship' of Tanganyika and other mandate territories, even if the period of transition was indeterminate. This set the tone for the Administration. It was also of course to be a useful rhetorical weapon in the hands of later nationalist politicians. Secondly, the Colonial Office in London agreed, when it took on the mandate, that Tanganyika should be a 'black man's country' along Nigerian lines rather than the 'white man's country' that it might have become if it had remained German and as Kenya and Southern Rhodesia were to become. European settlers were not to be encouraged, though neither were they to be debarred. The first British Governor, Sir Horace Byatt, cleared the country of German settlers in the period between 1917 and 1922. Although there was some backsliding under later Governors, including Cameron and Twining, Tanganyika never became a white man's country, which greatly simplified its politics.

It did, however, continue to exert a pull on the German imagination and, after the initial exodus, there was steady re-immigration from Germany, so that by 1939 there were again more German 'unofficials', mostly settlers, than there were British in the colony. There was even some talk in London in the run-up to war of handing Tanganyika back to the Germans as a sop to Hitler, though this came to nothing. When war broke out, the German 'unofficials' were summarily rounded up and interned. There was always a fear, though, that Germany would try to recoup its loss. Which was partly why my father spent his war teaching Africans how to shoot machine guns.

The colonial administrative structure was simple. At its apex was the Governor, who enacted laws on the advice of a Legislative Council, which he himself nominated. Beneath the Governor was a Chief Secretary, supported by a small central secretariat. The territory was divided into eight provinces under Provincial Commissioners

(PCs) and further divided into 56 districts, each under a District Commissioner (DC). A DC would typically have a staff of a district officer (DO), an assistant district officer and sometimes a cadet, all supported by a range of technical officers with expertise in agriculture, forestry, animal husbandry, healthcare etc. In 1939 there were 185 officers in the Administration in Tanganyika, rising to 194 in 1947 and 252 in 1957.[17] Not many to run a country the size of Britain and France put together. How was it done?

'These are liwalis and this is the DC and the DC is me. I tell them what to do. I don't do it myself. They do it. Indirect Rule.' This was my father's laughably brief introduction from his hard-bitten DC, Cecil Stiebel, to the system of government operating in Tanganyika in 1941. The concept of Indirect Rule is simple, but it has nevertheless given rise to intense controversy and voluminous literature. This is not surprising, because the debate over Indirect Rule[18] is fundamentally about the methods and conduct of British colonial policy, a proxy for British rule in large parts of Africa. It is necessary to understand the background, evolution and application of the concept to understand colonial administration in Tanganyika.

The concept was developed in West Africa, where the British found that territories taken by conquest had to be governed, initially at least, through indigenous institutions. When Sir George Goldie was carving out Nigeria in the 1880s and 1890s, he did so under the auspices of the undercapitalised and cash-strapped Royal Niger Company and had no option but to govern through local Chiefs. After his little army of 513 African troops, commanded by 30 European officers, had defeated the Emir of Nupe in central Nigeria and captured his capital at Bida in 1897, Goldie found himself without the manpower to set up an administration in the newly occupied territory. Following this experience he averred a year later that 'if the welfare of the native races is to be considered, if dangerous revolts are to be obviated, the general policy of ruling on African principles through African rulers must be followed for the present'.[19] The consideration for native races is a nice touch, a harbinger of the way in which the idea of Indirect Rule was to become subject to spin and ex-post rationalisation in the decades to follow.

Indirect Rule with capital letters was born in Northern Nigeria, and Sir Frederick Lugard was its midwife. Lugard was the man who took the idea and converted it into a system of government. Having subjugated Northern Nigeria by force of arms in 1903 he was in the same predicament as Goldie had been, with a staff of little more than four hundred to govern a population of ten million, inhabiting a territory larger than Germany. With limited excise revenue, he had little scope to increase the numbers of his staff in the short term. As it had been for Goldie, Indirect Rule was the only practical way forward. So he set up a structure whereby government would be conducted through Native Authorities. The Native Authorities would be three-legged, consisting of the Chief or Chiefs, native courts and a Native Treasury. The Chief (or emir) would be advised by government-appointed officials, whose role was intended to be purely advisory and not administrative, 'the whisper behind the throne, but never for an instant the throne itself'.[20] Lugard's innovation was to add a political rationale. Indirect Rule would be a means of defending and preserving African institutions, 'to retain and build up again what is best in the social and political organisation of the conquered dynasties, and to develop on the lines of its own individuality each separate race of which our own Great Empire consists,'[21] while at the same time bringing them 'into approximation of our ideas of justice and humanity'.[22] Britain's role was not just to govern its colonies, but to bring their mores and social structures, eventually, up to the same level as those of the mother country. This was what Lugard termed the 'dual mandate'.

Sir Donald Cameron brought Indirect Rule to Tanganyika when he was transferred from Nigeria to Dar es Salaam as Governor in 1925. He was keen to have it understood that he did not come to Dar es Salaam as an apostle of Lugard's, of whose style and personalised administration in Nigeria he disapproved. He claimed that his espousal of Indirect Rule or, as he preferred to term it, Indirect Native Administration, was a response to a situation which confronted him almost as soon as he arrived in Tanganyika, on which he had to make an immediate decision. Africans, 'tribesmen' as Cameron tellingly called them, were required by the British Administration to pay a hut and poll tax, as they had been under the Germans. It had been agreed by Cameron's predecessor that the tribesmen should no longer pay tribute to their Chiefs over and above the tax paid directly to the Government, because running the two systems of taxation together opened up too many opportunities for corruption and oppression. On the other hand, the Chiefs needed revenue and no one had addressed the issue as to how they would be compensated for their loss of tribute. Asked to decide whether they should be paid by central Government or by local Native Administrations, Cameron chose the latter. He did so on grounds of control and accountability: if the Government were to pay the Chiefs itself, it would have no way of checking the services performed by them on behalf of their people, whereas a locally-based Native Authority would be well-positioned to do so. This decision incorporated the Chiefs into the Administration, submitted them to the discipline of bureaucracy and committed Tanganyika to Indirect Rule.

In retirement, Cameron, like Lugard, put forward political arguments in justification of Indirect Rule. First, he reminded his readers that Britain administered Tanganyika as trustee under the terms of a mandate from the League of Nations. 'We should not be good trustees if we neglected to train people so that they may stand by themselves.'[23] He also made the much larger claim that Indirect Rule was the only way in which to preserve the integrity of African society and of preventing Africans from being reduced to servility. Both of these arguments are glosses on the truth, for the fundamental reason for Cameron's opting for Indirect Rule was the same as Goldie's and Lugard's: he did not have the manpower to run the country any other way. Indirect Rule was a solution to an administrative problem. This needs to be remembered in assessing its merits and demerits.

Despite his attempts to distance himself from Lugard, in practice the structure of Cameron's system in Tanganyika was much the same as the three-legged one developed by Lugard. The Native Authority itself would be constituted by a Chief or council or a combination of both, with legislative and executive powers. The Chief had powers to appoint Sub-chiefs and headmen, each of whom was responsible for a defined area or group of villages. If there was no obvious Chief available, efforts would be made to find a substitute, or create one. This would be a last resort, but unavoidable in the logic of Indirect Rule: if there was no Chief, there was no alternative to direct rule, which was what Cameron was trying to avoid. The native courts dealt with minor crimes and cases involving civil law or tribal custom. Initially, they were linked with the Chiefs, and responsibility for their operation was with the administration rather than the judiciary, in order to preserve indigenous legal practices. After

1945, however, they were brought progressively under the control of the professional judiciary. The third leg was formed by the Native Treasury, which collected taxes, remitting a percentage to central Government and retaining the rest to pay the Native Authority and finance local works and services. Tax revenue was derived from hut and poll taxes, court fees and fines, beer licences, market fees, cesses on local produce and local rates. The amounts going to each Chief varied, but in Tanganyika the norm was for the Chief to receive a rebate of 25 per cent of tax levied to cover the costs of paying his own stipend and local wages. Though in principle autonomous, the Native Treasury was overseen by the DC.[24]

Over most of the country the system was rolled out in as standard a way as local circumstances would permit. The exceptions were in large towns, such as Dar es Salaam and Tanga, where there were no obvious Native Authorities and direct administration by the Government was more appropriate. From 1926 until the advent of 'responsible government' in 1961 Indirect Rule formed the basis of Tanganyika's administration. It has been criticised on two counts: first, that it fostered tribalism, and secondly that it did nothing to prepare Africans to stand by themselves, to use the phrase employed in the mandate. These criticisms need to be addressed, because they have a bearing on the record of the colonial Administration in Tanganyika.

The criticism that Indirect Rule fostered tribalism is based on an oft-quoted passage in Iliffe's *Modern History of Tanzania*, to the effect that 'Europeans believed Africans belonged to tribes; Africans built tribes to belong to',[25] a process which led to a 'vast social reorganisation in which Europeans and Africans combined to create a new political order' in the period from 1925 to 1945. Iliffe goes on to claim that the new order was based on mythical history as the British sought to identify and revive structures that existed before the country became a German colony.

The implication of the formulation 'Europeans believed Africans belonged to tribes' is that they did not in fact do so.[26] Iliffe does not make this claim himself, though others have done so. It is hard to take seriously, since all observers from Burton and Stanley onwards have testified to the active agency of tribes in the region. Iliffe's argument, though, is more subtle, namely that the British misunderstood the concept of tribe in Tanganyika and what it was to

17

belong to one. The tribe did not have a tightly defined identity, like a football team, but a more open-ended one, with multiple identities, more like a football crowd. The individual could define himself or herself at one moment as the subject of a Chief, at another as a member of a cult, at another as part of a clan. The impact of colonisation, with its attendant processes of categorising, ordering and regulating African societies through tribes, was to crystallise tribal identities and to rigidify tribal structures. The definition and propagation of ethnic 'traditions' by anthropologists and administrators destroyed the fluidity and adaptability of prelapsarian African society and encouraged the growth of tribalism, which was judged to be a negative development. ('Traditions' is in inverted commas because the Dar es Salaam school came to hold the somewhat contrived view that the traditions were in effect invented by those who recorded them.)[27] The identification and appointment by the administration of Chiefs, who then built the tribes that Africans could belong to, initiated the 'vast social reorganisation'.

Very little supporting evidence is given for this thesis in Iliffe's book. It is of course hard to find reliable evidence on tribal structures prior to colonisation which is not based on the work of early-school anthropologists, whose testimony is of course suspect. (Terence Ranger, another leading light of the Dar es Salaam school, goes so far as to enjoin historians to 'free themselves from the illusion that the African custom recorded by officials or by many anthropologists is any sort of guide to the African past',[28] an extraordinary self-denying ordinance given the paucity of other guides.) For the same reason it is equally difficult to demonstrate in precisely what ways colonial administration rigidified tribal structures. The written material is almost exclusively from official records and, though there is some oral testimony from the African side, it should be treated as suspect, because it is delivered through an intermediary and often many years after the events to which it relates. With so little reliable evidence, it seems safer to conclude that, while Indirect Rule clearly had some impact in defining tribal identity through the appointment of Chiefs and Sub-chiefs, it was limited. In the southern part of the country, where for historical or cultural reasons tribes were not headed by Chiefs, administrators instituted chieftaincy structures which were as nearly authentic as they could make them, but for the most part Cameron and his officials were seeking to stabilise the country by building on *existing* institutions. To have gone to the extensive labour of introducing new institutions would have jeopardised the whole rationale of Indirect Rule, which was to provide quick and effective administration in the newly acquired colony. In the north-west there was remarkable continuity in chieftaincies between the German and British regimes and this is likely to have been the normal pattern.[29] Below the level of chieftaincies and sub-chieftaincies, the impact of the new Administration was slight. DCs and DOs were very few in number and scattered. They could influence the Chiefs and Sub-chiefs, and no doubt there was a trickle-down effect, but the bulk of society proceeded as if they were not there. 'In the normal way,' says my father, 'the Administration did not make much of an impression on the mass of the people. Whatever we got up to, the farmer in the bush paid his taxes so that we would leave him alone and got on with the job of wringing a hard living from his *shamba*' (plantation). There is no evidence of any vast social reorganisation, certainly no deep social reorganisation. The impact of Indirect Rule on tribalism in Tanganyika was marginal. The tribes were there before the advent of the Europeans and they are there still. Tribal identity may have become more distinct between the two periods, but it is difficult to ascribe this definitively to Indirect Rule or even to European agency.

My father and his colleagues would have found this entire discussion puzzling. Tribes were a given: his handover notes when he left the district of Mbulu in the Northern Province in 1956 start by describing the state of play in each of the four main tribal groupings in the district. He spent time delineating the border between the Barabaig and the Wanyaturu, not because of an anthropological interest in tribal definition, but because the border was in dispute and lives and welfare were at stake. He was absolutely not interested in inventing traditions. The discussion would have seemed to him of little value and almost meaningless.

There is more validity in the criticism that Indirect Rule did not prepare Tanganyikans to stand by themselves. Politically the concept of Indirect Rule was always an anachronism, based as it was on an essentially feudal and paternalist social model. In the 1930s and 1940s this was unexceptionable, because the British Government's conception of the political, social and economic needs of the colonies was so limited. Lord Hailey's *Native Administration and Political Development in British Tropical Africa* articulates the Government's

19

role as 'the establishment of law and order' and 'the provision of those requirements, such as means of communication, which would enable the population to satisfy its most elementary needs'.[30] These are very narrow aims, the unfortunate product of limited resources. To achieve even these small ends, the Administration needed the co-operation of its subjects, which it procured through the Chiefs and secured through the satisfactory operation of the native courts and treasuries, i.e. through Indirect Rule. However, the quasi-feudal system on which Indirect Rule subsisted did not marry well with the idea of representative democracy espoused by the nationalists after the war. 'Democracy demanded,' Nyerere said when he addressed the Tanganyika Chiefs Convention in October 1961, 'that the Chairmen of Local Councils should be elected,' despite the fact that this would 'place the Chief, who in the past had been the sole ruler of his Chiefdom, in an anomalous position'.[31] This anomaly was only ever likely to be resolved in favour of the democratic principle.

The Achilles heel of the system was indeed the ambiguous position of the Chiefs. In principle, they acceded to their titles on the basis of heredity, but the Administration always retained the right of removal for malfeasance or incompetence. Chief Fundikira, whose probation my father had to oversee when he was stationed in Shinyanga in the mid-1940s, was sacked by Cameron for embezzlement in 1937. This type of action showed where power lay. Moreover, with the passage of time the Administration became increasingly interested in appointment as well as removal. So, my father and the government anthropologist, Hans Cory, carefully orchestrated the appointment of their favoured Chief among the Wa'arusha in 1948. As the office became more bureaucratised and more closely identified with the colonial regime, the Chief's authority among his own people was inevitably diminished.

This process is well illustrated by the difficult negotiation between the Administration and the Wameru tribe, which is described by my father as a failure of administration and is worth considering in detail. The Wameru were a small tribe of some forty thousand people who subsisted on a mixture of agriculture and pastoralism around the base of Mount Meru in north-west Tanganyika. Having successfully negotiated the unification of the chieftaincy among the Wa'arusha, my father and Hans Cory attempted to achieve something similar among the Wameru in shoring up the authority of the Chief, Mangi Sante. Opposition to Mangi Sante was from a group of dissidents, described by the Administration as fanatical and intransigent, and led by one Baradau.

My father's analysis of why his opponents found Mangi Sante so unacceptable is puzzlingly superficial. A brief reference is made to the Wamerus' longstanding grievances over land and to the withering away of traditional tribal structures, but the quarrel with the dissident faction is mainly ascribed to its inclination to make trouble or 'fitina', which he describes as malice and persistence in stirring up a quarrel, to the point where original causes of the quarrel become forgotten and irrelevant. Other accounts, however, make it clear that there was a real grievance at the bottom of the quarrel and that it related to land. Land disputes are always bitter and the causes rarely forgotten or irrelevant. In this case the dispute went back over ten years to a proposal by a committee of Northern Province settlers and officials in the late 1930s that a corridor of land between Kilimanjaro and Meru, the so-called Sanya Corridor, should be made over to modern ranch farming, which in effect meant European farming. The proposal had been dropped during the Second World War, but had been revived when the war ended. The issue was referred to a committee chaired by Judge Mark Wilson in 1947, who recommended in favour of the proposal on the grounds that it would bring economic benefits that were in the national interest. Unfortunately, in order to create a block of ranch farming in the Sanya Corridor, two farms occupied by the Wameru in what they considered to be their ancestral lands in the Engare Nanyuki area would have to be repossessed and their inhabitants moved to an area of low-lying land further down the slopes of Mount Meru, at a place called Kingoro. The two farms to be repossessed by the colonial authorities, Kilimamnozi, No 31, and Legaruki, No 328, had originally been alienated by the Germans and had been bought back by the Wameru from the Custodian of Enemy Property after the First World War for a sum of £5433 over a period from 1925 to 1939. The money to pay for the purchase had been raised first by voluntary subscription and subsequently by a sale of land tax imposed on all adult Wameru.[32] It is easy to see why emotions might have run high at the second loss of lands so painfully re-acquired.

Mangi Sante apparently gave his approval to the resettlement plan in 1948, but a faction among the Wameru never accepted it and condemned Mangi Sante for having done so. A number of the dissidents, led by Baradau, refused to agree the introduction of the Cory-inspired constitution unless the Government revoked the appointment of Mangi Sante. This the Administration was not prepared to do. To have done so would have involved a significant loss of face, something which the regime could ill afford. Concluding that the dissident faction would have to be removed if the Native Authority was to operate effectively, conspiracy proceedings were instituted against Baradau and his allies. The Administration was successful in its immediate aims, in that convictions were obtained against the defendants, who were sentenced to a year in gaol and exiled to other parts of the country. However, success was short-lived because Mangi Sante's authority, far from being confirmed, was irredeemably undermined by his association with the Administration. He was eventually forced to resign in 1951, a year after my father had moved on to Mbulu. The Wameru were evicted from the two farms in November 1951, by which time several families had already moved to Kingoro. But ranch farming was not a success and the tribesmen were eventually able to repurchase and reoccupy the farms once more when the regime changed after independence.

When my father spoke to me as a boy about his tussle with the Wameru, the incident that he dwelt on was his dismissal of the recalcitrant elder Baradau during a disputatious *baraza* (public meeting) and his having to avoid following Baradau with his eyes as the latter walked away behind his back, not knowing what signal he might give to his excitable and hostile allies still arrayed in front of my father. His focus was on the drama of the contest and the need to maintain authority. This may explain the very little weight he attaches to the grievances of the Wameru. Although he was only two years in this particular posting, he cannot have been unaware of these grievances, because the land issue was a running sore in the Arusha district throughout the period from the publication of the Wilson report in 1947, the year in which he arrived in the district, to the eviction of the Wameru in 1951, and the main protagonists on the Government side, Donald Troup and Basil Stubbings, were both personal friends. But he seems to have concluded that the behaviour of the dissidents was vexatious and refers to the extraordinary patience of the Administration in dealing with them. Their behaviour may have been obstructive and perverse in the ways that he describes, but it is difficult at this distance not to sympathise with the understated

22

words of the UN Visiting Mission of 1951 that 'while there may be good practical reasons for the transfer…the removal of any land from the actual occupation by Africans in this heavily congested area is open to question.'[33] The use of repressive legislation to enforce the authority of the established Chief and the later eviction of the Wameru from their farms seem not only high-handed, but wrongheaded. In the event, the removal of tribesmen from the two farms in the Sanya Corridor became a rallying point for nationalist politicians in the Northern Province and a stimulus to the development of anti-colonial nationalist politics in Tanganyika. It led to depositions to the UN in New York and gave sustenance to Nyerere and other nationalist politicians who were pushing for independence. These were not the intended outcomes.

This episode illustrates the limitations of Indirect Rule. In the end, it diminished by association those whom it purported to promote, that is the Chiefs. As a school for government it was a failure. The proposal in the run-up to independence that the Convention of Chiefs might evolve into a second chamber under the new constitution, along the lines of the House of Lords, received short shrift from Nyerere, because it cut across his commitment to representative democracy. In November 1962, one year after independence, the new Government issued a memorandum on the 'Position of Chiefs', which ordained that after 1 January 1963, chiefdoms would no longer exist as units of local government. There was almost no reaction to this administrative fiat, which indicates how superficial had been the hold of the institutions of Indirect Rule on Tanganyikan social and political life. The idea that Tanganyikans might learn to stand by themselves through the gradual accretion of administrative experience to the Chiefs was never tested.

However, as I have argued earlier, the political and educational function was never the central rationale for Indirect Rule. It had been adopted by Cameron as the best means available for governing a large country with the very small staff at his disposal. As an instrument of government, despite its internal contradictions, it served the Administration well for thirty years. The Government's political, social and economic objectives had to be tailored according to its limited means. Politically, its overriding objective was to maintain peace and order; socially, it was content with gradual advances in healthcare and literacy rates; economically, investment capital was directed towards better communications and modest improvements in subsistence agriculture and the country's few cash industries. From 1926 until the late 1950s, Indirect Rule was entirely adequate for achieving these aims. It delivered political and social stability and modest economic advance. It enabled a small cadre of administrators to govern an alien populace many times its size without the use of force and with a degree of popular consent. As soon as that consent was withdrawn, it ceased to be viable, but up to that point it was an effective means of governing the country. To that extent, far from being a failure it was a modest success.[34]

One other factor in favour of Indirect Rule as it was practised in Tanganyika was that it insulated the people of the country against catastrophic errors of the type perpetrated by the direct rule introduced by post-independence governments. Villagisation is a good example. This programme was instituted by Nyerere in 1974 and required all of Tanzania's rural peasants to live in registered villages, known as *ujamaa* villages. These villages were larger than traditional ones, each containing a minimum of 250 families, usually twice as many. This made it easier to provide communal services, particularly education, but took no account of the logistics of agriculture. One woman in Songea complained that in order to harvest the crop from her acre of maize 5 miles away from her village, she had to make forty trips, each of which meant walking 10 miles. Planning was schematic and inflexible, with villages lined up close to each other along the roadsides, like soldiers on parade. The villages were run by elected councils, but decision-making was effectively confined to the Chairman and Secretary, who were in practice appointed by the CCM, the successor party to TANU, the original party of independence. Decisions were consequently arbitrary and autocratic. René Dumont, by no means a hostile commentator, remarks that villagisation was achieved by 'persuasion, but also sometimes with coercion; and not always with prior consultation with the peasants'.[35] The result was a catastrophic loss in agricultural productivity and widespread rural poverty and hunger. This is the type of measure, disastrous in its results, which could not have happened under Indirect Rule. As my father says, 'we could never have done what was done without the people's support'. Villagisation did not have the people's support, and on those grounds would not have got past the conceptual stage under Indirect Rule.

In 2005, my wife and I went to Tanzania on holiday. I went back to Mbulu, the small town in the Northern Province where my father had been posted for seven happy years and where I passed my early childhood. The Boma, the fine old German fort with its *Beau Geste* crenellations which had been my father's office, was gone, condemned as unfit for habitation in an earthquake zone. But the simple house that I grew up in was still there, darker now, because the glass doors had been replaced by stout wooden ones for greater security. Running water and power had been installed, so the taps no longer ran rust brown and the soft light of the hurricane lamp had been replaced by the glare of electric bulbs. It was still occupied by the DC, who greeted us hospitably, if warily. He was not from the region, and repaired to his own house in Arusha at the weekends, which he would not have been able to do in my father's day, since Saturday mornings were working mornings. The DC quietly detailed improvements in health and education and complained about poor roads strangling the development of the district. The preoccupations were the same, though some of the enthusiasm seemed to have gone.

My father expresses the hope in his memoir that if he were to go back after a couple of generations he would find 'traces of a more careful comprehension of what the land required for its care, and a touch more of kindly manners than might otherwise have been'. This scrupulous formulation reflects the colonial Administration's concern with the lives of African peasants and its aim to make two blades of grass grow where one had grown before. The daily round involved building roads, improving agriculture and administering the law. It was administration, not politics, and my father liked to quote Pope's *Essay on Man*: 'For forms of government let fools contest; whate'er is best administered is best.'[36]

I suspect that his response to the Mbulu that my wife and I saw would have been ambivalent. The town is bigger and there are signs of visible prosperity, including more cars and bicycles. But most of all there are more people. He put the population of his district at 175,000 in 1956. The DC told me that the figure in 2005 was not far short of a million, i.e. nearly six times as big in 50 short years. (The same is true of Tanzania's population as a whole, which was 7.5 million in 1948 and is 47 million today.) It is hard to see the land being treated with more care in the face of population pressure like this. As for manners, the people were kindly enough in their manners to us, as strangers, and seemed to be at peace with each other.

My father described his colonial career as hard, exacting, ill-paid and deeply satisfying. His emphasis was on the last phrase, though he thought that the privations were insufficiently acknowledged. But his strongest belief was that he and his colleagues had done a good job. They made mistakes, as we all do, but when they did, their actions were subject to process and eventually to the consent of the governed, which limited the gravity of any error. The intentions of the administrators were good. 'All were dedicated,' says Lumley, 'to the interests of the African peoples committed to their charge.'[37] In our more cynical times this sentiment sounds somewhat pious, but it reflects the ethos of the service, and my father would certainly have subscribed to it. The professors of the Dar es Salaam school would probably not, but they are biased in the other direction. The deficiencies of colonial administration have been widely broadcast, its merits less so. Like the ancient peasant in Sir Donald Cameron's anecdote quoted at the beginning of this book, recent historians have expected colonial administrators to have brought the rain as well as the roads and the railways. They were creatures of their time and they could not make the weather, but with limited resources, in a poor country, they succeeded in providing a form of government over forty years that was effective and fair. In Tanganyika they brought peace, the rule of law and steady development to a large region where the people had not experienced any of these benefits for centuries. They were not corrupt and did not govern in favour of factional commercial interests, considerable virtues, particularly in the light of subsequent history in Tanzania and elsewhere on the continent. And when they left, they left in peace and without rancour. Although colonial rule, as history has repeatedly shown, is an unsustainable form of government, it is an undertaking which can be done well or badly. Without being blind to the inherent flaws of the system that our fathers introduced and operated in Africa, we should not overlook the things which they did well.

I have added as appendices two annual reports, one for Maswa at the end of the Second World War and another for Mbulu in 1955, and my father's handover notes when he left Mbulu in 1956. The Maswa report would have been submitted by his DC at the time, Donald Malcolm, but has manuscript corrections by my father, which suggests at least that he was closely involved with drafting it. Though there may be more detail in them than the general reader requires, they are of abiding relevance to anyone interested in development issues in Africa. The tone is paternalist, but rarely patronising. It is not possible to read these documents without forming an admiration for the careful, pragmatic and disinterested character of the Administration they describe. They give a good flavour of a form of government which was cheap, efficient and just.[38]

Innes Meek

1

PROLOGUE

In every British colony that ever was, up-country officers hated and despised the Secretariat in the capital. So in Tanganyika, as elsewhere, we knew that it was only in the field, in the provinces and districts, that there were to be found dedicated administrators, close to the people, toiling away at the civilising mission which had called them so far from home. On the other hand it was the job of pertinacious bureaucrats at the Secretariat in Dar es Salaam to frustrate these noble fellows at every turn. The fact that we were all members of a single service and that the Secretariat at any given moment was largely populated by officers who had recently been colleagues in the field never altered these sentiments one whit. It was the general staff against the fighting soldier.

So there I was one day in January 1957, on my way back by air from long leave for a Secretariat posting.

Page-Jones,[1] under whom I was to serve, knew me well, for he had once been my provincial commissioner, and in his letter to me he had been at pains to point out, 'I do not suppose you will take kindly to Secretariat life, but I know you realise it is an experience you should not miss.' That was the rub. An effective spell at headquarters was a necessary phase of a successful career, and after 16 years in the field, nearly all in bush districts, I knew it was time that I broke my Tanganyikan record of having gone ten whole years without setting foot in Dar es Salaam at all. How was I to get on if the top brass did not even know me?

I suppose I must have reflected on that aeroplane how little equipped I was to deal at the centre of things with the full thrust of nationalist politics. It was to be three years before Macmillan spoke in Cape Town of the 'wind of change' sweeping through Africa, but many parts of the territory, and many other parts of Africa too, were already being shaken by the preliminary gusts. Yet this was not the case everywhere. On the whole the nationalist running was made among tribes whom we British administrators had traditionally regarded as the country's most tractable, such as the very large Sukuma tribe. There was a simple reason for this apparent anomaly. It was now not we but the agitators who were finding them tractable.

The peoples of our beautiful Northern Province, which my wife and I had enjoyed so long, were anything but docile. Competition for land on the fertile slopes of the great volcanic mountains of Kilimanjaro and Meru was intense, particularly since the best of it was in European hands. Nevertheless, the disposition of the dominant tribal groupings was capitalist, and while they would dispute forever among themselves and with the white settlers, the austere socialism of the nationalists held only a limited appeal. Thus our conflicts were intense but local, and right to the end the peoples of the province remained somehow outside the mainstream of the nationalist movement. Furthermore, in my own district of Mbulu, where I had been stationed for the unprecedented period of seven years, there was the additional insulation that came from physical isolation. Except where the Great North Road cut through the lightly populated eastern lowlands our high plateau above the Rift could only be reached by difficult escarpments, and during the rains it was often hard to get in or out. All in all, it was not a place for outsiders to preach in, and I never had more than two ill-run branches of TANU, as the Tanganyika African National Union was always known, on the fringes of the district. With their leaders I maintained a relationship of reasonably civilised antipathy.

I was not totally ignorant of what was afoot elsewhere. Of course I saw security reports and heard from friends more closely involved with TANU, and learnt a little from what we read in the *Tanganyika Standard* and a great deal more from the Swahili press. But still I must have thought to myself that I did not even know what Julius Nyerere looked like.[2] Here he was, for three years past the mainspring of TANU, the opponent of the colonial regime, the Enemy, and I would not even recognise him if I saw him. In those days, the *Tanganyika Standard* would no more have sported a photograph of him than *Pravda* would of the Queen, and the vernacular press could probably not afford photographs.

However, I was about to be relieved of my disability. The aircraft was not full, and presently I moved forward to an empty seat to make more room for my family to sleep. I was beside a diminutive African with a small Charlie Chaplin moustache. My curiosity was aroused, for an African traveller on an intercontinental flight was then unusual, since very few indeed could have met the price of a ticket, and strong organisations that could afford it were only just starting to be formed. But, as he and I exchanged courtesies, my curiosity was further stimulated by observing what he was reading. It was *The Approach to Self-Government* by Ivor Jennings.[3] Subversion. This could only be Nyerere.

Well, of course it was, returning from a lecture tour in the US and a second appearance before a UN Committee in New York, his fare largely paid by Dar es Salaam taxi drivers. When we arrived at Dar es Salaam, I was happy to have my identification confirmed by an enthusiastic crowd of ululating women there to greet him.

Such was Government suspicion of the nationalist movement at this time that on the following day Special Branch officers made a solemn note of what their target had been reading, and sedulous inquiries were made as to what else I had observed. Alas, I could only report that I had exchanged no more than the polite salutations with him, though as we all pulled ourselves together in the morning preparatory to landing, I had taken note from my seat back with my family of the indefinable charm this little figure could exercise. There had been an Englishwoman aboard, whom I subsequently got to know as the wife of an Indian, who had lost her shoe in the general mess that is created by a lot of people sleeping in an aeroplane. Nyerere eventually found it for her, but the finding of it and its return to its owner were marked by by-play so full of mutual allure that one could almost feel it. He had a cuddly quality which was as devastating to women as some of his other qualities were appealing to men.

In this prologue I have sought to reflect the mood and attitude of colonial administrators at that time, but I must not mislead the reader into thinking that we supposed the British were there for ever.

Just as the British administrators in India from far back knew that one day the Indians must govern themselves, so we had been raised in that tradition. Tanganyika must be for Tanganyikans. Where we went all wrong was on timing: we were going to work our successors out of jobs, but not ourselves. Apart from failing to appreciate the strength of nationalism and the political skill of Nyerere, we underestimated the mortal enmity of Americans to the whole colonial concept and the effect this hostility would have in the UN, and, above all, we did not understand the loss of the will to run an empire which sprang from the general decline of British power. But these were not ignoble misjudgments, for they were shared to an extent by everybody else concerned. At any time in the mid-fifties, Nyerere himself, like the UN Mission in 1954, would happily have settled for a 25-year period before handover.

How, amazingly, in that short space of time between January 1957, where I begin my tale, and 9 December 1961 we corrected our course and brought the ship to harbour and did so without bloodshed on the way is a significant story, and part of that story was to be the short, but strong, alliance between me and my travelling companion on that aeroplane. But I hope to illustrate the extent of change best by going back to the start of the story for me in June 1941, and setting the scene with a tale of what fun it was, and how fulfilling, to be an old-fashioned colonial administrator.

2

LINDI

Lindi was, and I suspect still is, a dump. A squalid little African township, a handful of Indian shops with little to sell as wartime shortages got worse; a fringe of European houses along an unappetising beach and some more straggling up the hill behind; a seedy little hotel and a club with a single tennis court and a parched nine-hole golf course; that was it. As I looked at the scene from the rail of the *Azania*, the little Government steamer that had brought me here, I could understand the looks of commiseration I had received in Dar es Salaam when I named my prospective post. Except for the occasional service of the *Azania* and another steamer, the *Tayari*, owned by one of the big sisal companies, Lindi was totally isolated. Here I was to be launched on my administrative career.

It was 1 July 1941. Long before, at Oxford, I had put my name down for the Colonial Service as a speculation for after the war, but I had not been many months in the Army when the Colonial Office started head-hunting, administrative strength in many colonies having been reduced to the point where breakdown threatened. When I finally received an offer in March, the only fighting in progress was in Abyssinia and the Western Desert, and, being young and innocent, I allowed myself to be beguiled by official assurances that there was every likelihood, on arriving in Tanganyika, that I would be exchanged for one of the older administrative officers presently seconded to the Army. This proposal sounded so sensible, since I was a fully trained soldier and certain to be of limited use in my new job for a couple of years at least, that I supposed it to be likely and, after much hesitation, signed myself out of the Army. To get rid of a subject that caused me much unhappiness in the next few years, of course this exchange never came about. In face of initial refusal in Dar es Salaam, I used influence to get myself applied for by GHQ in Cairo. When Government still refused to let me go, I sought to resign and was reminded that there was conscription and I was not free. So that was that.

The Colonial Office interviews were fun. For a start, each one gave a 24-hour break in London, which was a welcome change from a half-built barracks in Droitwich. Then it was easy to get on with the man in charge, who liked to pick recruits from families with a record of public service. Generations of colonial administrators had known Ralph Furse,[1] who bore the charming and misleading title of Patronage Secretary to the Secretary of State and who had indeed inducted my own father into the Nigerian service thirty years before me. He had an encyclopaedic knowledge of the colonies, and embodied in his person all recruitment policy and training programmes, but all training courses were naturally suspended in wartime and we newcomers were to learn our trade on the job.

Kitting myself out at Baker's in Golden Square in London had its lighter moments, for I had rather more help than I needed from an enthusiastic father whose ideas of tropical necessities were by now somewhat out-of-date. Instinct, rather than any contrary information, led me rightly to conclude that I would survive without spine pads, double terai hats and various other paraphernalia. I felt an equal aversion to sales talk when prompted to buy a safari lavatory seat, but here I gave way out of embarrassment when the assistant offered to erect it in the middle of his busy shop. It became in fact a prized and envied piece of equipment on long safaris in the bush without benefit of rest houses.

When I sailed from Liverpool on 1 May aboard the SS *Burma*, I formally joined the Colonial Service, and, being still a couple of months short of my twenty-first birthday, I believe I was the youngest cadet who ever did so. There were three others, all bound for Kenya, two of whom I had known well at Oxford, and one of these was a school contemporary too. We were in for a rough convoy. Liverpool was heavily bombed around the time of our departure, and the *Burma* was never victualled in a regular way, which produced some bizarre effects later on: plenty of gin, but nothing to mix it with, so we were compelled to follow the naval habit and drank it with water; mixtures at meals which no cookery book ever sanctioned. After rendezvous off Cape Wrath, the last land we were to see for six weeks, our forty-odd ships sailed north-westerly in glorious weather. But when we were a week out, with daylight stretched to almost 24 hours, those of us who had the duty of manning Lewis guns against the threat posed by the Focke-Wulf bomber which had shadowed us early on began to think we must by now be clear. It was at this point we came under wolf-pack submarine attack. Two ships went down directly on our port beam and then two more immediately to starboard within the space of ten minutes. There is a sombre finality in the sinking of a ship at sea. We had been told that no ships were to put themselves at risk by picking up survivors. Sensible orders, but we were proud that they were not fully observed. We lost seven ships in 36 hours by the time our escorting destroyer had to turn back with an incoming convoy, and ours dispersed. We pursued our way at a stately 10 knots in the *Burma* almost over to the Brazilian coast, and so eventually to Cape Town and Durban, with a welcome two or three days in each, and finally Dar es Salaam.

A regular bridge four kept me engaged for many hours a day on our long voyage. The master player, a bank manager, was a good teacher and keen to pass on his skills, including the use of a very precise bidding convention. A consequence was that I myself was a very good bridge player when I disembarked in Dar es Salaam, though many years of bush stations subsequently sent me downhill. But our teacher was also a pedant, while my partner Philcox, a delightful South African who was being sent home on the grounds that he was too old to join up, had a strong and mischievous sense of humour. There came one pre-lunch session, with a number of gins and water consumed, when Philcox and I found ourselves in command of the field and deploying all our new-found technique to identify every card of consequence in each other's hands until I confidently bid a grand slam in diamonds. There followed a long pause. What on earth was Philcox going to do? Surely not switch suits? Eventually, with a seraphic grin, he said, 'Eight diamonds, partner, I still had to show my Queen.' And at that moment the ship gave a heavy roll and over went Philcox, card table and all.

So in mid-June we steamed into the pretty harbour at Dar. First, the landmark of Government House, then a fringe of attractive buildings, the most important being administrative offices, all dating from German days, along the northern rim of the bay. In those days there were no deep-water berths, as there are now, and lighters came out to us as we moored in the middle of the harbour. Someone must have come aboard to take me ashore, for I recollect no confusion or difficulty in getting myself sorted out. There were only two hotels that were considered respectable for Europeans, the New Africa and the somewhat downmarket Imperial, and I was duly installed in the former. I was introduced to the Dar es Salaam Club, where I heard of Hitler's invasion of Russia and the news that the Governor, Sir Mark Young,[2] was to be transferred to Hong Kong, there, poor fellow, to face long years of imprisonment, and was to be replaced by Sir Wilfred Jackson.[3]

I reported to the Chief Secretary and was told that Lindi, the headquarters of the Southern Province, was to be my first posting. It would be a fortnight before I could get passage there by the government-owned steamer, the *Azania*. There were still some formalities in wartime Dar, such as dropping cards on official magnates and signing the books of the grandest, including of course the Governor, and in these I was instructed. Because Lindi was so isolated, there were basic supplies to be bought here and lines of communication to be set up with the local shops. But above all there was an active social life, for the war had cut men off from home and I was much in demand at dinner parties to give my account of the Blitz and conditions after Dunkirk. These early dinner parties exposed me to my first cultural shock, as the women retired at the end of the meal and the men promptly marched out to relieve themselves in the garden. (One might have thought that the arrival of flush sanitation would have led to the supercession of this up-country habit, but it never did, even in the august circumstances of Government House.) Almost the only night I was not asked out was that of my twenty-first birthday. Sitting on my own under the fans of the New Africa Hotel, sampling the hotel's cuisine and a bottle of Tusker beer, was hardly the celebration I would have planned.

For my two weeks in Dar es Salaam I was put under the wing of Andy Pike, the capital's DC. He was famous among other things for being the failure in his family: the story went that he alone of a clutch of brothers had to be content with a trial instead of an Irish international rugby cap. He took me out one Sunday to the old Arab port of Bagamoyo, where one of his formidable brothers, Ted, later Sir Theodore, was in charge and gave us lunch and a tour of the town's ancient graves. Andy cannot have found me useful for the time that he was saddled with me. Few creatures are indeed less useful than a completely green cadet, and I was the greenest ever seen. Not only was I the youngest in the history of the service, but I lacked all benefit of the year's training at Oxford or Cambridge that any peacetime intake had to undergo after their degrees. I had even squandered all those weeks on the boat playing bridge when I should have been mugging up on the basics of Swahili. In the two years of a cadetship it was necessary to pass a Swahili examination before one was confirmed in office as an assistant district officer, and thereafter Higher Swahili had to be taken within a stipulated period. In due course I spoke the language well, but in those early days I found that without reasonable fluency one was more of a handicap than a help.

So, after a bucketing voyage down the coast in the *Azania*, I came to Lindi, all too conscious of my deficiencies as a prospective administrator. But surely my training was about to start.

Formal instruction, as it transpired, was notably brief. Cecil Stiebel,[4] the Lindi DC, was a tough, burly fellow, reputed at one time to have been a bouncer in one of Mrs Meyrick's[5] London nightclubs. Be that as it may, he was one of a sizeable cadre recruited in haste after the Great War, when a civil administration was being knocked together in this former German colony. He had learnt on the job himself, and he was the last person to clutter anyone's mind with theory.

'It's like this, Meek,' was the guidance I got in due course. 'Indirect Rule, that's the system in this country, Indirect Rule! And this is the way it works,' taking a sheet of plain foolscap and drawing a large circle in the centre, with a series of spokes radiating out from it to a dozen or so much smaller circles around the periphery. 'These are liwalis,' indicating the small circles, 'and this is the DC and the DC is me. I tell them what to do. I don't do it myself. They do it. Indirect rule. Got it?'

'Yes, Sir.'

'Very well, you'll be taking over the Cash Office.'

I was trained.

After years of attempting to govern through a multiplicity of headmen, which in practice threw the burden back on the District

Office, local government in Lindi had been quite recently reformed in close consultation with the Muslim leaders of the community, a small number of Muslim magistrates being appointed as liwalis, each in charge of a group of villages. There were thus ten or a dozen subordinate Native Authorities, with a council of liwalis meeting at specified intervals as a superior body. As Cecil Stiebel had graphically illustrated, at the centre was the DC, usually supported by two or three district officers, according to the size and importance of the district. The DC was always the key figure: he could endlessly persuade, and in extreme cases he could direct, but he expected to have his way, and both Government and the Native Authority expected him to have it. It was a simple system: reasonably efficient, tolerably just, and cheap.

In my early years there were still some one-man stations, like the neighbouring Liwale District, where the DC was the only white official, but Lindi was a provincial headquarters and comparatively large. Apart from the PC himself, there were provincial staff, even in the run-down state of wartime, for the agricultural, forestry, game, medical and public-works departments, and, of course, the police. They were hard-pressed men, for the Southern Province straggled the whole 400-mile length of our border with Portuguese East Africa, and not only were travelling conditions difficult at best, but vehicles, tyres and petrol were all in desperately short supply in time of war. As for Lindi District, we had our team of the DC, the District Officer and me in the Boma. Every district office in the territory was called the Boma, literally a Swahili word for 'fenced enclosure'. The name stuck even when the Germans replaced the original enclosures with buildings designed to be defended, if necessary, as forts. In addition to the administrative staff we had our own medical officer and policeman in the district and probably our own Public Works Department officer. Besides all these officials, provincial and district, there were a couple of bank managers, the Imperial Airways man who serviced the splendid seaplanes which still used our harbour, and the businessman who ran a chain of lorries which held the province's commerce together from Lindi to Songea.

Very, very slowly I began to find my feet. The Desais and Patels, the Neronhas and De Mellos, those marvellously efficient and polite clerks from India and Goa who served us so well in East Africa, gave me the sort of instruction which I had thought I might have got from my DC, and in the Cash Office, where I passed two or three tedious months, I soon got the hang of Government accounting. More importantly, I got the hang of what the money was all about, how taxes were coming in and how the dirt roads were being maintained, two of the constant routine concerns of every DC.

In many parts of the territory at this time we were not really living in a cash society. In the poor Southern Province the annual African tax was then no more than six shillings a year, yet this demand was enough to ensure that many people from far up-country had to come down to the coast to earn their tax and enough for their very limited needs for consumer goods for their families. That was how the sisal plantations got their labour and so produced the country's main export crop. Sisal became in critically short supply later in the war when the Indonesian plantations were lost to the Japanese, and we had in the end to introduce conscription for labour on our big estates, but at this time that little six-bob tax did the trick.

Tax collection was the first litmus test of good administration, one of the basics, along with road maintenance and the smooth functioning of the native courts. If tax came in regularly and not too much was stolen on the way, if the roads were tolerable in the dry season and not too often impassable in the rains, if appeals from the native courts to the DC were not too frequent, then by and large things were in good shape and the DC a sound man.

Prompt checking of all tax collected against counterfoil receipts was one of a cadet's more boring chores, and it was a constant source of surprise to me to find how well our shoe-string system worked. It depended entirely on a network of peripatetic clerks, mostly no more than semi-literate, and in those days doing much of their travel on foot with minimal protection for what were by local standards very large sums of money. Yet, really very little went adrift by fraud or theft or accident. When it did, we were in trouble. Financial orders were very skilfully drafted, and the work must have been done by men who had never been in the bush in their lives, or who, having done their stint, were set on taking it out on their successors. There was prescribed protection against every human malice or folly and every stroke of ill luck that could be imagined, and whoever had failed to take the necessary precaution was liable to censure, and even surcharge. It was laid down, for example, that floating markers should be attached to cash-boxes when making a passage by water, an idiocy I recalled with a certain discomfort when crossing a river in spate with a tax collection aboard a canoe. Needless to say, all of us in the field became skilled and collaborative liars in the face of audit queries. Sometimes the auditors got their own back. A road inspector of the Public Works Department (the PWD, as it was known all over British Africa) was suspected of expanding his claimed mileage on a trip to pay road gangs. The query took the form, 'Would Mr So-and-so explain whether he travelled at 80 miles an hour and stopped at intervals, or whether he did a steady 40 and threw the money out of the window as he passed?'

This brings me to the second litmus test, road maintenance. Grade A roads were the responsibility of the Government in Dar es Salaam, through the PWD. (I should add that even Grade A roads at this time were dirt ones.) Grade B roads were also maintained by Government funds, but the allocation of funds was controlled by the DC. It was difficult, perhaps impossible, for the Audit Department to check that these moneys were devoted to their proper purpose, and in consequence the whole Administration in the field was joined in a covert understanding to raid Grade B road funds for projects dear to the DC's heart, but struck out from the estimates year after year by the heartless Financial Secretary in Dar es Salaam. Finally there were the local roads, for which the Native Authority was responsible. In all these cases the DC would have to see to it that labour was available for maintenance after the rainy season, and the state of the roads reflected to a considerable extent the vitality of the local Boma.

The third test of good administration was the efficiency of the native courts, which tried the bulk of cases of petty crime and all civil cases founded in tribal law and custom. From the inferior native court there was appeal to the superior and thereafter to the DC, always sitting with assessors where elucidation of native custom was required. Generally, appeals to the DC were limited in number where the system was working well. Later on I found immense interest in the process which took us so close to the daily concerns of the people, but in my salad days in Lindi I saw little of this aspect of the district's work. I can never forget, though, the incongruous response of a plug-lipped Mawiha woman who was asked what she was doing when her husband was killed by an arrow as he sat by the fire: 'I was cooking snake for his dinner.' (The Mawiha women wore wooden plugs in their upper lips, small in childhood and progressively enlarged as they grew older. The hideous duck-like appearance that resulted was the device of the tribe to make their women repulsive to slavers in order to avert captivity. They were a vivid reminder of the evils of the slave trade.)

The social life of our small British community centred on our tiny Club. That was where we got our exercise, had our evening drink, ran a monthly dance, but above all where we gathered at six each evening to listen to the BBC and news of the war. As junior boy, I was almost 'ex officio' secretary to the club committee, and I derived plenty of amusement from club politics. As in any small society, trivia could become matters of great moment, and I treasure the memory of a bitter row which divided the station for days about whether or not a penny should go on the price of a bottle of beer. My loyalties were deeply involved in this dispute, on the side of fiscal probity, and I called on the PC to enlist his aid. He was a teetotaller and had his own wireless, so he appeared at the Club infrequently, but on this occasion his vote would be crucial. To my consternation, I found him with no less a guest than Cardinal Spellman[6] of New York, on his way to visit American servicemen in Madagascar, but, nothing daunted, I launched into my appeal. His Eminence showed a proper appreciation of the niceties of my argument, and I like to think he was instrumental in pushing the PC my way at the vote next day.

The main business activity of the district was sisal, for it was in the light and sandy soils of the coastal belt that it flourished. Big sisal plantations were inherited from the Germans by the British Administration, and Lindi had a substantial share of them. They were owned by large companies, British, Indian, Greek, Swiss. Wages and conditions were poor, and the Administration kept a paternal eye on the estates and tended to side with labour when trouble blew up, as it did from time to time. Low wage levels were defended by the owners on the grounds that an African's cash requirements, including his tax, were low and he would be back off to his village as soon as he made his target figure, and production could never be maintained if labour turnover was too rapid. There was of course some truth in this, but it was a fundamentally disreputable argument and it was fortunately heard less often after the war as other areas of activity were opened up and sisal lost its predominance in the economy.

It was sisal that brought us Americans less welcome than Cardinal Spellman. American merchantmen would occasionally put in to pick up consignments of the valuable commodity. In our shabby little township there was nothing for roughish seamen to do but get drunk at our run-down hotel and consort with the local whores in a more public way than was consonant with colonial mores. The following morning would be disfigured by seamen, still drunk, weaving their way back to their ships with their arms around their tarts and a delighted crowd of townspeople enjoying the sight. Was the white *bwana*'s prestige, on which alone we depended, forever destroyed, we would wonder after each of these distressing visitations? Apparently not. It required other influences, years later, to upset the habit of authority on the one side and of obedience on the other.

Emaciated chickens, eggs, goats and *mchicha*, or native spinach, were the staples of our diet. Much else in this remote and ill-supplied place tended to be unavailable for long periods and then to arrive in small and unpredictable windfalls off ships coming to collect our sisal. Fairly unpleasant Bear cigarettes from Kenya were readily available, and smokers get used to anything. Favourite British brands were few and far between and were manna in the wilderness when they came. Local beer from Dar es Salaam was plentiful, at that time at any rate. Whisky was not to be had, and most of us relied for our spirits on a rather nasty South African gin. Not so Cecil Stiebel, that pillar of the *Serikali* (Government), who distilled a kind of potent and quite illegal rum for himself.

We drove nowhere for pleasure. Lack of petrol and tyres was so acute that motor transport was for safari only, and even there we were constrained to tour much less than we should have done. Later in the war we managed all these shortages much better. The deficiencies got worse, particularly petrol and tyres, but we developed surprisingly efficient rationing schemes for these and for many basic foodstuffs and textiles and liquor – surprisingly, because there were so few people to operate them, mostly the wives of officials.

Shortages of goods mattered little to most African peasants in their largely cashless society, though they were a hardship to the more privileged and a catastrophe to Indian traders, large and small. But the bulk of the population now became aware of the war in a much more direct way, for, before the Japanese attack in December, conscription was introduced. In theory Africans were not conscripted for the fighting services, presumably a bob of the head to Tanganyika's status as a League of Nations mandated territory, but for the Pioneer

Corps, wielders of picks and shovels. But in the people's minds this service was equivalent to the Carrier Corps of the Great War, whose members had died in their tens of thousands in the East African campaigns. So once they had been roped in for the Pioneer Corps, often quite literally, for many were brought in with halters round their necks like slaves of old, fit men made haste to volunteer for the King's African Rifles. So the Minister could say in the House of Commons, 'No, Sir, none are being conscripted to the fighting services,' with a colour of truth, while being wholly misleading.

Among a few tribes in Tanganyika there were plenty who were ready to go for a soldier, and there was no trouble in recruiting among the Nyamwezi, the Hehe, or, in my own Southern Province, the Ngoni of Songea. But the predominant tribe in the districts near the coast and near the border with Portuguese East Africa was the Makonde, who had no sort of military reputation and who proved themselves expert at avoiding service. No use in *baraza* to ask the Makonde if they felt no *haya* (shame) at shirking – 'We Makonde have no word for *haya*,' the interpreter would say. Men took to the bush and stayed in the bush. And their Native Authorities sent us their sick, men with gigantic hydroceles dangling between their legs, men with hernias, unfit men who did not mind a long walk to the coast, medical rejection, and a long walk back, all at Government expense. The rate of medical rejection was always high, and I can remember one extreme case when 38 men were sent back out of 40. Of course, the fact was that it was not their war, for a generation later their fellow Makonde on the other side of the Ruvuma River were to fight for years to rid themselves of the Portuguese.

However, we got our quotas of men in the end, and, since Lindi was the gathering point for recruits from all eight districts of the Southern Province, the presence of several hundred men at any one time awaiting medical examination, documentation and then one of our occasional ships dictated a pleasant change in my circumstances. They were housed in what we called the Central Civil Depot, a specially constructed mud-and-wattle encampment 2 miles out of town along the beach, and this establishment I was sent to run. There was plenty of paperwork to meet the Army's requirements, and I had the help of an English-speaking clerk with that. But I was not having the recruits sitting around idle all day, and I kept them busy with the rudiments of drill and discipline, helped by the small police detachment I had with me. Inevitably, given the circumstances of their conscription, there was a steady trickle of desertions, but on the whole the drafts I shipped away were reasonably content.

During the three months or so these agreeable duties lasted I was having my first taste of life in safari conditions, and I took to it. I lived in a small one-roomed mud hut with a coconut-palm-leaf roof, from which just above my head I was one day disconcerted to find a snake dangling, as I lowered a forkful of bacon and egg into my mouth. On another occasion, washed shaved and dressed in the morning, I reached for my pile of copies of *The Times*. My father kept me supplied with these, and all through the war I read one copy a day and did the crossword in it, even though the exigencies of the mail meant that I was sometimes eight months behind. In this instance my hand was checked just in time, as I went for the top copy, by the sight of a malevolent hunting spider perched on it. These incidents aside, I found that in two important respects safari life did not differ from routine domestic life, in that oil-lamps and a 'thunder-box' were part of the scenery on most stations, where we had neither electric light nor domestic running water. It was to be years before I enjoyed these amenities, and I have never since lost my respectful regard for a light switch and a pull-and-let-go.

My British colleagues largely left me to my own devices at the depot. I had no car, and every evening I would make the 2-mile walk along the beach and back by moonlight, with little crabs scattering under my feet, to hear the news at the Club. But during the day I was bound to learn Swahili, and my grasp of the language naturally came on apace. For this reason, and also because we were living cheek by jowl, I got to know my servants very much better. Phillipo was my boy, to use the term now considered opprobrious but which I shall stick with because it was current throughout my time in East Africa, without a touch of offence on either side. He was a tall, dignified fellow, not much older than I, and he, more than anyone, set about educating me in the language. He had the good sense to speak slowly for my benefit and, since he had no word of English, I was compelled to pick it up. For business purposes in a later career I treated myself to a Berlitz course in a foreign tongue; my progress with Phillipo was less concentrated, but the principle was the same – there was no option but to talk the lingo. When I left Lindi, Phillipo was not willing to leave the coast, and we parted company. I did not see him again for nearly thirty years. In December 1971, my wife and I were Nyerere's guests for a fortnight to celebrate ten years of Tanzania's independence. We came out of a banquet in Dar es Salaam on independence night, and among the crowd outside was Phillipo, still tall and handsome and wearing the extra years remarkably well. He had heard I was back in the country and had come to say 'Jambo' and to meet my wife. We embraced with much feeling.

Omari, my cook, was much older, a wisp of a man, but a vigorous personality and by no means too bad a cook. Above all, he was a dab hand at curry, which was about as far as bachelor entertaining was expected to stretch, invariably on a Saturday when work was over and beer could flow. If the curry were good enough, it did not matter that caramel pudding was the only pudding, absolutely the only one, which cooks in bachelor establishments would produce. Omari not only stayed with me in my later postings, but his wife became our first child's *ayah* until Omari died and she reluctantly returned from Arusha to her Lindi home.

Presently a permanent commandant for the depot was dug out of retirement, a house was built for him and a telephone installed, and I went back to the Boma. In due course I saw a lot more of my recruits as they started to return for leave. With their heads full of army teaching that 'the *askari*, as a soldier, is the salt of the earth, tough and a killer of men', a thoroughly ill-disciplined lot they turned out to be. Badly behaved soldiery on leave was a problem everywhere, but most of all in Lindi where they would have to hang about for days, or even weeks, waiting for a boat to return them to their units. Since they treated the Indian clerks with contempt, I used to deal with their pay and rations myself, and more than once I had a fight on my hands, while there were constant incidents in the township to tax the resources of our small police force.

Meanwhile, we used to play at soldiers ourselves, for after the Japanese came into the war we formed a local defence force. The rank and file were mostly loafers from the *pombe* (native beer) market, joining for the sake of the sixpence we paid for each training parade, and on the whole it was as well that we were not required to test them against marauding Japanese. However, at least these diversions took me away on a couple of courses. The first, in Dar es Salaam, was memorable only for the instructing sergeant blowing a large hole in our gymnasium wall with an Italian anti-tank rifle with which I presumed he was not familiar. But the other course took me to the Kenya Highlands, where the country and the teeming game one saw from the train on the way were enchanting to anyone who had seen no more of East Africa than a strip of dreary coastline. Getting back was quite complicated. At Nairobi, for a start, I was put in charge of the troop train on which I was to travel. I had been required by the authorities to travel in uniform and on military rail warrants, and it proved useless to protest that I was really a civilian and was not going through to Mombasa, but getting off at Voi. I was the only officer travelling and I was to be in charge, and that was that. The responsibilities would have been minimal if some of the soldiers had not started blazing away at antelope grazing nearby, while the train was halted to take on water. Reasoning that if the authorities in Nairobi took me for the real thing, so might the soldiers, I took names and numbers. I did nothing with them, but the firing stopped. Voi, on the Nairobi–Mombasa line, was the junction with a spur connecting with our own northern line from the port of Tanga to Arusha. I had to take whatever was on offer, which proved to be the guard's van on a goods train, designed like a vacuum cleaner. I have been as dusty since, but not often. Eventually I got to Korogwe and its filthy hotel, where I passed the night with bed bugs and the mosquitoes which made a happy passage through the rents in my net. Nowadays the railway runs from Korogwe to Morogoro on the central line, but at this time the connection between the two systems was by an atrocious dirt road. The day before had been all dust. This one was all mud, for the heavens opened and it took 12 hours to cover the 120 miles of our journey. Even the company of two delicious Greek girls did not make up for the toil as the male passengers put their shoulders to it time and again to heave our lorry out of the ditch and to get something, anything, under the spinning wheels to give them grip.

By this time Cecil Stiebel had been posted elsewhere and I had a new DC, but not before he had provided us with yet one more anecdote about his style of life. A quinine injection in his backside had gone wrong, and the local medical officer decided that the resultant lump must be excised. This called for anaesthetic, but Cecil, with a show of bravado, declined to have it administered. He bore the painful little operation very well, stifling any groans with heavy puffs on a cigarette. Looking for somewhere to pitch the stub, he spotted a slop basin and cast it in, and proceedings were promptly disturbed by a sheet of flame from a residue of ether in the bucket. The rest of us suspected that Cecil, extraordinarily tough as he was, was not just demonstrating the fact. In a hard-drinking service he was outstanding, and it was commonly believed that on this account he was not amenable to the anaesthetics of the day.

Cecil's wife was not with him in Lindi, and when I next saw him, some years later, there had been a divorce and he had a new one. She was affectionately known to him as 'the dik-dik', after the tiny antelope. She was indeed minute, and as quiet and demure as he was rowdy and rough, but her dominion over him was absolute and effortless.

His successor, C.B. Wilkins, left little mark – indeed he is only really memorable to me for his prodigious capacity to snore. Our houses were all very open to whatever breezes might blow, and they were fairly close together, so this capacity was by no means a private vice. The palm trees shook, mosquito gauze rattled, birds took wing when Wilkins slept. No wonder his wife seemed harried and intense. Yet I remember him kindly, because quite soon he began to let me loose on safari. Before that, however, I had had one or two day trips with departmental officers, one which sticks in my mind being with my close friend Harold Gillman, always known as Gilly. This was on a visit to the liwali of Mingoyo, and I had some fairly detailed instructions from the DC as to the matters to be raised with him. By this time I had mastered the basic structure of Swahili and, knowing what I needed to talk about, some hard swotting the previous night had produced what struck me as quite a good speech. Indeed it went down very well. I was impressed. Gilly was impressed. So was the liwali, but of course the wretched man launched into a torrent of cross-examination and I was undone. Gilly to the rescue!

Touring was the mainspring of effective district administration, listening to the people, talking to the people, transacting as much business as possible on the spot instead of compelling clients to come in to the Boma to bring us their troubles. Foot safari was best of all, for it provided intimate accessibility on the march as well as in camp, and I managed a good deal of touring on foot in the next few years. But even then the foot safari was a declining practice, and it declined much faster as motor transport slowly became freely available after the war. But what really transformed the nature of touring was the advent of four-wheel drive. In the wet season, before Land Rovers were with us in plenty from about 1950 onwards, one struggled along main roads or one walked. But, once one could get anywhere at any time, a new dimension was added to administration. It was good in a way: much more could get done, and in all one saw far more people. But it was a pity: a certain closeness was lost, and too many saw us as birds of passage covering them with dust or mud according to season.

By this stage in my cadetship I was modestly useful on safari. The DC, to our Africans, was the 'Bwana DC', but his number two, or, in my case, his number three, was the 'Bwana Shauri'. '*Shauri*' is one of many useful omnibus words in Swahili, meaning 'business', 'affairs', 'complaint' or 'trouble', according to taste, and I could now deal with, or at least pursue, the petty *shauris* which mean so much to many peasants, usually accusations against the local headman or Sub-chief to whom in the ordinary way the complainant would look for redress of grievance. Then there would be road work to be inspected, native court records to be examined, the old and infirm to be exempted from tax, the state of the crops to be assessed, perhaps above all the endless gossip to be indulged, for chatting gave one the people's mood.

There were excitements from time to time. I was on foot safari once, with my twenty or so porters strung out in a long file behind me, passing through tall grass at the height of the dry season, when we were all but enveloped by fire. On another occasion I was travelling in the rolling, lightly wooded country inland, and was about to have my tent pitched in a glade outside a village when the local people gave emphatic warning of a man-eating lion in the neighbourhood. So I made camp in the middle of the village square and passed a good night; but there in the morning were the pug marks of a lion entering the tent and then retreating from it, not the first time a sleeper has been grateful for an animal's suspicions of what may be concealed under a mosquito net.

Lions throughout this area tended to be man-eaters, chiefly because there was relatively little game for them to prey on, and partly, it was said, because the lion population of 1905 had become accustomed to human flesh in the slaughter of the Maji-Maji rebellion, with the taste being passed on to succeeding generations. Certainly the Southern Province had been the main centre of the rebellion and had suffered accordingly in the Germans' ferocious suppression of it. At all events man-eaters were by no means uncommon, and the local people had evolved a drill for them. Where a lion had made a kill and was sleeping off its meal in a known spot, the word would go out and, in that fairly densely populated countryside, a crowd of men would throw a stockade, sometimes astonishingly extensive, around the area, and then they would send for help. Two or three years previously just such an appeal had come in to C.P. Lyons, then the DC in neighbouring Mikindani. He got to the scene that evening and entered the stockade with a local tribesman leading a goat. They found themselves a tree. It was a slim tree and C.P. was a big man, but it was the best tree they had, so they tethered the goat nearby and up the tree they both climbed. Darkness fell, and ants attacked them so painfully that the African was disposed to come down until a low growl inclined him otherwise. Presently there was a roar and a rush and the goat went down. C.P. switched on the torch lashed along his rifle barrel, saw with a shock that there was more than one lion on the kill, and fired, but the concussion extinguished the torch. There followed an interminable night, full of sinister growls and rustles. Dawn revealed a dead lion and a dead goat, but nothing else stirred. Infinitely cautiously the two men edged their way out. C.P. sent for reinforcements in the shape of his DO, and the two of them in due course accounted for another half dozen lion within that same stockade.

East Africa had a very full share of hard-bitten and eccentric characters. Now that elephant poaching across the Ruvuma in Portuguese East Africa was a thing of the past, we did not see many of them in the Southern Province, but there were one or two. C.J.P. Ionides,[7] the 'Snake Man', would walk into Lindi once a year from Liwale, where he was game ranger. He was very deaf, but more or less deaf according to his taste for his company. In any event we saw little of him. He would buy, or order, his stores for a year ahead, come into the Club bar for a drink or two, and walk the hundred miles back to Liwale. Then there was 'Dynamite Dan' Eldridge, whose nickname dated from ordering drinks on the Lupa goldfields with a stick of explosive in one hand and a lighted fuse in the other. He had been poaching on the Ruvuma a generation back in German days; but later on I was to learn much more about that from another engaging rascal. 'Dynamite Dan', whom we were by then employing

– because by that stage of the war everybody was employed for something or other – was best remembered for shooting his cook and being acquitted of murder. He had heard a scuttling outside his tent, claimed he thought it was a hyena, shot and killed the man. The cook was known to have a pretty wife.

A character of a very different sort was Thomas Marealle,[8] who came to the Lindi Boma as a clerk. He was the first sophisticated young African I had met, a Chagga tribesman from Kilimanjaro. Tom was to play a prominent part in the territory's affairs in the fifties, and even more in Chagga affairs, since he was elected Paramount Chief in 1952. But despite an early taste for politics when he was a government servant, his chiefly position, once he had acquired it, prevented him coming to terms with the TANU nationalists, and he was eventually swept from office. All this lay in the future, but during the war he became the first Tanganyikan to be sent by the Government for a course at an English university. I was able to help him with introductions, including one to my father. He was grateful and was a faithful correspondent, and I was amused to trace the growing sophistication in his letters by slow gradations from 'your loving son, Thomas Marealle' in the first to 'Yours, Tom' in the last.

Having written of the African peasantry as a largely cashless society, I should mention what remarkably little need of the stuff we ourselves felt at that time. I spent my two years as a cadet in Lindi on £350 a year, and for a lot of that time £10 a month went home to pay off the last of my Oxford debts and my military tailor, and yet I never felt hard up. This was chiefly because there was so little to buy in the shops, and what there was was kept cheap by a surprisingly effective system of price control. On safari a sheep or a goat was to be had for a couple of shillings and it was hard to persuade anyone to take money at all for a chicken or eggs or some mangoes. I probably paid Phillipo 25 shillings a month and Omari, the cook, 30, though with servants there was always an unacknowledged understanding that a 'reasonable' proportion of your food went to them too.

By the middle of 1943 my two probationary years as a cadet were up, and, with Swahili and law examinations behind me, I was a proper Bwana Shauri. It was decided I was due for a change of scene, and I was posted to Shinyanga, a thousand miles away in the Lake Province.

3

SHINYANGA

Bridge and Bols gin with the Dutch Captain and officers during a rough passage on the coaster, the *Tayari*, took me to Dar es Salaam and the central railway line for Shinyanga. This was the railway by which the Germans had bisected the country from the east to Kigoma on Lake Tanganyika in the west. I used to enjoy my train journeys. Old-fashioned puffers drew us, stopping from time to time to replenish wood and water for the boilers. There was plenty of dust, and the scenery was hardly uplifting, for much of the way was through dense, waterless thorn bush. But even that could fire the imagination, as one marvelled at the skill and determination with which the Germans had driven the railway through, with the limited resources and wholly untrained labour available to them.

However, I was never in all my time to get as far as the central railway's western terminal, for Shinyanga lay on the long northward spur of the railway, built by the British from Tabora to Mwanza on Lake Victoria. Sukumaland, where I was to be stationed for the last four years of this six-year tour of duty, then comprised the four districts of Mwanza, Kwimba, Shinyanga and Maswa. Mwanza, prettily situated on the shore of the lake, was a very large station, being the headquarters of the whole of the extensive Lake Province. As time passed, I made many friends there, and it was a congenial place to pass the Easter and Christmas holidays on occasion. But my postings were to be in Shinyanga, the most southerly of the four, and in due course Maswa, the most easterly, stretching away into Masai country.

I took my first look at Shinyanga and felt that after two years in Lindi I might have done better. It was a squalid, dusty little place, with barely a tree to be seen. The official houses were British PWD rather than the higher, deep-verandahed German houses which made up the best of those in Lindi. There was a large, sandy square in the centre of the little township, bounded by shabby, little shops and houses. They included a single general store catering for us officials, where Sulemani, a genial and astute Indian, maintained a good business despite all the difficulties of wartime trading. There was a tennis court for recreation, so that in retrospect the meagre resources of the Lindi Club seemed lavish. Indeed, Shinyanga's social centre was perhaps the railway station. Twice a week the train from Dar es Salaam would make a long stop there and we would gather to collect library books, cases of beer, and to have a drink in the dining car. The Greek chief steward was a friend to everyone along the line. He was, or rather had been, a tremendous gambler, like so many of his countrymen. For this reason it was better to meet him over a glass in Shinyanga, when he was always happy, than it was to travel with him on the central line, for somewhere near Morogoro he could not fail to catch sight of the sisal estate and its handsome house which he had lost at poker. Gloom would fall.

Merely looking at the station, then, might have made me feel that everything had changed for the worse, apart from the difficult decision as to whether Lindi's heat and humidity was better or worse than the dry heat of the Sukuma savannah. This was not at all the case. From the start, now that I had a grounding in my trade, there were clear jobs to be done which I could understand and do something about. Then, although to begin with the only other British on the station were my DC and his family, there was none of the extreme isolation that characterised Lindi. The railway brought visitors from north and south, provincial staff came frequently on tour, but above all there were a variety of other European communities in the district, with a good deal of social interchange between them all. Close by, at Lubaga, Alex Prentice ran experimental cotton plantations. There were missions of various persuasions, and perhaps above all there were the rapidly developing mines at Mwadui, where diamonds in quantity had just been discovered.

The Tsetse Department had their headquarters, with a scientific staff of six or seven, at Old Shinyanga a few miles away. The tsetse fly would not normally have been much trouble in a heavily populated district like Shinyanga, where it was easy to call out the people and eliminate the fly by cutting down the bush which harboured it. However, it was the department's duty to seek means of getting rid of this pest which did not rely on the easy availability of manpower, for that resource was not forthcoming in most areas of Tanganyika where tsetse-borne trypanosomiasis made it impossible to keep livestock. The department thus required blocks of fly-infested bush to be retained in country where it could easily have been cut down, so that scientists could experiment with more economical clearing methods, such as rendering the insect infertile or clearing only certain sorts of bush. Not surprisingly, this policy was much resented by Native Authorities and was a constant source of complaint to the Administration.

There were about a million Sukuma at this time, making them, together with the closely related Nyamwezi to the south, much the biggest tribal group in Tanganyika. Some two hundred thousand of them lived in Shinyanga District, which was mostly heavily cultivated and grazed steppe, getting on for 4000 feet above sea level. Everywhere the eye lit on those remarkable granite outcrops which Stanley[1] had remarked as distinctive of Sukuma country when he passed through in 1875. But the countryside in Shinyanga never appealed to me as it did to him. True, it must have been in much better heart then that it was in my two famine-stricken years, but it lacked the woods and the spaciousness which I was to find in Maswa. But the people were bright and engaging, and a pleasure to work among.

The Sukuma were farmers first and foremost, with millet and maize as their staple food crops, cassava as drought-resistant provision against shortage, and cotton as a cash crop. But they were also cattle-owners, there being at the time about twice as many head of cattle as there were people. Much of the land was good and fertile, but the lack of rain and density of people in many places were creating dusty scars, and the need to spread the populace over the land was clear, but to do that watering places were essential and so was space, and space was lacking in Shinyanga. It was not until I came into the much larger district of Maswa later on that I was able to participate in a deliberate effort to make more land available to ease the pressure on the fertility of overcrowded soil.

Even in the relatively easy-going days before the war there had been close investigation of the way the Sukuma managed their land, and a lot was known of how their agricultural practices might be improved and overstocking of cattle reduced. This was reflected in Native Authority legislation, which was largely directed at agricultural improvement. There was insistence on the laborious business of making ties of earth at intervals between ridges as the people cultivated, so that the resulting bowls would hold water when the rains fell. There were attempts to prevent cattle trampling the fields into dust by feeding on crop residues after harvest. There were provisions against the parasitic striga weed. All this went well or not so well according to the strength and authority of the Chief. All of it was good common sense. All of it was the first thing to come under attack from nationalists as a colonial imposition, enforced by toady Chiefs upon the people. I wonder, do the farmers tie-ridge now in Sukumaland or is erosion let rip?

But, as elsewhere, such problems in 1943 and 1944 took second place to supporting the war effort and operating all the essential wartime controls. So, when we persuaded the people to sell their cattle, it was to provide bully beef for the Middle East and not to reduce cattle densities for their own good. And in any case, we had a famine on our hands, and to begin with there were only Colin Macpherson, the DC, and I in the Boma, although in due course we had our agricultural officer restored to the district, and a cattle buyer from Liebig's[2] was sent to us.

Colin was as straight and decent as people come. He was also almost as solemn as his Irish wife, Violet, was witty and gay. They had two daughters with a full ten years between them, and since they were infinitely kind and hospitable their bachelor DO was soon very much part of the household. But I got no more formal guidance from Colin than from either of my DCs in Lindi. The only piece of information that I can recall came as we were walking away from the Boma one evening, and he suddenly stopped and said, 'I must tell you. I really must tell you.' I stood transfixed. What frightful error had I committed? 'You simply must keep the racket head higher on your forehand,' and he demonstrated before we walked on.

Other friends were the Findlays, Victor and Bunny, at Old Shinyanga. He was well known as a big-game hunter, and I took every opportunity to pick his brains on the subject, since my thoughts were beginning to turn in that direction, though Shinyanga District held out no prospects. But our shared interest was in Napoleonic history, and I made full use of his distinguished library. After I was posted to Maswa and had not seen them for some months, it happened that I was in Mwanza for some weekend jollification, where Bunny was waiting one evening for Victor to join her from safari. Alas, I was in her company when news came of his death. It was an old story, a rhino wounded at the first shot, a determined pursuit into heavy bush, the fatal charge. It was just as well that I was there that sorrowful night, for poor Bunny was otherwise among strangers.

Dave, the Indian sub-assistant surgeon, looked after our little hospital. Thanks to him, I made up slightly for one of Lindi's many deprivations, bridge. He had a couple of friends who ran the largest store in Mwanza, and they would come to stay with him once or twice a month, when we would make up rather a high-class four. And the conversation was good and lively, almost entirely devoted to Indian politics and, on their part, the sinfulness of colonialism; and when the venue was Dr Dave's house rather than mine the Indian food was equally good and it made me a lifelong devotee. I had a regular New Year's Day tryst with Dave. On all stations, boards were appointed to account for all Government stores. Most of these were awful chores, but the hospital board everywhere was ameliorated by a popular tradition that the champagne stock, held at all hospitals then as the only alleviation of blackwater fever, must be tested to be sure it had not gone flat or otherwise deteriorated. Colin and I had to share all boards between us, and fortunately he was at that time teetotal. I always did the hospital, and I am glad to recall the champagne was always in good condition.

The Native Authorities in Sukumaland were very different from those in Lindi. Here were no appointed headmen, but powerful Chiefs, heirs to a substantial tradition. There were 14 Chiefs in Shinyanga District and, though they varied greatly in ability and in standards of integrity, they could never be taken lightly. Little could they have dreamt that their future authority was to be as brief as our own: Nyerere was to blow all the territory's Chiefs away like chaff before independence came. Nevertheless, so long as we believed, as we did, in working through indigenous institutions, in the Chiefs of Sukumaland, as in many other parts of the country, we had institutions of substance. The Chiefs in theory owned all the land, but there were many indigenous checks and balances; and, quite apart from the ultimate authority of Government, no bad Sukuma Chief would get away with too much for too long without his own people calling him to account. Chiefs of course might offend us, the immediate administrators, by weakness, ineffectiveness or persistent drunkenness, none of which vices would necessarily trouble their immediate subjects; and to get rid of a bad Chief for such reasons was by no means easy. They were not to be dismissed at a wave of the hand: the PC at least would be involved, and sometimes the highest reaches of Government.

Indeed, there was an example of the implications of dethroning an important Chief living in the Shinyanga District. Saidi Fundikira had been leader of the Nyamwezi to the south of us, and he had been Sir Donald Cameron's star when that great Governor brought Indirect Rule to Tanganyika from Nigeria. As the tale went, at a great *baraza* at Tabora in 1929, Sir Donald had shaken Fundikira by the hand and said before the assembled thousands, 'I am proud to call this man my friend.' A few weeks later he was found to have made away with £14,000 of Native Treasury money, a great sum in those days. No criminal proceedings were ever taken, presumably for reasons of what one may term decorum, but he was deposed and exiled to Bagamoyo on the coast. When the war came, Fundikira's German sympathies – many Chiefs had nostalgic memories of the simplicities of authoritarianism and the *sjambok* – suggested that he would be better isolated far inland, and his place of exile was fixed at Lohumbo on the railway line in the south of my district. This proved a nuisance, though not for the sort of reason anybody had in mind when he was sent there. The PC was Geoff Webster, Uncle Geoff, a most kindly soul and an old friend of this engaging villain. Fundikira, having been convicted of no offence, was in receipt of a respectable pension, but he was used to high living and from time to time ran short of cash. Nothing was easier than for him to jump on the train and repair to Uncle Geoff. A few days later I would get a telephone call from the PC. Could I deduct £20 from Saidi's pension that month and send it back to Uncle Geoff to repay his loan. 'Yes, of course.' With great diffidence, 'Excuse me, Sir, but Saidi is not allowed out of Lohumbo without permission.' 'Oh well, Meek, I've known him for years...'

Saidi Fundikira, apart from being remarkably good company, was interesting to me because of his Arab cast of countenance. A number of the chiefly families among the Sukuma and the Nyamwezi showed in their faces, and sometimes in their lighter colour, that they were originally outsiders, Arab in this case but more usually of Hamitic stock from Uganda or north-west Tanganyika. A predilection for stranger Chiefs made sense. A new Chief would have to be found as groups of Sukuma moved into fresh country and there would be a much better chance of impartiality in the allocation of land and stock from an outsider than from one of the local families.

Corruption in the important Tabora chiefdom sadly did not end with Fundikira's exile. In 1957 the son who had succeeded him shot himself as police were moving in to arrest him for embezzlement. He was then succeeded by a friend of mine. This was Abdullah Saidi Fundikira,[3] and our paths crossed many times. I knew him in Maswa District as an agricultural officer, the first Makerere graduate to be appointed to our civil service. We started badly, with a stupidly touchy row of the type which characterised the period of adjustment we were all entering upon. I had sent Abdullah a note, addressed to him by surname alone, as was the convention among my British colleagues at the time. Back it came with its answer at the foot, but with 'Mr' inserted before his own name and underlined several times. We had words. But we became friends in 1953 when we were together at Cambridge for a fortnight on a course on local government in the colonies. I was later to have dealings with him on the Chiefs' Convention and in the Council of Ministers in the run-up to independence.

When I arrived in Shinyanga, by far the most important Chief was Makwaia of Usiha, who presided over the Shinyanga federation of Chiefs which made up the district's supreme Native Authority. He had a counterpart in Maswa in the person of Chief Majebere of Mwagalla, and the two were rivals in the moves that were being tentatively made towards a federation to embrace all four of the Sukuma districts. Both were men of the old school, of no education, great common sense, vast experience and commanding personality. There had been a recent attempt at reconciliation between these two powerful characters, in the furtherance of which Makwaia had married off a daughter to Majabere; but she was an educated girl who soon ran away, leaving relations between them worse than ever.

However, soon after I came on the scene this rivalry was ended by Makwaia's death. The old man was a Muslim and had left a number of sons, more than one of whom had pretensions to the succession and a faction to support him. The power of the *Serikali*, was always decisive in a disputed election, but we set great store on securing the full backing of the elders for a candidate, and much lobbying on our part followed. In fact I doubt if the lobbying was needed, except that discussion gave pleasure to the elders, for both character and education made the claims of Kidaha Makwaia[4] outstanding. Here was another product of Tabora School, Tanganyika's Eton, which catered particularly for the sons of Chiefs, and of the University College at Makerere in Uganda, where he had just completed his second year. Here was just the sort of progressive, well-mannered, aristocratic young man we were delighted to deal with, and it soon became clear that the elders were of the same opinion.

In fact, Kidaha's career to independence was a sad one in many ways. He proved as good and progressive a Chief as we had hoped, but some years later he resigned the office. Then we ourselves pushed everything his way: first African on the Legislative Council, first on the Executive Council, then in the fifties membership of the Royal Commission on Land and Population, all of which stamped him as the favoured son of Government and in due course prejudiced his position with the nationalists. Nor could he ever bring himself to throw in his lot wholeheartedly with TANU. 'Our Hamlet' was Nyerere's apt description of him. As far as Nyerere was concerned, he was never more than on the fringe, and the wrong fringe, of the eventual struggle for power, and he rapidly faded from political significance.

Shinyanga was in the grip of famine when I got there, as it was to be again in the following year. Failure of the rains was something to be dreaded when war made outside help difficult or impossible to get and when, for the same reason, transport was so badly impaired. But we managed pretty well and, though people went hungry, nobody died. We had our main food depots in godowns[5] at the railway stations, whence trucks would shift supplies to the affected chiefdoms, and after that transport was by donkeys or porterage. At numerous *barazas* Colin and I would stress that this food was free, and that knowledge reduced the peculation that assuredly went on, as did the rough checks on the distribution system that we constantly made on safari. On the whole it worked, but success in distributing famine relief had its own dangers. People knew that a kindly *Serikali* would not let them starve; and among the indolent this confidence did not encourage timely planting for the next season's crop. Neglect to plant was an offence chargeable in the native court, but a fine in the court weeks after the planting season was over would do nothing whatever to reduce the risk of food shortage next year. Most good administrators and all the local headmen believed in a spot of rough, immediate justice when the planting season was on and a farmer was drinking *pombe* by his unturned field.

Famine relief meant much safari, and I was soon on terms with Chiefs and headmen all over the district. They varied greatly in style and ability. Shoka of Uduhe lived in a European style of house, and his wife, who was as charming as he was, always insisted on a formal tea party, short of cucumber sandwiches maybe, but basically the authentic ceremony. Kapella of Tinde, on the other hand, lived the life of his forefathers. Unfortunately, his only son, Massanja, was a bad hat. He traded in *moshi*, the lethal, local bootleg spirit, he had fields of *bhang*, above all he was a master of *fitina*, the peculiarly African compound of plotting, intrigue and stirring things up. One day Chief Kapella had not long left me after an interview in the Boma, when an excited messenger rushed in to say that his lorry had overturned and the old man was dead. Were we to be landed with Massanja as successor? I made my way to the scene, to find the lorry in the ditch, a man with a broken neck alongside it and beyond him the still figure of Kapella. But I no sooner approached than the old fellow, frail at the best of times, sat up, and in due course stood up, apparently none the worse, and I put the problem of Massanja away for another day.

No two days in African administration were ever alike, and there was plenty of diversion in Shinyanga. Much of this was provided by Violet Macpherson, who had become an important part of the Boma team. From an office adjoining mine she dispensed all the various permits for war-rationed goods, petrol, tyres, flour, cloth, liquor and so on. This was by no means the boring task it may sound, for the controls she was exercising were over the lifeblood of every store and shop in the district, and a great deal of heat could be generated over allocations between one trader and another, so that from time to time I had to go to her rescue. But there was one occasion when she had to come to mine. Somali cattle traders were considerable buyers on our markets and were continually on the move around the district.

They are very handsome people, and one afternoon my door was unceremoniously burst open by a stunningly pretty Somali girl. Eyes flashing, she poured out a torrent of complaint about the thrashing she had had from her husband. I tried unavailingly to soothe her and direct her to the native court, which Somalis tended to regard as below their very considerable dignity. Feeling I was insufficiently impressed with what had been done to her, she abruptly turned her back, bent forward, flung over her head a cascade of white cotton skirts, and exposed to eyes by no means unimpressed her mangled but comely behind. This was no situation for the entry of a pursuing husband, and I let out a yell for Violet.

Shinyanga was at this time a focus of interest all over East Africa, because diamonds had been discovered on a large scale at Mwadui some 20 miles away. There were plenty of indications that the area might be diamond-bearing, so that there had been a lot of prospecting over the years. One of these prospectors was a Canadian geologist, Dr Williamson.[6] He was originally working for a large company, but he hung on when the company and other prospectors had all dropped out. He was more or less broke, and at times almost starving; indeed he could not have carried on if he had not been grub-staked by Sulemani, the Indian trader in Shinyanga, who was in due course well rewarded for his faith. Eventually Williamson's persistence was justified, he found diamonds, and by the time of my arrival the mine was being developed at frenetic speed considering the extraordinary wartime difficulties of getting equipment and transporting it to so remote a place.

To begin with I was on friendly terms with the mine management, sufficiently so to have sold Williamson a valuable shot-gun to finance a local leave. I can remember too being out at the mine on business one day when Williamson, in his cups as he frequently was, elected to show me the previous day's takings. Opening an old cigarette tin full of diamonds, he scattered them across the billiard table. At that moment the telephone rang outside, and without a glance he marched out to take the call, leaving me, somewhat unnerved, to stare at this scattered and unchecked fortune.

Illicit diamond broking, IDB, was bound to be a problem from the start. Recovery systems in those days were simple and manual, giving every opportunity for theft and concealment, while techniques of checking and searching had none of the sophistication that I saw when I returned to the mine as Government director many years later. Additionally, there was a much smaller mine alongside Williamson's, and nearby an ex-jockey from Johannesburg claimed to be sitting on a diamondiferous pipe. So there were easy outlets for diamonds, and the Sukuma soon realised they were onto a good thing. In short, there was a serious security problem, and at that stage few ideas as to how to deal with it.

One April day Colin and I were brought a disturbing story by a Mwadui mineworker. In the previous month a gardener called Zolo was said to have had his house and person searched for diamonds by Sackville Scott, the mine manager, and a group of mine *askari*, in Williamson's presence. Scott, when nothing incriminating was found, had hit the man and kicked him. He then had him stripped of his trousers, put down on the ground and given, it was said, something like a hundred strokes with a hippo-hide whip, Scott stopping proceedings at some point to rub salt in Zolo's bleeding wounds. The man was in a very poor way for a couple of days, but Scott, perhaps not surprisingly, refused transport to take him to Shinyanga hospital. But ten days later he was sufficiently recovered to make himself scarce to Tabora, his home, paid of course to do so and escorted by a couple of *askari* from the mine to see him onto the train without any chance of his coming to us in the Boma.

I held relaxed views, which are highly unfashionable today, about a modest use of corporal punishment where an immediate effect is wanted, as I have indicated, but this tale appalled me. If it were true that there had been quite so brutal an assault on mere suspicion and without a tittle of evidence, here was something to make the gorge rise. But was it true, and could we even find a complainant? As luck would have it, our hearing this story coincided with the arrival of Major Scarth, the very experienced labour officer from Tabora, on a visit to Mwadui. We briefed him and sent with him our senior policeman, the honest and sensible Sub-Inspector Amri. When they came back a few days later, Scarth was convinced of the story's truth, and determined to find Zolo at Tabora, while Amri was armed with an impressively convincing set of statements from witnesses of the beating.

By the time this affair moved on it happened that I was on my own in Shinyanga. Since no one could take home leave during the year, officers, after a certain period, were sent on so-called special leave, either to Kashmir or to South Africa, for three months, and Colin had taken his family off to the latter. I was much too junior – still only one off the bottom of the staff list – to be gazetted as DC, so Shirley Hopkin from Maswa, of whom more anon, became for the time being DC of both districts. But he left me almost entirely alone, and I was on my own when Scarth came up trumps and sent me the injured party, Zolo, from Tabora. I promptly installed him in the police cantonment, where he would have at least some protection from whoever might try to get at him. The state of his backside said all that was necessary about his beating.

Looking back with the worldly-wise eyes of later, how naive I was, at rising 24, to suppose that this could ever be handled as what it was, a straightforward case of assault against Williamson, Scott and the *askari* who had used the whip. But I had the sense to realise that things were likely to go wrong unless the case was handled urgently, and I proposed to summon all three men to my court in the following week. But here I struck a snag. There was bound to be a skilled Nairobi lawyer defending, and Sub-Inspector Amri could not be expected to cope with him. So I really had no choice but to ring up the Superintendent at Mwanza and ask for the loan of an experienced prosecutor. Of course the cat was now out of the bag. Within half an hour Uncle Geoff was on the telephone. How could I take the case when, as officer in charge of police, I had had a hand in framing the prosecution case? I saw no force in that and said so, for this was a dilemma which frequently arose and we were trained to wear our two hats quite separately. Well, it was invidious for me when I knew the parties so well. Yes, it was, but that was my bad luck, and I rubbed in the need for speed when all the essential witnesses were employees on the mine and open to pressure. 'I will send our resident magistrate, and there won't be any delay.' 'Very well, Sir.'

Of course there were delays on one specious excuse or another. Weeks went by, and I exercised my right to protest direct to the Chief Secretary in Dar es Salaam. All that happened was that Sub-Inspector Amri was transferred to Kilwa, about as far from Shinyanga as could be. Gavin Faringdon, a Fabian peer on an official visit to see how we ran a League of Nations mandate, stayed with me for a few days and I enlisted his help. (Lord Faringdon[7] had recently been on a parliamentary delegation to Moscow, and I looked forward eagerly to slaking my thirst for firsthand news from Russia. 'Moscow?' he said. 'We went to the ballet. Charming, but charming.' Thus was encapsulated the entire struggle of the Red Army.) He was a decent chap, and I have no doubt did his best in Dar, to no avail. He acquired a mistaken impression that I was, like him, opposed in principle to all corporal punishment, which produced a desultory correspondence until I returned to England in 1947 and he repaid my hospitality with an old-fashioned country-house weekend – except that the other guests were mostly Labour ministers and the entertainment was opera at Swindon rather than field sports.

My final effort was made when the Governor, Sir Wilfred Jackson, was halting at Shinyanga on his way to Mwanza and I solicited an interview. Colin, now back from his leave, escorted me to the august presence and I delivered my complaint. 'My boy, the law will take its course.' And so it did in November, five months after I had been ready to proceed. By then every witness of any consequence had been got at, with the Indian medical witness happy to testify that Zolo's injuries could have been caused by the poor fellow sitting on something sharp. But it was established that an assault had taken place, for the wretched *askari* was fined 40 shillings, while Williamson and Scott were acquitted. Zolo too must have given the defence good value, for on his return to Tabora he was able to blossom out in new suits and hats and shoes. I never lost my youthful disgust at this shoddy affair. But at least we now got a strong police presence at the mine, which both improved security against IDB and insured against such atrocious behaviour recurring. But my own relations with the people at the mine were far from cordial thenceforth.

In August, Shirley Hopkin was to take his own special leave and I went to take over Maswa for a couple of months. Handing over took four or five days, and I appreciated the opportunity of observing one of the last eccentrics in our service. He only worked for about three hours a day. In the early morning, feet on desk, he would read the latest consignment of newspapers from home. In the afternoon, he had better things to do than show up at the Boma at all. But between ten in the morning and lunch everyone knew who was DC. He had a strong personality, a sharp tongue, an acid pen and a mischievous sense of humour, so that the more pompous of his colleagues found him a bad man to tangle with. He was overdue for retirement, but was soldiering on while the war continued; when it ended, he was stationed at Bagamoyo on the coast and, the story went, he thereupon motored into Dar es Salaam, handed the Boma keys to the PC and departed. Shirley had an astounding appetite for women, but not for the white variety, whom for the most part he cordially detested. It was just as well, therefore, that he had been on bush stations all his service, where he could indulge himself without having to put up with the social round associated with the *memsahibs*. Not surprisingly, the territory was spangled with his bastards, about whose progress and well-being at school or in work or in matrimony he pursued a wide correspondence, and about whom he was only too ready to chat with his companion of the moment. But in other ways he could be a very private man. He and I both liked to walk around the station in the hour before sundown, but for him this had to be a solitary indulgence, and one looked away on any chance encounters. Come sundown, all this changed and he was an exceptionally amusing drinking companion, as we foregathered at his house or at mine.

There had been several drinks taken one night on the broad open stone verandah that jutted out from the front of the DC's house when we were interrupted by a swishing sound. Peering into the shadows, the source was identified as a night adder making its way towards us across the rush mats. I grabbed my bull terrier, the snake coiled itself up and considered us, and we stood up and shouted for his servant, Musa, who in due course produced Shirley's gun. Somewhat tipsily he took aim, but decided the Dietz oil lamp was too far away. 'Closer, boy, closer. No, closer than that.' The reluctant Musa inched it to within a foot of the still-passive snake. All was ready at last, and Shirley fired. The light went out, and with one accord he and I and the servants cleared the verandah wall into the night. Cautious reconnaissance presently revealed a dead night adder beside the shattered lamp, but whether it was slain by shot or by splinters was questionable.

Maswa was a splendid district, but my couple of months was spent quietly enough in getting to know the people and the country, very useful occupations as it turned out when I was posted there in 1945. Shirley returned and I went back to Shinyanga, not without getting stuck for five hours in the flooded Manonga River. That taught me a lesson, as the sun burnt the tender skin behind my knees. I never felt it, with the river flowing over my legs, and by that night I was painfully blistered and in bed with a soaring fever.

More pleasantly, I got back to find Dick Gower in my house. He was being posted to Mwanza, but in my absence life had been particularly hectic for Colin, and Dick had been pulled off the train to plug the gap for the last three or four weeks. This was a great reunion, for I had been Dick's fag at school, where he was captain of every sport, despite the poorest eyesight and a remarkably unathletic physique.[8] As I was on my back with sunstroke, it fell to him to go alone to the Indian tea party given in honour of the Maynards. 'Nangi' Maynard, 'nangi' being the Sukuma word for teacher, and his wife, a doctor, were famous American missionaries with the Africa Inland Mission. At Ibadakuli, some 10 miles away, they had done wonderful things educationally, vocationally, medically. But they had never been back to the States since they came out a quarter of a century before. Leave, or rather Nangi's furlough, as it was always termed, had for years been talked about as something in prospect but which never actually happened. But now they were to go, so the Indians threw their party, and Dick came back to tell me of the highlight, the presentation to Dr Maynard, preceded by long speeches, of a quite valuable trinket in a wooden box. She waved it away. 'No, thank you,' she snapped. 'I don't smoke.'

Misunderstandings about the giving of gifts were a hazard in Tanganyika. When one was on safari, African Chiefs and headmen in most parts would have taken offence if one sought to pay for a few eggs or a scrawny chicken. In the same spirit Indians on their own days of celebration, or on ours, would come along with trays of sweetmeats, which we were expected to accept. But things could go wrong in these simple ceremonies. One Christmas Day an Indian trader turned up at Colin's house with his offering for the DC, and was casually waved in by Violet to the bathroom where Colin, stark naked, was contentedly shaving. I heard the roar from a hundred yards away. Of course there were rules about gifts, as there were about everything, but the essence lay in what was understood in them. Thus a bottle of whisky was in order, provided the Indian trader (Africans had no access to spirits until very much later) was not about to appear before one in court. A bottle of whisky was 'perishable', and 'perishables' could be accepted. But a case of whisky, equally perishable, was not at all legitimate. And from time to time we all had to cope with much more than that. Years later in Mbulu I returned from safari to find my wife admiring various positions in front of the fireplace for two small but handsome Persian rugs. As they would have been the first pretty things we had ever had in the house, she has never forgotten the mortification of their instant return to the Greek farmer who was at that time seeking an extension to his farm.

Dick went on his way, and I settled back into the Shinyanga routine. That routine included, in my spare time, my discussion group. I thought Africans poorly served by the Swahili press of those days, and once a week I had a gathering in my garden open to anyone with an interest in the outside world – Boma clerks, policemen, veterinary guards, agricultural instructors. No topics were off limits, and any views could be discussed. It is strange that this was considered a very radical experiment, and visitors from Mwanza would ask to attend in the sort of tone they might have used if they wanted to come to an orgy. Indeed, at these meetings the stirrings of political thought among these fairly unsophisticated people were clear enough, but for the most part in a very innocent way. Particularly as the war moved towards its close they wanted to know what would follow. They were remarkably well aware of how little Britain had done for the territory in the decade before 1939, first because of the Depression and then because of the possibility of reversion to German control. What was likely to follow this time, when Britain would be exhausted and ruined? And did I think that India would govern itself, and what would happen to the colonies conquered by the Japanese?

Yet there were no high aspirations expressed about an African place in the political scene. They were well enough aware of our general obligation to lead them to self-government somehow at some time, but fortunately, for that was the way I saw it too, they never asked me to offer a little precision to the notion. But they did want to know about prospects for development in general and education in particular, and here at least I could show our good intentions by pointing to the Colonial Development and Welfare Act, passed at the war's darkest days in 1940. There was a touch of much sharper political thinking, though, when Hamsa Mwapachu[9] joined us over the Christmas vacation from Makerere, where he was in his last year. Hamsa was a half-caste. His father had been a Dutch diamond prospector, recently down on his luck. I had him brought in from his camp when his servant reported that he had not long to live, and had him put in my guest house, where I saw him through his last day or two. He was a giant of a man and we had a terrible struggle to get him out of the narrow guest-house door when he died; and I had an even greater struggle at dead of night (one buries people quickly in the tropics) to persuade Nangi Maynard to let him rest in consecrated ground. He was an evil liver in Nangi's book, and I hope I may be forgiven the lies I told. Anyway, though I did not know what sort of bond there was between father and son, this made some sort of tie between Hamsa and me. Unlike his father, Hamsa was a little slip of a man, but brimming with intelligence, and a sharp questioner in my meetings. I never knew it at the time, but he was my first link with Nyerere, for they were both at the centre of the small group of Tanganyikan students at Makerere who were already, albeit not quite deliberately, laying the foundations of the political case against continuing colonial rule.

The foot safari which brought an end to my time in Shinyanga seemed unremarkable. Indeed, it appeared so ordinary that there stays in my memory nothing more than a dust storm blowing my tent down while I was in my hip-bath. The combination of exposed nudity, a wet skin and a great deal of dust is mortifying for the victim, but good for gales of helpless laughter among the African spectators. But when I got back to Shinyanga I felt ill, and soon was very ill. We were well disciplined over prophylactics and mosquito boots, but most of us suffered fairly regular bouts of malaria, and that, to begin with, was what I insisted on being treated for. But when I was finally taken off to Mwanza for more expert medical attention, I turned out to have both typhoid and paratyphoid, no doubt picked up from contaminated water on that same safari.

A liquid diet was then, and for all I know still is, the only treatment for typhoid, and I got bored to tears with milk and beef tea, but it soon transpired that I had been through the worst, untreated, in Shinyanga. One Sunday I was well enough to play truant and take a canoe with a veterinary friend for a picnic on an island in Lake Victoria. This produced a touch of sunstroke and a high temperature that evening, and I had some embarrassing explaining to do to avoid being treated as a relapse. Meanwhile a medical argument was going on to establish how to get me to Dar es Salaam, where alone it could be established that I was clear of infection and not a carrier. So potentially plaguey was I held to be that for a time the experts sounded as though whatever conveyed me there, railway coach or aeroplane, would have to be immediately burnt thereafter. A slightly less dire solution was eventually agreed, namely that I must take my own eating and drinking utensils, and, thus equipped, I set off by train.

In Dar es Salaam I was tested and cleared, and took myself off for a fortnight's sick leave with my old friends from Lindi, the Gillmans, who were now stationed near Tanga. The high spot of that visit was a trip to the lovely hill station of Amani, where the Germans had established a famous botanical station. Alas, it was marred. These were days when a decent bottle of spirits had become harder to lay hands on than ever, and we had rejoiced in somehow procuring a bottle of Gordon's Gin. As we established ourselves in the rest house, I looked out of the windows to see Mbango, my boy, emptying a bottle on the ground. How conscientious, I thought: Mbango knew that bad water had nearly done for his *bwana*, and here he was refusing to put up with any water which had not been boiled and filtered under his own supervision. This of course was exactly what was in the good fellow's mind, and it was not until the last glug of the emptying bottle that Gilly, Rosalind and I realised that we would have to make do with the scenery and no gin.

Back in Shinyanga I had no more to do than pack my kit, say a sad goodbye to the Macphersons, for he was about to retire, and take myself off to Maswa. I was changing places with a friend, Dick Dewar. He was newly wed, and some nosey parker of a colleague had suggested to the PC that Drena, his bride, should not be exposed to the bachelor goings-on in this remote station. It did not, of course, matter what a bachelor was exposed to, so off I went with high delight at the thought of a district I had taken to so keenly the year before.

4

MASWA

When I got to Maswa, Donald Malcolm was in charge, Shirley having for some time been posted away to Bagamoyo. The two men were as different as chalk from cheese, had a cordial dislike of each other, and had taken over districts, one from another, before. On each occasion trifles were employed to demonstrate how different things now were. Office furniture was moved from here to there, whitewashed stones in the forecourt were shifted into different patterns. Africa remained unmoved.

Shirley, as I have related, was the laziest of men, though highly effective in the short daily spell that he devoted to work. Donald on the other hand, never stopped working but largely, as it seemed to me, at the wrong things. He was a splendid amateur combination of architect, draftsman, engineer and builder, and the dams and roads and bridges and houses that he left as his memorials made him worth several times his stipend as a DC. But the ordinary running of his district attracted only a small part of his attention. This suited me well. I was more than happy to get on with the district's day-to-day administration, while he had the fullest scope for his own particular talents. He had had years of experience in Sukumaland and had in 1938 produced an authoritative report on land usage in the whole area, and he had now, after a spell in the Colonial Office, been commissioned to bring that report up to date as a guide for action after the war. Perhaps more importantly, from his point of view, the principle of a federation of all the Sukuma Chiefs as a superior

Native Authority had now been accepted, and a headquarters required to be built for them on a 'green field' site at Malya on the railway line. This was right up Donald's street, and in consequence I did not see him at all for long periods at Nyalikungu, the district headquarters, while he was busy creating at Malya, 30 miles away, a new township, with council chambers, offices, houses and roads. We had a most happy relationship in our respective slots.

I can have wasted little time in getting out and about, for about a month after I arrived I was camped with the Superintendent of Police from Mwanza in a remote spot on the Masai border, presumably in connection with stock theft by those marauders.We were comfortably ensconced by the camp fire that night, with endless space around us, an infinite ceiling of stars above, and no sound except occasional animal calls and quiet African voices at their fire in the background. It was an unlikely setting in which to hear on the wireless the news of Hiroshima.

Peace brought no easing of our burden of work. In a country of some 375,000 square miles, with a population which was probably by then around ten million, the Administration was by 1945 reduced to under two hundred British officers, and departmental services were even more depleted. But on this occasion the Colonial Office did not make the mistake of recruiting anyone who came to hand to fill the gaps in our ranks, as they had done after the First War. They proceeded slowly and methodically to select first-class material from the forces, which was the sound way to do things, but the price was continuing shortages of staff in the field for another three years or so. Meanwhile all the material deprivations of every kind continued or got worse, not only in the stuff of daily life but in transport by sea and air, which was of course devoted all over the world to getting the armies home. Work was in many ways more pressing. The tasks of demobilisation replaced those of recruitment. Bully beef for Britain became necessary instead of bully for the forces in the Middle East, so we still had to struggle with the Chiefs to get the people unwillingly to sell their cattle, their own store of value. And, in addition, in the Maswa District we were starting to find money to spend as a foundation for some of our post-war plans.

These pressures reflected themselves on me in various ways. Perhaps the most obvious was when 'Daisy' Cheyne, who had replaced Geoff Webster as PC, paid an official visit in 1946. By then my tour had lasted five years, in insalubrious districts. I had declined the chance of three months special leave in Kashmir or South Africa, the option exercised by most of my colleagues, because by the time I qualified for it I thought I might prejudice my chances of home leave, so the only respite I had had was three separate fortnights of local and sick leave, and I had had bouts of malaria as well as typhoid and paratyphoid. I was summoned with same formality to the PC's presence: 'Meek, would you mind doing another year?' and he explained all the staffing difficulties throughout the territory which it appeared that only I could alleviate, so persuasive was he. Of course I had no real choice, and I accepted with pardonably good grace, but I thought of that interview in later years when sometimes people jibbed at a month's or a fortnight's delay when their normal 30 months were up.

We were set on greatly improving the quality of Native Authority staff, and in Maswa at this time we had the money to do it. We even secured a Makerere graduate to take charge of the Native Treasury, but for artisans and clerks and senior messengers we plundered the ranks of the returning soldiers to great effect, and we soon had what must have been one of the most efficient local-government machines in Tanganyika.

That was one small local aspect of demobilisation. A much more general one was the extraordinary ease with which, on the whole, the entire operation was completed. Here were tens of thousands of African peasants, plucked only three or four years previously from a life which for most of them was little removed from the Iron Age, taught the use of modern weapons, transported hundreds of miles across a sea they barely knew existed, introduced to new societies, plunged into a war whose origins they could not comprehend; and then they faded back into the bush. Some political activists; sharper questions at *barazas*; a consciousness that Indians, whom they had hitherto known as very, or relatively, rich were mostly as poor as they were; khaki greatcoats and *askari* hats; very soon there seemed little else to show for the exposure to the great, wide world, though perhaps the leaven worked beneath the surface.

We despoiled the Army in another way. We were building Malya, houses at Nyalikungu and dams in the bush, and we could not do so without transport for materials, tools and food, and of this we were desperately short. We persuaded military headquarters at Mwanza that in so large a district we needed trucks to help get the returned soldiers back home, and two were seconded to us with a small detail to run them. We made shameless use of them as two more units in our spare and dilapidated transport, and well they served this purpose until disaster struck. One of them, loaded with building tools, overturned and an unfortunate *askari* was killed. A military court of enquiry into the improper use of the vehicle seemed bound to follow, but at the critical time the headquarters at Mwanza was dissolved and responsibility passed to Tabora; and they had no sooner caught up with the situation than demobilisation overtook them too, and in the end we heard no more. The lorries stayed with us for good.

Maswa had great areas of good land which only needed water to enable the people to move from the overcrowded parts of Sukumaland. Once there was water for people and stock, they would move in and clear the bush which harboured the tsetse fly which killed their cattle. But first the water had to be there, and the Sukuma tribesmen had a splendid system of voluntary and unpaid labour, ten days at a stretch, to build dams and roads and clear bush. Here Donald Malcolm was the perfect DC for them. There would be long discussions and arguments with the Native Authority as to which areas were most suitable to be opened to settlement. The subject was a thorny one, for population meant prestige and pay, and Chiefs were therefore in intense competition with one another; but, in the African tradition, agreement would eventually be reached. In a given year there might be eight dam sites selected, and tracks had to be cleared to them so that wheeled traffic could get in. Then Donald would survey the sites, identify the spillways, peg the banks and get us all involved with the Chiefs in supervising the work and making sure the tribesmen carried earth from the excavations in the direction which meant they trampled the earth already laid and so helped consolidate the banks. He wrote an invaluable little guide to this practical amateur approach. Of course, as he readily admitted, he remained an amateur, and we had our casualties; if one dam failed out of eight built in a season at virtually no cost in cash, we were left with seven and perhaps another couple of hundred square miles opened to cultivation and grazing.

Maswa was a district of rolling, wooded country with thin populations, and my recollections are of safari tales and a rapidly developing passion for hunting elephant in days when it was respectable to do so. But even in Maswa the Boma was always full of bizarre incident. There was Edward Halwenge, our head clerk, an extremely sophisticated Luo from Kisumu in neighbouring Kenya, who was eventually to become a permanent secretary in independent Tanzania. He thought himself several cuts above the local tribesmen. 'There's a native to see you, Sir.' Words passed. The implied contempt touched me on a raw spot. It was besides a reminder of how watchful one had to be with all the Boma staff, clerks and particularly messengers, to ensure that humble petitioners did indeed gain access and gain it without paying bribes for the privilege. To us the average Boma was a very rough-and-ready workplace, but to the ordinary tribesman from the bush it was a place of wonders where he was easily open to being dominated and swindled by those who knew their way around.

However, it transpired that the sophisticated Halwenge, tower of strength as he was in daily administration, had his own Achilles heel. He developed jaundice, an illness which was well understood after all, but he was wasting rapidly away under the treatment which, with Western confidence, was prescribed for him. I watched his decline with increasing concern and made no resistance when, through his growing weakness, he insisted on being returned home to Kisumu for the sacrificial goat and the witch-doctors. It worked, and within a remarkably short time he was back with us and well on the road to recovery. And this was not the only time when I had recourse to the power of faith in native medicine. Shortly afterwards I had on my hands one of our little group of police *askari* also wasting away under a prolonged attack of unceasing hiccups. I was persuaded to send him to a bush doctor when all our own efforts had failed, and back he came recovered.

My attempts to treat Micky Norton were less successful. He was a famous figure, who had been a great elephant hunter and notorious poacher from the turn of the century onwards. Of the many stories of his exploits the best known was of how from the north bank of the Ruvuma River, which separated Tanganyika from the former Portuguese East Africa, he shot an elephant on the Portuguese side, saw it drop, and swam in pursuit, crocodiles notwithstanding. But the beast was only wounded, and it caught him as he came up the bank, tossed him into a tree, pulled him down again and left him for dead, first covering him with palm fronds, as elephants sometimes will. But he survived. Now at the time of which I write he was employed as a game observer, looking for signs in wild animals of rinderpest, the cattle-killing disease which the Veterinary Department had virtually eliminated in a very successful campaign in 1942, and he was due to come to Maswa for a safari along our eastern border. Unfortunately, before he could leave Mwanza he went on a formidable drinking bout, which in Micky's case was always something very formidable indeed, and had to be taken into hospital to dry out. But the hospital was hard by the hotel, and no sooner did he improve than he would repair there and was soon as bad as ever. After some days of this the doctors decided the bush might suit him better, and I was asked to take him anyway.

I arranged his camp and porters in Kanadi, some 40 miles away, and gave the Chief the strictest instructions not to let him have any native beer, still less *moshi*, the illegal and lethal native spirits, and then telegraphed Mwanza that all was ready. In due course he arrived at Nyalikungu in a lorry with an astonishing quantity of liquor, considering the acute shortage that still generally prevailed. He was wildly intoxicated, and I sent him on to his camp. I had arranged an intelligence service, and runners kept me informed. At first he was just drinking and carrying on as before, with no question of setting off on his safari. Then hopes rose as he finished the spirits and started on his beer supply. But then the beer too was gone, but with no sign of improvement. At this point I took alarm and sent a truck for him. He arrived at night and was quite out of his mind, and was clearly a menace to the driver by whom he was sitting, so I resolved to escort him to Mwanza, collected a few things and jumped into the cab alongside him. It was a nightmare journey through the dark. The rains were on and we slipped and slithered off the road at regular intervals. Each time Micky would get out and, since he was an enormous man, it took almost as much physical effort to get him back into the cab as to get the lorry out of the ditch. And all the time he talked, stories of the Matabele rising, tales of the Maji-Maji rebellion, accounts of the bush and the chase. I was not expected to reply but he would get aggressive if he did not at least receive appreciative grunts, and he was not a size of man one wanted to tangle with in the cab of a truck. It was only 90 miles to Mwanza, but it was full morning before we got there and I deposited my charge at the hospital and turned straight back. Two days later he was dead, but he had had a good run since the elephant thought he had done for him forty years before on the banks of the Ruvuma.

The Sukuma had continuous trouble from Masai cattle-raiders, not infrequently accompanied by blood-letting, and at one point a meeting with my opposite number from Masailand became desirable and fairly urgent. There was, however, no road communication, although I believe there had been a motorable track before the war and distances were too great for a foot safari within the time available. I therefore resolved to try and take our most battered Native Authority truck along the stock route through Kimali to the Ngorongoro Crater, and a difficult journey it turned out to be. In the course of it I had my first encounter with the Bahi, a tiny tribe, apparently not more than forty or fifty souls all told, of bushmen pigmies, speaking a 'click' tongue and living entirely from what they could kill or gather in the bush. They had the prominent buttocks which distinguish the bushmen of the Kalahari, to whom one must presume they were distantly related. They existed quite outside our system, although I was told that years ago some officious DO had had one of them imprisoned for failure to pay tax, but he had been over the gaol wall and away in a twinkling. I shot them a zebra and gave them salt, and they did me a little shuffling dance, while far overhead an aeroplane passed. I asked their leader, who spoke Kisukuma, what they thought of that modern miracle, and received a nobly indifferent shrug.

Late on the second day we came in triumph across the Masai steppe to Endulen, and there joined one of the Masai District roads to climb, as darkness fell and mist descended, to the 8000-feet rim of Ngorongoro's vast crater. The cab of the lorry had no window, and I shivered in a thin shirt and shorts and rejoiced when eventually I reached the cluster of log cabins which served as rest-houses, and the warm fire by which Jimmy Rowe, the DC – and in due course a close friend – and his party were gathered.

I was to come to know Ngorongoro very well, both as DC Masailand and as a visitor, but the first delight in that spectacular view across the crater's 10-mile diameter stays fresh in mind. The magnificent crater floor far below, later reachable by road but then only on foot, was open savannah, alive with game, but the rim and its southern flanks were covered in heavy montane forest. On a misty evening, dripping with moisture and draped in old-man's beard, the mighty fig and pillarwood trees crowded round the road in pregnant stillness. This was a new African experience for me, and I was very excited to see elephant, rhino and buffalo in great numbers against a background so different from Maswa's open bush. I particularly remember encounters with buffalo: rounding a bend in the dirt track, we would suddenly come across a solitary bull standing in the middle of the road, head held high, eyeing our oncoming vehicle with immovable indifference.

But for now, there was work to do, and in due course we set off back on the track to Endulen, and on to the border, where we made what were doubtless only temporarily efficacious arrangements to restrain the Masai from their national pastime. After the bitter cold of the night before, the trip across the Masai steppe was marked by a following wind like a puff from a furnace, and every few miles the truck would boil and we would have to face it into the wind and stop. It took hours to cover 40 miles of that wild track.

Every dry season considerable numbers of young men from all over Sukumaland make a safari for salt from Lake Eyasi, the large undrained basin which was bordered by four different districts: Maswa, Masai, Mbulu and Singida. Salt prices in the shops were thought high by the natives, but I believe their journeys to get it for an illusory nothing were primarily an observance of a longstanding tradition. For some of them the round trip could take six weeks, and I knew it culminated in some hardship, so I decided to go and see the scene for myself and to earn some money for the Native Treasury at the same time. So here was another trail-breaking trip through the bush which eventually brought our truck to the lake, continually passing little groups of Sukuma with panniers for the salt slung by a yoke across their shoulders and supplies for the journey carried in their hands or slung around their waists. We camped for the night on the edge of the lake, which at this season at the western end was dry as far as the eye could see. We carried water with us, but the salt pilgrims had to spend that last night with only the little they could carry with them, for there was no fresh water near the lake. So, already thirsty, they had to make their way over the white shimmering heat of the lake surface to where the best salt was to be found. Here in due course we came upon them as we nervously inched our lorry over the yielding surface – once through the crust and there was no hope of retrieval before the rains came and our conveyance was engulfed. They were almost hidden by a cloud of salt as they dug it out, the sun blazed down and they would have another night without water before they got on their way home. For us it was easy, if anxious. We assessed the effect of each bag of salt loaded, judged the wheel impressions to the half-inch, moved a little nearer shore, repeated the performance again and again, and eventually decided to risk no more. Off we went and sold our salt in the fullness of time for the treasury's benefit, without, I trust, damaging the market that the stout-hearted tribesmen had created for themselves.

There was a meeting in the bush with that great Afrikaner hunter and expert on the Masai, Willie de Beer, then a temporary policeman, on his fruitless search for a young warrior who had run a spear through Hugh Grant, the Kenya DC Masai, at a cattle market and then was thought to have taken refuge in Tanganyika. There was an evening drink in the rocky *kopje* where the Ntuzu rest-house was perched, while Charles Zech, the German Jewish refugee stock inspector, told tales of adventure in Abyssinia and the stars shone down and the hyrax played around us and a leopard called in the distance. There was a jolting ride in the back of a lorry around the Malya construction site while, with all the confident opinions of youth, I explained to Creech Jones,[1] the Labour Secretary of State, just how Africa should be administered. In remote Kanadi there were pot-shots in the early morning at the baboons which were such a local plague, as they sat in a long row along the rocky skyline like targets in a shooting gallery at a fair. There was the huge plantation of *bhang* we discovered in a distant village in Dutwa, which I was visiting to oust a drunken Chief and propose a new one to the people. I sent the owner, an imposing figure covered in bells and clashing bangles, to prison, but he developed such acute withdrawal symptoms that I eventually allowed him a daily ration of the stuff.

5

ELEPHANT

It was above all in Maswa that I took with passion to elephant-hunting. There was no such sense of guilt then as the mere thought induces nowadays. Elephant were abundant and strictly protected, hunters immediately after the war were few, poaching was negligible. As residents, we were allowed two licences a year, no more than visitors, but we got them at a much cheaper rate, £15 for the first and £30 for the second, if my memory serves me. But that came to £45, which was a tenth of my annual salary, so that it was a big investment for a young DO, and it was very important not to go to bed with an unused licence at the end of its year's validity. This could happen more easily than might appear, and not only because one could simply lack adequate opportunity to hunt. All tusks weighing under 30 pounds were forfeit to the Government. This was of no consequence early in the life of the licence when one was looking for a big bull with tusks of upwards of 70 pounds a side. But if one were in one's last hunt during the licence's currency, one could no longer afford to be choosy, and the hunter would then be ready to shoot at any bull that looked comfortably above the legal limit. Here it was quite easy to make an error, particularly if the more slender ivory of a cow were mistaken for a bull's.

These mercenary considerations were important to hard-up young men with licences and porters to pay for, but it was the sport itself that consumed one. It was a hard game. The old hands always said it took a hundred miles an elephant, and this was a hundred miles in the harshest physical conditions. One was usually up at five in the morning and often not back in camp until nine at night, and sometimes sleeping on the trail. In between was a mixture of hard slog over appalling country, through taxing bush, wrestling perhaps with the relentless wait-a-bit thorn and periods of extreme activity as one got into position to study the quarry and assess whether the trophy was worth a closer approach. It was also a dangerous sport. With reasonable luck, most of the reconnaissance could usually be done at a little distance, particularly if one carried binoculars, an extra burden which I preferred to do without. But closing for the kill was a different matter. Once I can remember a clear shot from forty yards, but on most occasions found myself having to get to between fifteen or twenty yards, usually in light bush with nothing on which to rest a heavy rifle. There are various shots that will kill an elephant, but I nearly always went for the brain from a flank. This was a much smaller target than heart or lung, but, unlike these, one knew exactly what one was aiming for. Where heart and lung were concealed in the vast body, the brain, from the side, was clearly indicated by the small depression between eye and earhole. If you hit it, he was dead. If you missed, you were likely to give your intended victim nothing worse than a short, severe headache, the honeycomb of bone in an elephant's skull being notably insensitive. But a wounded elephant one was honour bound to pursue to the end or until all trace was lost. I had a friend, a professional hunter, who followed and eventually killed an elephant whom he had wounded 80 miles away.

One's companions were important. In Maswa, Masailand and Mbulu I always had a favourite office messenger who acted as gun-bearer, which meant that he carried the rifle, an oppressive burden in great heat, when the going was open, and I carried it in bush where one might at any time stumble on rhino or buffalo. And there were always a brace of local trackers, men of superb skill in following the spoor over the most stony terrain, or in judging to a nicety the distance between us and a herd ahead by testing with a hand the heat of the animals' dung. The four of us could usually get a break towards the middle of the day, sitting companionably on thorns under inadequate shade, while we ate sandwiches from camp and made disciplined use of the water bottles. This pleasurable interlude could be revealing of doctrinal laxity. Two or three years after

Maswa, when I was hunting in Masailand under conditions of great hardship for both food and water, there was nothing at all to hand for the midday break but sardine sandwiches, and fish was *muiko*, or taboo, to the tribe to which my messenger belonged. In the straits that we were in, he made no difficulty about eating then, so long as he did so behind a bush where the rest of us could not see him.

Then gear was important. First, the rifle. I always shot with a Holland and Holland .375 magnum. The .375 eventually became the lightest rifle allowed by law for shooting big game, and I always longed for, but could never afford, something with much more stopping power, like a double .500. It was no comfort to remember that Karamojo Bell,[1] greatest of elephant hunters, had regularly shot with a Rigby .275. He always took the brain shot, and if one could shoot as he could shoot that was all one needed. Not being so skilled, I always had to make do with something a good deal lighter than I would have wished.

Footgear posed questions which I never answered. Karamojo Bell, again, used to hunt in plimsolls. For stealth and speed they were doubtless ideal, but I found they got sliced to pieces in no time and were all too apt to encourage a blackjack thorn through the sole and into one's foot. So it had to be boots for the march, and with them one could not wear the ordinary stockings that accompanied our shorts, because the sharp grass-seeds penetrated them and drove one slowly crazy. Puttees saved one from this torture, but the toil of removing the seeds from yards and yards of puttee at the end of an exhausting day was more than could be readily endured. So I settled for boots and gaiters, despite the disadvantages of clumsiness and noise. I used to carry plimsolls in my haversack, but time was usually too pressing to make the change when reconnaissance turned into a serious hunt.

I always carried a little muslin bag of ash. Wind was crucial; one whiff of us and the quarry was away, and the wind can be extraordinarily treacherous in the bush on a broiling African day. So I would shake the bag every few paces on the close approach and was able to measure every slightest shift in the breeze. While the elephant's sense of smell is the main danger to the hunter, it is wrong to suppose, as so many people do, that his sight is very poor. It is true that my life has been saved by an elephant's indifferent vision at close range. Nevertheless, I once emerged with my party on an open plain with the wind blowing dead in our faces and saw a small herd some half a mile away. We were, as always, quiet, but we did not attempt to conceal ourselves, because we knew they could not get our wind and they obviously, as we assumed, could not see us at that range. They saw us at once and were off.

In my few years' experience of elephant-hunting I certainly did not learn anything about them that would compare with the deep knowledge acquired by the lifetime professionals, but I did encounter another myth, comparable to that about their sight. It was widely held that elephants sleep only on their feet. This is not so, as I suppose most zookeepers could tell us. I once had the uncommon experience of coming on an entire herd asleep at noon in a cluster of doum palms on the banks of a river in Maswa. We wandered foolhardily among them, some standing, others lying down, and, to say we had done it, each of the four of us came within a pace of a cow asleep on her side. It was curious, as aggressive hunters, to find ourselves in a scene of such peace.

I have in fact spent a lot of time at peace with elephant. There were hours passed on top of a rock or up-wind of a water-hole or just standing behind a tree when I almost felt myself sharing in their family life and the cheekiness of their young and the cows' protectiveness of their calves at the first whiff of danger. Not so peaceful was an occasion when I was hunting with Ken Flood, a policeman friend, in very harsh country in Masailand. We were far from the Pangani River, the nearest water, and had no more for our two selves and our posse of four Africans than the 44-gallon drum which I could carry in the back of my Bedford box-body. So all washing and shaving was forbidden and we became pretty objectionable company; but the elephant were feeding in the area, making the long trek to the river only every third night. To add to my own discomfort, in reaching under my bed for my bush-jacket in the pre-dawn darkness on the first morning of the hunt I was stung in the thumb by a scorpion, and so acute was the pain that I did not realise that the poultice we misguidedly applied was so hot that it was stripping the skin off. So for the rest of the safari handling my rifle was an uncomfortable business. After three or four fruitless and exhausting days, the rumble of great stomachs told us one morning of the presence of elephant, and we shortly found that a fine bull and his mate were grazing slowly towards us. When he was some twenty yards from us, he half-turned and offered me the brain shot. I fired, and he dropped like a stone, and Ken and I turned to cover the cow in case she came for us. She came all right, but not for us. In a trice she had her shoulder to her mate and had him on his feet and shakily away without presenting another opportunity; and though we followed most of the day, they were shortly going like the wind so that in due course we lost their trail. I was delighted at this vindication of the theory that a missed brain shot is unlikely to do much damage, but even more exhilarated to see evidence of what I had been told of the faithfulness of these marvellous animals one to another.

A much more successful hunt was also in company, this time in my earlier hunting days in Maswa with Deric Broadhead-Williams, a prospector. This was a full-scale local leave for me over Christmas in 1945, in good elephant country in the east of the district. A full complement of porters took us and our tent and gear a day's march from where we left our truck, and then departed to return in two weeks' time, leaving us with our cook and two gun-bearers and the usual pair of skilled local trackers. We had three licences between the two of us, and not long to go before their currency expired, but a fortnight seemed ample time in view of all the optimistic reports from local people.

Sure enough, on the very first day we came upon what, at a distance, seemed to be a fine bull; but on closer examination the tusks showed up as unduly thin, perhaps fifty pounds a side, and, since we hoped to do much better than that, we rapidly made ourselves scarce when he showed signs of aggression. For day after weary day thereafter we saw every other kind of game but never the elephant we wanted. Everywhere there were signs of great numbers of them, but always the spoor was stale, the droppings cold. Late every night we would be back in camp for a dejected glass of rum and a boring meal of bully beef, since we avoided shooting for the pot because of the risk of warning off our quarry. But on one such occasion, when we had only some three days left, we returned to hear from Omari, my cook, that a local honey-hunter had come in to camp to report a large herd some 2 or 3 miles away. It was extraordinary how even in apparently unpopulated bush someone would always turn up with news, just as when one shot an elephant in the remotest spot, in no time at all there would be a small crowd of men and women to carve up the carcass for meat. On this occasion our honey-hunter's news was no more than a rough guide, for illiterate bush dwellers are no judges of distance in European terms, and in any event the herd might have covered many miles since he saw them. But his was our only pointer and we resolved to go where he had indicated.

At first light next morning we were on the ground and soon found ample signs of many elephant, and set out to track them, but by then they were well ahead of us and there followed some hours of fairly rapid pursuit with barely time for a rest in the intense heat. In mid-afternoon we were rewarded with the familiar sound of tummy rumbles, and shortly the dim shades of grey in the great expanse of thick bush ahead told us that we were approaching a very large herd indeed. As we drew nearer, continually re-checking the wind, we could see that the herd was slowly grazing from left to right across our front and that the bush was punctuated by narrow open glades, offering us a field of vision. We hastened accordingly to our right to get ahead of the herd, while staying to its flank, so that we could observe individuals crossing one of these glades.

Numbers of cows and calves and a few young bulls passed before us. At last there came sedately a single big bull who paused for a moment to feed. There was no doubt of the size of his tusks, and, since a bush concealed his head, Deric and I fired almost simultaneously for his heart and saw puffs of dust rise from his hide where our bullets struck home. But he was off at once into the shelter of the bush ahead, while we pelted up the edge of it, trusting that another glade would give us a further chance. So it transpired in half a mile or so, and once again the tell-tale dust showed that we had hit him hard. Another desperate rush followed and then we saw the unmistakable wide arc of his tusks as he stood behind a bush and waited for us. We paused to gather breath and then slowly approached, certain that this time we must drop him with a frontal shot. We were wrong, and for the third time he turned and took off.

Much chagrined, we took to the trail in country now much more open, and soon drops of blood confirmed that we had a wounded elephant to follow and made sure that we would not be misled by other tracks. The trackers had times of hesitation over rocky surfaces, but as the afternoon wore on we were closing on our quarry and more and more frequently came upon shady spots where he had paused for long periods. As evening drew near our trackers were confident we were on his heels, and now some heavy bush loomed ahead where it seemed likely our elephant would pass the night, but the light was gone before we could go in after him. There was nothing for it but to eat the little cold food remaining, wrap ourselves in a blanket apiece against the night chill, and sleep where we were.

Following a wounded elephant into heavy bush at dawn on an empty stomach is not on the whole to be recommended, and I for one nearly jumped out of my skin when a partridge rocketed up at my side. But our nerves were not stretched for long. Our quarry had indeed been nearby all night long, and we shortly had a good view of him just ahead of us. This time there was no mistake, and he fell to a single shot. Now we wanted to discover why we had failed to bring him down the day before, and at once were taken aback to discover that our prize had not been hit where we had seen bullets strike home. Clearly we had not, as we had supposed, been firing on a single bull, and it looked as though we might have another wounded beast on our hands. But before we could do anything about that we had to get the handsome tusks out of our quarry and then make our way back to camp for a combination of breakfast and lunch.

There a man had just come in to bring the startling news that two dead elephant were lying in the bush where our engagement had taken place on the previous day. A quick bite of food and off we set, and there we found them in thick bush, in each case dropped by a heart shot within a hundred yards of where we fired. That evening over a happy drink by the camp fire it was easy to see, as we looked at our six tusks, how we came to make our mistake. One identifies elephant largely by their tusks, and all of these were of approximately the same weight and length and shape. So there we were at the very end of a hunt which had seemed set for frustration with all the trophies for which we were licensed as a most acceptable Christmas present.

But mostly I hunted on my own, enjoying my African companions, the bush and the infinite variety of wildlife. There was no such magic about shooting in populated areas. I did it once when it was necessary to kill one of a small herd of crop raiders. I did it on another occasion when unfitness and haste nearly cost me my life. I was just up from malaria and was sitting in my office about four o'clock one afternoon when an African came running in: 'Bwana, you've got a licence and there's an elephant just up the road. Huge tusks.' I should have reflected then that Africans were rarely good judges of the weight of ivory and that the place he named, a few miles away, was quite densely populated and that it was highly unlikely that a big bull would have strayed there. No such cautious thoughts stayed me. I armed myself in haste, forgetting my invaluable little bag of ash, jumped in a truck and got myself to the scene.

When I arrived, there was little time left before the light went, and again I was pushed into undue haste. I was shown a patch of very dense bush some half a mile off the road in which I was told my quarry was. The local people were all gathered on top of a *kopje* as though for a show. I should of course have guessed that they had been teasing the beast all day with arrows and stones, and I would have been right if I had made a further guess that this elephant was in fact a cow with misleadingly long, but slender and light, ivory. I did not stop to think, but, with the light fading fast and with none of my usual meticulous care for the wind, I began to skirt the bush and try to get a sight of those tusks.

The rest is soon told. She got my wind and charged. I was on the very edge of the bush, which I could hear being smashed down as though by a tank, but I could see nothing of her for a stopping shot. I turned and ran back, perhaps with some thought of getting up-wind of her, but in truth running for my life. But I had my head cocked back to watch for her, and as she emerged from the bush, fury and power incarnate, so, not a dozen yards ahead of her, I put my foot in a hole and fell, my rifle flying far out of my hand.

Fear, in my experience, depends entirely upon the element of risk. I have often been frightened, but not at all on the two occasions in my life when death seemed certain and imminent. A moment before I had been terrified. As I hit the ground I was entirely calm. I thought of my parents, I remembered women. Because of my haste in leaving the Boma I still had in my pocket the strong-room keys, and I wondered if they would be trampled out of shape and, if so, how Donald Malcolm would get access. But then it did not happen. She must have charged entirely by scent, since she could no more see me through the bush than I her, and perhaps she never saw me at all, or perhaps she just lost sight of me as I fell. At all events she blundered past me, her huge feet within inches, and stopped. I could look straight up at her stern and past it to where I could see her raised trunk testing the wind for my scent. I had a chance, I was once more at risk, so fear revived and I thought that every elephant in Africa would hear my newly thumping heart. And thus we stayed as the tropical darkness quickly fell. I do not know how long I lay, perhaps fifteen minutes, nor whether she had in fact moved off with that extraordinarily silent gait that elephants have; but in due course the thorn bush in my crutch outweighed all fear and I inched my way on my belly to my rifle and rejoined some surprised African companions. Back home that night I drank as good a drink as would ever pass my lips and reflected on life on borrowed time.

Well before the end of 1946 I had been told that I could take home leave any time I could get a passage after the following January. This was easier said than done. There were of course no scheduled air services in those days, or for a long time to come, and shipping was still desperately short and irregular. One half-promise after another fell through until in the latter part of January I lost patience at waiting for a telegram from Dar es Salaam and set off on a foot safari in the north of the district. There had been much unseasonal rain at the time, and after two or three days my porters and I found ourselves crossing a plain up to our knees in water. At about noon a figure appeared in hot pursuit of us across this soggy scene. Our caravan stopped at his shout, and up he came to me, bearing, according to the very best tradition, a note in a cleft stick. It was from Halwenge at the Boma to tell me that if I could trek back and reach the Boma tomorrow, hand over, pack my house up, and be at Malampaka to catch the train two days later, then I had the prospect of a seat in a Groundnut Scheme charter plane from Dar es Salaam. A lorry would be waiting for me at the Bariadi River.

I turned all the porters round for a forced march through our swamp until at evening we reached high ground and pitched camp. Off we went at crack of dawn, and by mid-afternoon we came to the Bariadi. There was our lorry, but between us and it, over the long concrete drift, flowed a hundred yards of river in full and violent spate. I waited an impatient hour before we were all able to struggle over, barely maintaining our footing on the drift against the waist-deep tide of water. I was on my way.

The journey home from Dar es Salaam, which it turned out that I was visiting for the last time in ten years, was a saga of its own. We were travelling in a converted Lancaster bomber, with seats for 13 passengers, although in fact we numbered only half a dozen, so that we were comfortably uncrowded. We had a two-day stop in Nairobi, and, since baggage was virtually unlimited, I was able there to fill up a trunk with everything of which my family would have been most short: hams, butter, cigars, whisky. But as we pursued our leisurely journey, with nights in Khartoum, Cairo and Malta, we were getting worse and worse accounts of the weather ahead in Western Europe, for we were arriving in the middle of the worst of post-war winters. Sure enough, when we took off from Malta we were ordered to join the immense number of weather-bound aircraft at Marseilles; and, since nobody at home was expecting our arrival on any particular date, our little party set about enjoying this unexpected taste of French life.

It was not until long after dark the following day that we were advised that London was usable, and off we set once more. No doubt it had been, but by the time we were overhead it was snowing hard again. The pilot made three hair-raising attempts to land, the very pretty girl in our party fainted and I set about reviving her with enthusiasm, and then we were redirected to Paris. With the city looking lovely in its blanket of snow, we arrived well after midnight at Le Bourget. Astonishingly, there was no one on duty and we simply lugged our bags through the airport, hailed taxis and drove to the best hotel we could think of. The next day the charter company offered to send us back by rail and boat. I led a passengers' revolt: 'You contracted to deliver us by air.' They acquiesced, and to my astonishment continued to pay our hotel bills for the three days we were there. What fun to be in Paris again, even in the bitter cold, even with so little heating, even with the relatively shabby people.

When we finally got to Heathrow I opened my array of gifts in customs with a degree of trepidation. 'How long have you been away?' 'Six years.' He waved me through.

6

ARUSHA

We were still so short-handed in Tanganyika that none of us got more than four months for our first post-war leave, no matter how long the wartime tour had been. I used this spell to good effect by embarking on my only continuously successful venture. I got married. My bride, Nona Hurford, was the sister of my closest friend at school, but I did not re-meet her until well into my leave, so we decided to be engaged for no more than a week. We had a Scottish honeymoon in pouring rain. We fitted in a Commemoration Ball at my old college, Magdalen College, Oxford, white tie and tails and flowing champagne for the first time since the war, another at Brasenose, where my father was a don, and yet another at New College, where my younger brother had returned after naval service. And then my four months was up and I had to fly back.

It looked like a long separation. Nona was to come by sea with our heavy baggage, and merely rejoining a husband gave her no kind of priority. Bureaucracy, however, proved no match for her. The Crown Agents left her to make her own booking, and she met nothing but frustration with every respectable shipping line. So she took herself to the disreputable and got booked on a Greek line out of Marseilles of a reputation so awful that P&O felt bound to do something when she innocently reported her success and asked to be taken off their six-month waiting list. 'Oh no, Madame. Of course, if you could leave on Friday...' This was Tuesday, with all the packing to be done. 'Certainly.'

I have never been sure she would not have been better off with the Greeks. The *Empire Brent* was no longer a troopship, but the passengers could not tell the difference and the East African press was full of stories of the horrors of the voyage for mothers with young children, resembling, I suppose, Heathrow on a strike-bound holiday weekend, prolonged for a month. But I collected her at Mombasa after less than two months apart.

The Northern Province had four districts, Arusha, Moshi, Masai and Mbulu. All were beautiful, healthy and bristling with varying challenges, and it was to be my good luck to spend more than nine years serving, at one time or another, in all four of them. My present posting was to Arusha, where the provincial headquarters also were, and the Arusha District was in trouble. Curiously, since I was only to be second-in-command, I had been summoned to the Colonial Office in the course of my leave to be told what was expected of me. I was ushered into the formidable presence of Sir Andrew Cohen,[1] later Governor of Uganda. Presence is hardly the word, for during the half hour of our interview he seemed to be as much absent as present. Restless energy drove him here and there for a quick word with a colleague, a snatch of dictation, a telephone call. But in between all this activity he gave me his message clearly enough. The Arusha District was of great importance because, although it was small, it was the heartland of Tanganyika's white settlers, whose farms were highly profitable and whose political and economic influence were such that the two local African tribes were truculent and disaffected. Wartime stresses and staff shortages had resulted in years of administrative neglect. Matters were now to be set to rights, and the team to do that would be Donald Troup, as DC, and I, as his senior DO. Most of the day-to-day handling of the tribesmen would fall to me, and in this I would have the help of Hans Cory's[2] vast experience. Hans was an Austrian Jew who had recently become government anthropologist. The establishment at the Arusha Boma would be increased by an extra DO, so that there would be no excuses if Donald and I did not make a proper job of sorting out the tribal grievances. All this sounded interesting and exciting.

My years in the Northern Province accounted for the decade that I passed without visiting Dar es Salaam. Arusha is hard up against the Kenya frontier, so that if one returned from leave by sea one took the train from Mombasa or Tanga; and if by air one flew into Nairobi and came on south by road, which is what I did in June of 1947. Soon after leaving Kajiado, the district headquarters for the Kenya half of the Masai tribe, the vast mass of Kilimanjaro dominates the eye, with its great snow-cap on the 19,000-feet peak of Kibo and the lesser Mawenzi, rocky and more daunting to the climber. But soon, as one heads south for the Tanganyikan border at Namanga, the steep volcanic cone of Mount Meru looms above its forest line some 50 miles to the south-east of Kilimanjaro.

Arusha District was Mount Meru, just as Moshi District and Kilimanjaro were synonymous. It was true that in the west we stretched out to the forested flank of Monduli Mountain, close to the Masai headquarters, where Wa'arusha tribesmen had settled in some numbers; and in the south our area impinged upon the edge of the great Masai plain, where some limited European settlement was opening up new wheatlands and where a number of sisal plantations were longer established. But basically the district was the mountain. The whole area was small, as districts went, and effectively much smaller than the boundaries would suggest, since most of the real business was concentrated in the extraordinarily rich volcanic soil on the southern slopes of the mountain above the Arusha township. The population too consisted of not much over a hundred thousand Africans and a few hundred Europeans and Indians making up the official, commercial and settler population. But, at the same time, the scale of our job was much more than square miles or census returns would suggest. Indeed, the small physical scale in Arusha compressed and made more potentially dangerous the issue of whether rich white settlers, providing much of the country's economic backbone, could continue to prosper in close propinquity with overcrowded but productive and efficient peasant farmers.

Meru was a dartboard. At the centre was the bare, rocky summit, around which ran the first concentric circle of a thick belt of heavy, tropical forest, the living guardian of the water on which the thriving agriculture below depended. Then came a belt of African *shamba*, the tribesmen being basically cultivators, with cattle as a sideline. They grew their own food, of which bananas were the staple, but they also raised a variety of profitable cash crops, coffee being the most significant. But their plots of land were getting smaller and smaller, for each son was expected to have at least a patch on the fertile, volcanic soils, and room for expansion lower down was barred by the final belt of white settler farms, mostly devoted to highly profitable coffee. These lands had originally been alienated when they were empty and when there was no pressure of population on the higher mountain slopes, but now things were very different and the Africans felt hemmed in. Some of the richer ones ran their cattle with the Masai in the plains, but they really needed corridors of escape to be bought for them through the European farms. This was a solution not to be tried by government for some years yet, and meanwhile ways had to be found to appease the resentment of two sullen and almost mutinous tribes.

There were some seventy thousand Wa'arusha on the south-western slopes of the mountain, and thirty thousand Wameru to the east of them. The Wa'arusha had close ties to the Masai, sharing Hamitic blood and a similar social structure, and they had sheltered the starving nomads when rinderpest had almost destroyed their herds in the 1890s. In appearance, with their blankets and spears, red ochre in their hair, they were virtually indistinguishable, though the mountain water made a Wa'arusha's teeth blacker and a more varied diet put a fatter calf on his leg, or so old hands contended. The links between the two tribes were maintained by giving and taking in marriage, which always seemed curious to me when the two ways of life were so markedly different. No Masai, living as he did by blood and milk and meat, ever put a hoe in the ground, whereas the Wa'arusha were farmers, and the meat they regularly ate was bought. Indeed, by this time half the families in the tribe owned no cattle at all and an average holding among the rest might be a dozen head and a few sheep and goats. Anything above such numbers would be lent out to Masai partners. The economy of the Wameru was similar, though more dependent on the banana and even less on livestock. What is it about the banana? All the brightest and most thrusting tribes in East Africa relied on it as their staple food.

These two tribes had suffered not so much from bad administration as from a lack of it. There were too few staff in wartime, too many changes of administrators, that old besetting sin of our service, too much concentration on the needs of productive European farmers. The Wa'arusha were very present among the European population. Every day their men and women would swarm in their hundreds through the town of Arusha, with its considerable commercial and official European population, on visits or journeys or to sell their produce. Contact was close and continuous with the European farms which hemmed them in on their tribal lands. They worked for the farmers, indifferently, stole from them, disputed water rights and grazing rights and rights of way with them. They had a reputation for lawlessness and indiscipline. For their part the Wa'arusha felt they had been neglected. I could feel it too on my evening walks out of the township and up the foothills among the banana groves. There were sullen looks instead of cheerful greetings, and it was clear at once that there were things to be set to rights.

However, there was a pause before we set about tackling the tribes' political problems, for Donald Troup was not due back from leave for six weeks, and my old friend Dick Gower was holding the fort as DC. He was also in the house intended in due course for my wife and me, so we set up home for the first time in temporary quarters. As it turned out, we were to have seven different homes in that 30-month tour of duty, which perhaps explains why we have been gypsies ever since – we are capable of settling down, but not without feeling that several years in one place is itself a sufficient reason for moving on.

I had had my own experience of kicking off in Tanganyika with no knowledge of Swahili at all, and I watched with interest and sympathy to see how Nona would cope. Her team consisted, first, of Omari, my old cook, who had made the long journey from Lindi to rejoin ship, together with his wife, Fatima, who later became our *ayah*. I had not, however, asked Mbango, my houseboy, to come back. I liked him immensely, but he was too far set in scruffy bachelor ways to adjust to a '*memsahib*'s rule', so we recruited one Kassum from the coast at Tanga. He was a tall, genial fellow, whose toes on one foot had been completely destroyed by jiggers, apart from the big toe, so that he left disconcerting footprints when he washed down our stone floors. I felt for him about jiggers: on local leave in Lushoto during my last tour I had had 28 of these nasty little parasites dug out of my toes in a fortnight.

The last of our entourage came to us by way of a temporary 'perk'. People imprisoned for relatively venial offences were often allowed to work out their sentences extramurally on any tasks that improved government property, and official gardens counted as government property. So we had Shabani as our gardener, and of course he got roped in for a lot of odd jobs, for he was a gentle obliging character, notwithstanding that he had been convicted of a *crime passionel* of great violence. He had the most divergent squint I ever saw in a man, a flaw which somehow seemed out of harmony with a violent affair of the heart. We never forgot him because of the prominent part he played in Nona's first dinner party. As newly-weds, we had been much dined around the station in our first few weeks; and presently, once we were out of our original shack and into the pleasant little stone house which Dick Gower had been occupying, the bride had to face the ordeal of returning hospitality.

Dinner parties had to be handled with a certain amount of care. Tanganyika was relatively free of snobbish class divisions between officials which marred social life in some colonies, but there was plenty of sense of hierarchy and precedence, and even the least respectful of us kept an eye on the staff list for a seating plan at dinner where there was any question as to who was senior to whom. However, there were no difficulties of that sort on this occasion, merely anxiety on Nona's part that things should run smoothly, the food be good, her husband's career not jeopardised. Drinks passed happily, we all sat down to table, conversation flowed, first course good, main course up to standard, Kassum served impeccably, and I could see my wife gaining confidence by the minute. We awaited the pudding. Now the pudding was a splendid iced meringue concoction which Nona had put together that morning and had despatched to the nearest refrigerator in the Troups' house some hundred yards away – we had no fridge of our own, partly because they were not to be had so soon after the war, and partly because we could not have afforded one if they were to be had. Shabani, we shortly discovered, had been deputed to collect it at the appointed moment. Presently we heard a dreadful crash outside. Then the door opened. But it was not the immaculate Kassum but Shabani, eyes askew, in his garden-stained *kanzu*. With a touching air of duty done, he silently proffered to Nona a pudding like a collapsed snowman encased in a jigsaw of glass fragments. She stared, appalled, but it sealed the success of the evening.

We were soon close friends with Donald and his wife Phyll. He was an Oxford rugby blue, a no-nonsense, jolly extrovert with plenty of sense and experience. Phyll was as good-hearted and sociable as he was, and the four of us spent many evenings in each other's company. The two of them had a remarkable capacity for generating noise, not least in their fairly frequent disagreements, which we, until we got to know them, mistook for violent rows. We came back with them for a nightcap late one night after a dance at the Club. Because the Troups had two young daughters, their *ayah* was on duty, which meant she was stretched out fast asleep on their sofa. The African capacity for deep sleep is a marvel. I have known night watchmen who would not waken unless one actually stumbled over their recumbent forms. Phyll and Donald were having an altercation as we walked in, and I thought the din would rouse the entire neighbourhood, but the *ayah* never stirred until Donald, forgetful of her presence, sat down on her.

Donald needed his solid common sense when he first arrived in Arusha, for he found Dick Gower and me longing to lay our hands on the Meru dissident faction who were already giving us serious trouble in their agitation against Sante, the established Chief. Donald quite rightly insisted that, with Cory's help, we must try to appease them before we got rough. Meanwhile Dick took himself off to a fresh posting and I set about trying to ensure that our cadet, John Vinter, got rather more by way of guidance than had come my way in Lindi. John was a mature man with a fine war record, and he soon made a very good fist of the Boma routine. With Donald looking after broad policy and keeping the politically powerful European farmers reasonably sweet, I was left free to concentrate, with Cory, on the deep-seated grievances of our two tribes. We in fact tackled them both over the same period, dividing our time between them, but I will tell the two very different stories separately.

Hans Cory was a dumpy little man with a thick German accent, a large collection of obscene African figurines and a remarkable gift for winning people's confidence. Government inevitably used him as a fire-extinguisher in difficult situations, and poor Hans must often have wished he could pursue his anthropological studies among tribesmen who were not at odds with each other or with Government. Trouble-shooter he might be, but he gained African trust because he always came to them as a seeker for truth and never as the champion of any particular government line. He always looked behind what might seem to busy administrators to be mere recalcitrance or bloody-minded folly. He would seek out a widely representative group and deploy with them a patience in discussion as inexhaustible as the Africans' own. He used many little oratorical tricks, among which coarse and very funny sexual allusion worked as well as it would have done with most comparable British audiences. He did the colonial Government proud, his eccentricity as a servant matching ours in taking him on. He was never a man to be overlooked.

The Wa'arusha at this time were divided into two chiefdoms, Ilboru and Ilburka, under Chiefs Simeon and Simon respectively. Simeon was a wise and firm old man, Simon weak and ineffective. The two chiefdoms only existed because of a forgotten quarrel between two powerful people, now long dead. That the division was contrary to the natural tribal structure was clear from the fact that the clan and age-grade organisations were common to the whole tribe and took no regard of the chiefdom boundary. It was obvious that putting them together would make more than a sum of the parts. So Hans and I had this object in mind as we set out on the main task of framing a constitution that the Wa'arusha could understand and use. This was to prove a long task, given the people's sullen mood. The tribe and their customs had never been the subject of study before, and we needed a group of all social levels and ages to consult, but first a degree of trust had to be established. We had to persuade the people that we wanted to know all about them because we were out to help them, not manipulate them for the Government's benefit.

I left Hans to do his part in his own idiosyncratic way while I went back to basics by going on safari. This was more of an innovation than it may sound. The populated part of the district was so small and so full of comfortable settlers' homes where a visiting DC was more than welcome that no ordinary touring had been done for years. It may have seemed absurd for me to be pitching my tent, as I often did, within an hour's walk of my own home, but it gave all sorts of people the chance to stop by the camp fire for a chat. Gradually I got a reputation as an approachable sort of Bwana Shauri, and more and more people would stop complaining about grievances and talk to me about what lay behind them, often the styles and attitudes of corrupt headmen or arrogant settlers. The people of the district were terrible fellows for nursing a grudge, and the first stage in the cure was to let them talk about it.

Hans Cory and I would compare notes at weekends about our various informants, and we started to sort the trustworthy from the placemen. After some weeks our group began to take shape. I suppose there must have been about twenty of them, and in due course we began our discussions, always in the most informal circumstances under a tree right on the boundary between the two chiefdoms. Small symbols are important in Africa, and our meeting place indicated that neither chiefdom was being preferred to the other. We made it clear that the members of the group were not representatives, so that they were not answerable to anyone for whatever they chose to tell us, but we cast our net wide to include old and young, traditionalists and educated, animists and Christians. So with them we set about exploring the structure of tribal custom and organisation in the hope of finding a pattern which could be used to build a local administration better suited to the people's needs than the arbitrary system of Chief and headman. It was an education to me to watch the patience and persistence with which Hans set about his job. Long discursive chats very slowly broke down the aura of suspicion with which we were confronted at the start. Slowly a mood of good humour replaced the doubts about what these meddling Europeans really wanted. Gradually the group began to meld and move with us in the same direction, so that misleading answers to questions carried scornful exposure by the respondent's fellows.

So in due course Hans's penetrating investigation of the sources of influence within the family, clan and tribe yielded their fruit. Flourishing below the Administration's threshold of vision and dealing with a great variety of business beyond the Administration's ken was a lively indigenous social structure. Clans were significant, but, as with the Masai, Wa'arusha society was founded on age-grades. An age-grade covers roughly half a generation, and thus for practical purposes there are always three current grades to consider – the youth, the middle-aged and the elderly. Members of yet more senior grades have usually retired from active life. The lowest unit of tribal life is the area known as the *balbal*; this is also the administrative area of the *jumbeate*, or headman's area, and, despite the absence of a church, is perhaps best translated as a 'parish'. Each age-grade has in every parish four elected leaders, called *laigwanak*, controlling the affairs of that age-grade within the parish. This structure conferred genuine status on the *laigwanak* of each age-grade, so that it was quite wrong to suppose that all affairs of consequence must be dealt with only among the elders, as was so often the case with African tribes. Furthermore, the age-grades naturally ran right through the tribe as a whole and the more one founded a system on the age-grades, the less the logic in maintaining two separate chiefdoms.

After some weeks of discussion there emerged proposals for local administration which seemed attractive to our group and which were therefore likely enough to seem sensible to the people at large. It would be tedious to describe it in detail, but it was founded on councils made up of the age-grade leaders in each village, with some representation for Christians who were outside the age-grade system. The councils had the duty of assisting their village headmen, but there was also special provision for them to be available at stated times and places to hear complaints against a headman, because the lack of machinery for ventilating grievances, except by agitation, had been a recurrent theme in our talks; and with the Chief's approval a council was to be able to elect or depose a headman. We went on to propose that there should now be only one Chief for the Wa'arusha and he was to be assisted by a tribal council, mostly chosen from the village councils in prescribed ways.

There were arrangements again for complaints against the Chief himself to be properly aired, and the procedure for choosing the Chief was elaborately designed to involve the village headmen and councils. It was laid down too that the Chief's election must be unanimous, an extreme provision to British ears, but in African debates the minority will almost always rally to the majority opinion in the end.

At about the time our proposals were knocked into shape, Hans was moved to deal with some spot of bother elsewhere and it fell to me to take our ideas to the people at large. My many *barazas* made for fitness, since most meetings could only be reached by stiff climbs up Mount Meru's steep foothills. The debates themselves made a happy change from the sour disputes with the Wameru which were going on at the same time. Our proposals were so clearly founded on tribal custom that they were accepted with only slight amendment, and I had no difficulty at all with the most potentially contentious issue, the unification of the two chiefdoms. Soon I was able to move on to launch the new ship with the election of the new councils and, with some careful timing, I was able within a week to visit the inaugural meeting in each of the 25 village areas. I felt sorry for my excellent messenger, Meagi, who had the job of translating 25 identical speeches and 25 identical sets of jokes from Swahili into the vernacular.

Once the village councils were in being, the tribal council could be formed and we could move on to the delicate task of the selection of a Chief. From the start, every care was taken that one chiefdom should not feel that the other was being preferred to it. Hans had a group of a score of advisers in all that he did. They were of all ages and they represented all the main interests of the tribe – the clans and the age-grades, the Christians, the wheat- and coffee-growers – and they were drawn in equal numbers from the two chiefdoms. The meeting place was on the boundary, at a spot customarily used for gatherings of age-grades and clans from both sides.

In the end the amalgamation was brought about without incident in January 1948. One Chief retired a month before, and the other voluntarily stood down to allow of a free election for the Chief of the united Wa'arusha. The procedure for this election was prescribed in the constitution so laboriously hammered out between Hans and his elders. First the tribal council, augmented by the headmen, met, discussed possibilities and agreed on a candidate. They called an *engigwana o balbali*, which consisted of the headmen, the tribal council and all *laigwanak* of all age-grades of each *balbal*, and secured unanimous agreement to their nominee. There was then a gathering of all the Wa'arusha, attended by the PC and other officials to give the Government's blessing. It was an impressive occasion. The PC, Donald and I were all in full dress uniform. The people were gathered in large numbers, and the proceeding began with a senior *laigwanan* praying for blessing on their deliberations. The members of the original *engigwana o balbali* then went into *engiliwata*, that is, went off into a closed session by themselves on one side. This, of course, was pure formality, for it was known to everybody there that the choice of a Chief rested with them and that they had already met and made their choice; indeed, it was probably very well known whom they had chosen. But ceremonial plays as important a part in Wa'arusha coronations as it does elsewhere, and this departure before the whole tribe was intended as a visible witness to the people that their own representatives had received full opportunity with all other *laigwanak* of having their say in the choice of the Chief.

All went as we had hoped, the ineffective Simon was pensioned off, Simeon was chosen and was duly installed. After that, for my last year in the district, it was just a matter of oiling the wheels. One or another of the Administration and departmental officers made a point of visiting a good proportion of the monthly meetings in the villages and all of the tribal council meetings. The former were much preoccupied with the apparent trivia which are the real stuff of peasant life, wild pig in the fields, the closure of a cattle track by a European farmer, squabbles over water for irrigation, the neighbour's wife. The tribal council was soon established in a new headquarters, known as *Enaboishu*, or 'union', built at that point on the old boundary where Hans and I used to meet our consultative group. Simeon's own position as Chief and head of the Native Authority was paradoxically strengthened. The Chief had never been an autocratic tribal 'boss', as he is often conceived to be by Europeans, but something midway between that and the purely spiritual leadership exercised by the Masai *laibon*. The elders of the tribal council were very much his men and, perhaps to his surprise, he found his acts and opinions invested with a force and weight which he had never experienced in the old days. Under Simeon's wise direction the members of the tribal council soon showed themselves strong leaders. For their Native Treasury's benefit they introduced progressive taxation in the form of a cess[3] on coffee, by far their most valuable crop. I expected desperate argument over this issue, for the coffee cess would fall most heavily on the rich and influential, and therefore by definition on many of the councillors themselves. Indeed, this issue was for that reason at this very time causing us most bitter contention among the Wameru. But the Wa'arusha leaders saw the justice of the rich paying more than the poor, backed it up and took the people with them. Before I left they had also introduced ten days of free labour, on Sukuma lines, for public works. The result was a substantial earth dam in an expansion area for the tribe on the slopes of Monduli Mountain, which they could never otherwise have afforded.

I made many friends among the Wa'arusha. What had seemed bloody-minded, stiff-necked arrogance in mid-1947 appeared as forthrightness and decent pride in the changed attitudes of a year later. At all events, there came the time when Dar es Salaam abruptly ordered me to Kongwa, headquarters of the Groundnut Scheme, to open a new administrative district there. To have a district of my own was enormously appealing. On the other hand, I wanted to pursue my happy relationship with the Wa'arusha, and I did not want to leave the fight with the Wameru. So I held my peace. Donald protested vigorously that he and I had been sent to Arusha as a team to sort things out, and here was I being removed after a year. Tim Revington, the PC, supported him. Dar es Salaam did not respond. Out of the blue came Chief Simeon's Swahili plea to the PC. Bwana Meek knew the people, the constitution was new and fragile, the tender plant needed to be watered by someone who knew the traditions, customs and, curiously, the temperament of the Wa'arusha. I still held aloof from the argument, but, even at the price of my own district, I was rather glad and certainly considerably touched when this appeal found a response and I was left where I was for a further six months.

So here was a tale of sympathetic, skilful and successful colonial administration[4] at its very best, and it is clearly time that I turn to a very different story. Perhaps it goes too far to call the case of the Wameru insoluble, but it certainly proved beyond our powers and the powers of our successors to solve it, despite the skills of Hans and the infinite patience which we in the Administration exercised. The Wameru and their suspicions about our intentions towards their land were to be a thorn in our flesh right up to independence.

There were, I think, two main reasons for their intractability. In the first place, the indigenous tribal structure which had survived so robustly among the Wa'arusha had withered among the Wameru, and, hard as Hans and I laboured to produce an equally acceptable system based on their own *washili*, or clan leaders, it never caught the enthusiasm of the people. Secondly, there was a small but powerful faction in the tribe who were, irreconcilably as it transpired, opposed to the Chief, or *Mangi*. Mangi Sante was not an outstanding Chief, but he was by no means too bad. He was stupid, but he was tolerably honest and he was orderly in his conduct of business and, as events were to show, he was brave. But there was at a place called Akheri on the mountain a rich and influential group, with adherents elsewhere, who would not have him at any price.

I forget now the original reasons for the feud, but they really do not matter. The Arabic-derived Swahili word *fitina*, which I have used before, again comes to mind. The word is not readily translated but it encompasses both malice and persistence in stirring up and pursuing a quarrel. The original causes of the quarrel become quite inconsequential. When Africans indulge in *fitina*, they do so with a whole heart, and Sante's enemies proved unrelenting. Everything that we were to do to assuage the quarrel was to be consistently misrepresented as a triumph for the agitators.

When Hans Cory left us, I had a very different task on my hands with the Wameru from the wholly successful undertaking among the Wa'arusha. I was trying to breathe life into an insecurely founded constitution at a time when hostility to the Chief was being lashed up to a point where we had either to conclude that the Chief could no longer be effective and must be replaced, or we had to proceed against the troublemakers. At the same time I was advocating all over the chiefdom a cess on all primary produce sold which the Wa'arusha had already accepted for the benefit of the Native Treasury. The constitution, the Chief's position, the coffee cess, all were inevitably pulled together by the Akheri faction, although it was the last of the three which became the initial flashpoint. Africans are susceptible to the most bizarre and improbable tales, and the proposal to tax coffee production was represented by the anti-Chief party as a plot by Mangi Sante to sell their coffee *shambas*, to the KNCU, the big Chagga coffee co-operative on Kilimanjaro, and we began to receive reports of meetings held by the agitators to propagate this unlikely story.

I accordingly arranged to come out to Akheri and meet the Chief there to hold a *baraza* and make one more attempt to explain to the people what was really proposed. When I got there, I found some three hundred or more people gathered. The tension was palpable, and it was obvious that Mangi Sante, in the heart of enemy country, was under great strain. He and I took our seats, with the people in a half-circle facing us, and the leading dissidents, all by now well known to me, prominent at the front. I opened proceedings with an account of exactly what was proposed. Coffee *shamba* owners were the richest of the tribe, at present the Native Treasury's reliance on a flat-rate head tax weighed unduly hard on the poor, and a larger contribution to the revenue from the wealthy was fair. Having made these simple points in several different ways and having attacked the way the proposal had been transmuted into some sort of machination against his people by Sante, I called for comments. Up got Baradau, the leader of the opposition. His theme was that all people were people, and all should be treated alike and all should therefore be equally taxed. I interrupted. 'Baradau, I hear you telling me that all people should be taxed alike, and Mangi Sante can hear you, and your coffee-owning friends sitting here at the front can all hear you. But I am used to hearing you at meetings speaking with a great voice, yet here today you speak surprisingly quietly. Now away at the back of this *baraza* I see many poor people in ragged clothes who would be glad of your advice, and yet I doubt that they can hear you. I therefore entreat you to repeat loudly and clearly the words that the Chief and I have had the benefit of hearing.'

Baradau refused. 'Very well. Those who come to a meeting should speak so that all can hear, particularly those who lay claim to leadership. If you will not do this at my meeting, you have no business to be here. Go at once.' Immediately a lot of those in the front jumped to their feet with sticks raised threateningly, and I had a potentially nasty situation on my hands. Baradau and I stared at each other for a long, long spell. Then he turned and walked away behind me in the direction of the courthouse. Now I had to outface those on their feet, while resisting the temptation to look around and see whether Baradau was disposed to give the signal which would set them all at Sante and me. Slowly they sat down. The meeting proceeded, and in due course concluded, but I returned to Arusha to report to Donald that the dissidents would never be assuaged and that we should now proceed to prosecute the leading agitators for attempting to subvert the Chief. But after long discussion, into which we brought the PC, it was concluded that we should make one more effort to appease, in the best sense of that misused word, the opposition.

Accordingly we arranged a big *baraza* at Akheri, where Tim Revington, a tough but elegant ex-Coldstreamer with an impressive command of scholarly Swahili, reminded the dissidents that they had a new constitution, in the devising of which they had themselves participated, and that under it there was an explicit procedure for getting rid of a Chief where the majority disapproved of him. This was the procedure they should follow if they were acting in good faith, but nevertheless he would arrange for the DC to hold a meeting at Pole, Mangi Sante's headquarters, in ten days' time to hear each and every complaint that anyone cared to prefer against the Chief, and that none need fear retribution for so doing. That sounded very well, but his speech was punctuated by Baradau and his intimates chanting slogans against the Chief and clapping hands as they did so, a highly insulting gesture by Wameru custom.

Donald and I were in for a hectic three months. We started by arranging for the 'complaints *baraza*' to be held over two full days in March at Pole and we provided for the whole Meru tribal council and independent Wa'arusha elders to help us as assessors. But before the appointed day we heard prognostications of trouble, since Sante's supporters believed that it was time the other side had its say for a change, so we took with us a young police officer and half a dozen *askari* with rifles and bayonets, the police in Tanganyika being a paramilitary force. At first this seemed an unnecessary precaution. There were only a few hundred people on the grass outside the courthouse and they were mostly from Akheri and the other two parishes where Baradau's supporters were strongest. However, we had only been there a few minutes when a warlike chant could be heard and shortly we could see climbing up from the valley in an ordered throng several hundred young men armed with spears and sticks shouting slogans on behalf of the Chief. Obviously we had far too small a force, so how were we to use it? The prudent course was to keep them together, but then there would be little chance of keeping the two sides apart. So we interspersed the *askari* with uniformed tribal messengers and strung them out in a line across the front of the oncoming band, while we ourselves went forward to meet them together with Sante, who survived this test with credit. The young warriors had worked themselves up into a fine state of fury and for a while it looked as though we and the flimsy line behind us would all be brushed aside or submerged as they went for their opponents. But slowly the authority of the *Serikali* and the Chief prevailed until at length we had them seated to one side while they chose representatives to come and listen in the courthouse to see how fairly proceedings would be conducted.

In fact the complaints turned out a mish-mash of rubbish. Many related to events so distant in time that there was no possibility of arriving at the truth, many more involved allegations of petty corruption which proved baseless and should in any case more properly have been directed at various clerks. The only solid case was about possession of a piece of land which had been originally heard in a native court and had then passed up the whole appellate process to the Governor himself, being at every stage decided in Sante's favour. At the end of two tiresome days (we took a much stronger police escort on the second) we, with the full support of the assessors, had thrown them all out as baseless. Before returning to Arusha we left instructions for the 11 principal agitators to come to the Boma next day. Our last hope was that they might yield to Dutch uncle treatment away from the heady atmosphere of Akheri.

When they came, Donald reminded them that they had nearly all been members of Cory's group, and had thus had full part in framing a constitution to which they had subscribed; that that constitution provided a procedure for getting rid of an unpopular Chief; and that an elaborate hearing of complaints against Sante had exposed them all as groundless in the judgment of ourselves, of their own tribal council and of independent elders of another tribe. Much old ground was gone over, and it was getting dark before we warned them that there must now be a stop to agitation or they would be prosecuted. Since they had some miles to go back through the forest, I crammed them all into my Bedford box-body truck and drove them. So relentlessly perverse were they that even this small courtesy was used as a weapon. Within a couple of days there had been yet another subversive meeting. The Chief was on his way out, their views were prevailing with the Government, see how soon the Bwana Shauri had been their chauffeur. We decided to prosecute.

The charge of attempting to subvert the power of a Chief was a little used provision of the Native Authority Ordinance, and one which required the Governor's authority to prosecute, which we duly secured. It only carried a trifling maximum penalty of a year's imprisonment, but conviction under it meant that we could seek the banishment by the Governor of those found guilty to other parts of the territory, and months of struggle to sort out Meru politics had convinced us that the chiefdom could not at present be at peace so long as these men were there. In the ordinary way, the preparation of the case would of course have rested with the police, but this sort of highly political business was much better in the hands of us in the Administration who alone had the whole background, and so Donald and I and the new cadet, Stevenson, spent days in camp at various centres in the chiefdom collecting statements from a great number of people who could give particulars of subversive behaviour by any of the 11 people we intended to charge. Meanwhile, the political importance of our difficulties on the mountain in Arusha had continued to be appreciated in Dar es Salaam, and there was no difficulty in arranging for crown counsel to be sent to us to prosecute the case in court. The sharpest of the local lawyers in private practice, Alec Reid, was certain to be engaged for the defence.

It was possible to swear complaints on the basis of the statements we had collected against all 11 accused by the middle of April, and in due course they were arrested and remanded in custody. Reid applied for bail for them on 1 May. Donald and I were not disturbed. The nature of the charges, the seething state of the chiefdom, the near certainty of interference with witnesses all made it certain that bail would be refused. Theeman, the same resident magistrate who had heard my case against Williamson and his mine manager in Shinyanga, granted it. There was no doubt at all how this would be regarded on the mountain, and within hours Donald and I were packed and off with a force of police *askari* to camp at Akheri to keep the peace. Uneasy days followed, for it was now a truly hostile place, but within ten days Freddy Southworth, the crown counsel, succeeded in reversing the bail decision before Stanley Walden, the Deputy PC, who was eventually to hear the case, and we had our men back in prison and were able to return home.

The case came to court on 19 May, 1948 and it lasted a month. This was scarcely surprising. For a start, there were 11 accused and 13 different charges. One was a general conspiracy charge joining all 11, and there was one particular conspiracy alleged against three of them. Then there was a single charge against each accused separately as illustrative of the nature of the conspiracy in which they were engaged. Our prosecution witnesses numbered 23, for the defence there were 25, and in addition there was the evidence of the 11 accused themselves. The charges themselves read oddly to a European eye. There was the allegation that the Chief had sold the coffee plantations, there was the insulting hand-clapping at the Akheri *baraza*, there was a death threat to the Chief. At a circumcision ceremony there was the Chief's traditional apportionment of beer, consumed on this occasion, the charge alleged, by Baradau. One of the accused was stated to have urged his hearers 'to burrow under the Chief like a mole beneath a banana tree to bring him down'. Another charge put in one man's mouth a rather disgusting phrase about the Chief's supporters being made to 'sniff our shoes' once Sante was removed.

During the whole month I was scarcely out of Southworth's company. Freddy was an extraordinary fellow. He had been blown up in the terrorist attack on the King David Hotel in Jerusalem and had survived a coma of weeks, with a steel plate subsequently implanted in his head which used then to cause him severe headaches. As an advocate he was relentlessly pertinacious, and accordingly tailor-made for a case of this complexity. Being fresh from Palestine, he had little Swahili, but neither – curiously, since he had been many years in the country – did his opponent, Alec Reid. Here my presence in court alongside Southworth gave the prosecution a great advantage. In a case that was so remote from the normal run, there were many nuances of translation which were well outside the bounds of the court interpreter's skills, and I was able to ensure that muffed passages did not put our side off fruitful lines of questioning, while my intimate knowledge of the entire case and all the personalities came in equally handy. Reid was conscious of this, and tried various shifts – without success – to get me out of court. One day he was questioning one of our witnesses about the circumstances in which his original statement had been recorded, obviously seeking to imply in characteristic fashion that the witness had been in some way coached. It so happened that it was I who had recorded this particular witness's statement, and it was at once obvious that, if this came out, Reid would apply to have me removed on the score that I was a potential witness whom he might himself wish to call; and, no matter how specious the argument, it was one which Stanley Walden might find very difficult to refuse, since, as a very senior Administration officer himself, he had to be particularly careful to avoid even the appearance of bias to our side. I tilted my chair back so that Reid's body was interposed between me and the witness. When the inevitable question came, 'Who took your statement?' the witness could not see me to reply 'This Bwana.' He merely said, 'The Bwana Shauri,' and Reid did not think to ask him which Bwana Shauri. He sensed he was on to something in the charged court atmosphere, though he did not know what, and he nagged away at the same topic with one witness after another until he got bored and dropped it. It was not until that happened that we reintroduced any witness whose statement had been taken by me rather than by Stevenson or by Donald himself.

Our work by no means ended in the courtroom. We had a large selection of potential witnesses to the various charges, from whom Freddy had to pick each evening those who seemed likely to present their testimony most clearly on the following day; and there were always tactics to be discussed over a drink subsequently. For a month one lived and breathed the case, and I got a better insight into the legal mind than I ever had until many years later in a different career I spent two and a half days in the witness box before the Restrictive Practices Court in London.

But finally there came the day when the last examination-in-chief, cross-examination and re-examination had been concluded. Freddy Southworth and I repaired to my verandah and, sustained by Nona's coffee and sandwiches, by two o'clock in the morning produced 52 pages of typescript for his closing address the following day. Re-reading it now in the recollection of the circumstances in which it was produced, I can still admire the clearness of Freddy's description of the elements to be proved in a conspiracy charge, the lucidity with which he analysed the evidence of such a host of witnesses to prove the individual charges and meshed it all together to demonstrate the common course of action, the cogency with which he refuted the defence argument that the accused had justifiable grievances and that in any event they had only engaged in legitimate political activity. It was a *tour de force*. Stanley Walden adjourned the court for a few days to consider his judgment, and then convicted the accused on all counts and sentenced them all to the maximum one year. Inevitably there was an appeal to the High Court, but Walden's judgment was upheld, and we were then able to get the Governor's agreement to banish all 11 to other parts of the territory on the expiry of their sentences. In the whole of the British era in Tanganyika I do not think there was any court hearing which resembled this one in the combination of legal complexity and good old African *fitina*. Its successful conclusion gave us peace and order in the tribe after many, many months of agitation and riot. That was as much as we could hope for.

These strenuous administrative times with the two tribes were not of course the whole of my horizon, though I have recounted them in detail because at the time that was precisely what they seemed. One of the many rewards of district life was that at any given time there was always some cause or other which filled the whole field of attention and was for a time one's entire preoccupation. Everything else was small change.

But there is plenty of interest in small change. We held a census that year, and it fell to my lot to enumerate the South African farmers on the wheatlands to the north-west of the mountain. We had a considerable South African population in the Northern Province as a whole. They were the descendants of Boers who could not abide the defeat by the British at the beginning of the century and shipped themselves and their families and their ox-wagons and oxen too up the coast to the port of Tanga in what was then German East Africa. From there they trekked inland to settle under a no-nonsense German regime which would suit them better than a British one. Poor fellows, a decade later they were saddled with the British again and this time there was nowhere to run to. Some of them prospered, and one of them in my time associated himself with Government by accepting nomination to the Legislative Council, but they were mostly poor and they kept very much to themselves. Their view of the African was so antipathetic to our own that there was a gulf between them and us, but when I appeared as a census official they had to give me access to their homes and I saw some very squalid scenes. One family of ten in a windowless house of corrugated iron had a single living room and two small bedrooms, and many others were scarcely better provided. Signs of too much in-breeding were often plain to see in children's faces, and all in all they were often living in conditions which the Africans they despised would never have tolerated.

Dick Gower turned up again. He had a three-month assignment in southern Masailand which kept him mostly on safari, but when he came to town he used our house as a base. When he arrived, he was fresh from Dar es Salaam, whither he had been summoned to be instructed about his new job. There he had found the only two reputable hotels full, and he was wondering along Acacia Avenue in some doubt as to where to lay his head when he was hailed by a Greek whom he had known in Arusha. It transpired that this acquaintance now owned the Central Hotel, an establishment patronised by poor Greeks and Somali cattle traders and not at all *comme il faut* for administrative officers. 'But Bwana Gower, you must come to me.' On arrival, a boy was summoned and told to take the distinguished guest to the hotel's best room. 'But,' he protested, 'there is someone asleep there.' 'Then,' said the Greek 'he must go.' And upstairs he went, woke his compatriot and ordered him out. He supervised the tidying of the room, the provision of a fresh jug of water, and paused to consider what supreme touch of hospitality he could add in Dick's honour. 'Boy,' he finally declaimed, 'Tia shiti safi' – 'Put on clean sheets'.

I have mentioned before that Dick was an astonishing athlete despite very poor eyesight, but his eyes did for him when it came to shooting. This was a real handicap in the Masai bush, for on safari one's retinue rely very much on the *bwana* shooting for the pot. Guinea fowl were very plentiful in Masailand and, whenever Dick came in for a break, he had more and more shaming stories of being urged to stop and have a go, and the misses that inevitably followed. Until, that is, his final safari, from which he returned wreathed in smiles. On the penultimate day there was yet another large flock crossing the road. 'Simama, Bwana, simama,' cried the boys – 'Look, look'. The hell with it was Dick's first thought, but his second was that he had no more face to lose, and he obediently stopped and crawled up the short slope over which the guinea fowl had passed. Poking his head over the top, he found them grazing in a little dell below him, heads turned inward. He loosed off both barrels, 13 birds lay dead, honour and pride were restored. We took Dick with us that night to dine with Locke, our local game ranger, and made him tell the story. Locke looked appalled. 'Dick, do you mean you shot them sitting?' 'Don't be a bloody fool! Do you think I could hit a bird in the air?' Poor Locke overdid a passion for snakes, and died a few months later as he fumbled for one he had put in his jacket pocket.

We were so hard up in those days that we could not make much use of the fortnight's local leave we got each year. An exception was a trip up Kilimanjaro, when a scientific friend from old Shinyanga days got me commissioned and paid for by *Nature* magazine to plant some photographic plates on the top of Kilimanjaro to be bombarded by cosmic rays for purposes obscure, but connected, I believe, with nuclear research. It is a five-day trip, three nights up and one down, but Nona was expecting our first child and I had to leave her at the hotel from which climbing parties depart. She had a tougher time than I did, for my old friend from Lindi, Thomas Marealle – now very much a figure on the Chagga political scene, where he was eventually to become Paramount Chief before being voted out of office – insisted on taking her under his wing. This was very well up to a point, for she saw much of that beautiful mountain, but there came the moment when a kindly Chagga woman, learning of the pregnancy, insisted on sour cream in a gourd as the sovereign assurance of a safe delivery. Having somehow survived her nausea, she got back to the hotel, only to have our bull terrier slay the little monkey which the German proprietrix kept on a string in the garden. She was glad to see me back.

So, to replenish the coffers I had to stick to hunting elephant. One long weekend I took Nona and Innes, now safely delivered by the sour cream, to a settler friend, and set off myself on a nag lent to me by Mangi Sante for a hunt on the slopes of Mount Meru. I was riding up a steep slope through thin regenerating bush when I glanced to my right and saw a rhino a cricket-pitch length away. At that moment the saddle girth broke and I subsided over my animal's tail to the ground. Uncomfortable, but the charge never came. I had an unsuccessful hunt, but got back to Nona to find that elephant were raiding her host's plantations and shot one of them to put a stop to it.

We were sad to leave Arusha for Moshi – for a rather pointless follow-up study to a major investigation of land problems among the Chagga – but that was followed by a direction to take over Masailand as DC for six months from mid-1949 while Jack Clarke was on leave. For me, this was bliss.

7

MONDULI

The matters I had to deal with in Arusha, and also in my three-month sojourn in Moshi, were primarily those which arose from congestion, with the tribesmen squeezed between the forest and the white settlers' farms, and the settlers in turn feeling the weight of swelling populations on their boundaries. In Masailand, by contrast, one had to deal with space and emptiness. With fifty thousand nomads in twenty-five thousand square miles, it required a lot of hard travel by the DC to look after his parishioners, or even to find them.

The thrill of being DC of one's own district for the first time takes a lot of beating. When I got my orders, we had barely put the last ornament on the mantelpiece of our new house in Moshi, whither we had just moved from the pretty mountain base of Lyamungu, but I think we had packed and got under way within 24 hours, so keen was I to get myself in post before anyone changed his mind. The 50 miles from Moshi to Arusha, long since under tarmac, was then notorious as the most rutted and potholed main road in the territory, but on this occasion we bounced over it in my uncomfortable truck as though on air. A further 25 miles to the west and we turned off the main road to the headquarters station of Monduli, lying at the foot of the mountain of the same name and made pretty by the blue jacaranda trees lining the main street.

Most British administrators fall in love with the Masai, as indeed they tended to do with all tough nomads: Turkana, Somali, Bedouin. I expected to do the same after my own love affair with the Wa'arusha who had such close ties with the Masai and who so exactly resemble them in appearance and dress, but I found in fact that I never really took to them collectively, fond though I was of certain individuals. Perhaps it was because the Wa'arusha, without realising it, had badly needed help of a kind which I was able to give them, whereas the nomad Masai merely wanted to be left alone, and I dare say I found their robust independence somewhat frustrating. But how would a man not be happy who had to drive 200 miles north and as far south to reach his district boundaries, and whose writ ran over both the Serengeti Plains and the Ngorongoro Crater?

Masailand was obviously more of a man's world than a young mother's. There were rest-houses, it was true, but they provided the minimum of comfort, added to which the sight of her precious babe encrusted with the dust which smothered us on the road in the dry season was another deterrent. However, I took Nona up to Ngorongoro once to give her a first experience of big game at close quarters. We arrived in thick mist which gave no views at all. In the night a sinister little sound awakened us. Torchlight revealed the source to be a mouse drowning in a basin, and since the mist held next day that was as much wildlife as she saw on the trip. More ambitiously, I once took her all the way to Kibaya in the south. Kibaya had once been a sub-station with its own DO, one of whom had been killed by an elephant and was buried there, and what used to be the DC's house was a great deal better than a tent or the usual two-roomed rest-houses. Then we went on further south to Kongwa, where Robin Johnston was setting up a new district for the headquarters of the Groundnut Scheme,[1] to discuss a plan, which happily came to nothing, for the scheme to operate over a large block of South Masailand.

Routine administration, whether holding court, collecting tax, hearing appeals, discussing affairs in *baraza*, could only take place where the nomad Masai congregated, and that meant at cattle markets. Except for some special purpose one could not see the people in any other way, except family by family in their *manyattas* scattered widely over the pastures. So one did the rounds. I had six weeks once when I had only a single night at home in Monduli, and in my six months I certainly spent much more than half of my time on safari. There were two DOs, Vinter and Stevenson, both of whom I had known as cadets in Arusha. Vinter was with me at Monduli, and he and his Australian wife, Helen, looked after us for the first day or two as we were settling into the DC's house, a rambling bungalow quite unlike the usual PWD pattern of house. Stevenson, however, had a sub-station at Loliondo in the far north of the district across the Serengeti Plains, where he and his wife were quite on their own. Then we had a vet, Keith Thomas, who had fought at Arnhem and whose job was of course of great importance among a pastoral people. Mattis Möller was our doctor, a Swede who had been working in Ethiopia until his lovely wife, Ulla, found the country too hard as a place to raise their children. So Mattis came south to Tanganyika to look for work. But our Government, who were able to take him on some months later, were short of funds at the time and could not give him a place. Indeed, they were so short of funds that they had just withdrawn our doctor from Monduli. This deposition was unimportant so far as we officials at Monduli were concerned, since Arusha was only 25 miles away, but the Masai relied on a doctor turning up at their cattle markets. So, as the Masai Native Treasury was comparatively rich, I took him on as their employee, probably the first white public servant of any treasury in the territory. Then there was Hopwood, the district foreman, who looked after our roads and bridges and buildings and, finally, another Swede, a colourful eccentric called Lale Ekmann, whose job it was to supervise the running of the cattle markets. Lale came, I believe, from an aristocratic background in Sweden, but he had lived a rough life in Tanganyika for very many years, poaching elephant, trading ineffectively, and now farming on Mount Meru so precariously that he needed our job to make ends meet. He had married quite late in life, and raised a brood of famously handsome and talented daughters, all of whom in due course married friends or acquaintances of ours.

I write of places like Longido, Naberera, Kibaya, where our cattle markets were held, as though they were considerable centres, and indeed they do figure as village names on maps, but in truth there was almost nothing there. One drove 50 miles, or 100, or 200, and then, with very little change in the aspect of the bush all around, there would be a courthouse and a house for the clerk, a rest-house, a couple of Indian shops, a dispensary, the cattle-market enclosures and a complex of wells on which everything else depended. Here Mattis and Lale and I would descend one evening and set up camp and sit around the fire after supper while Lale told some of his vast fund of highly improbable stories. Then in the morning the cattle would be driven in among choking clouds of dust and Lale would get on with the market while Mattis saw to the sick who had been saving their afflictions for him since he was last there a month before. Meanwhile I did business with the local clan heads, held court if there were cases to come before me, or heard appeals from the native court. A couple of days of this, and then we would pack our traps and go on to the next market for a repeat performance.

There was a fund set aside in the Native Treasury for ranching, which had long been talked about but never tried. It seemed to me that this was worth a go, and I resolved to make use of the cattle markets to buy up young stock, run them for a while and sell them off. Looking back, I had no business to commit large sums in this way when I was merely standing in for the incumbent DC, and I later avoided asking Jack Clarke whether the undertaking made money or not; but, since we remained very good friends, I cherish the thought that my ranch was a good commercial venture for the Masai.

Because of the shortness of my tenure, and apart from my ranch, Masailand stays in my mind as a series of incidents. When I think of Masailand, it is synonymous with dust, and yet I was there in the rains too. I remember coming down the hair-pin bends from Ngorongoro in such wet mud that all I could do was to let my Bedford slide at each corner and fire it off the moment we were pointing in roughly the right direction. At the bottom my faithful boy, Saiboku, had as green a face as an African can have.

It was in the rains too that Stevenson had a small crisis in Loliondo. He had his sergeant in charge of police under close arrest for some alleged offence to do with illicit *pombe*, all much to the fury of the Superintendent in Arusha. One way and another a personal visit was desirable, but getting to Loliondo posed problems. The normal route was by Ngorongoro, up the mountain's southern face, round the crater rim, and then down by the Olduvai Gorge, which L.S.B Leakey[2] was to make famous as the cradle of mankind, and northwards across the Serengeti. But the rains had made Ngorongoro impassable and the only alternative was through Kenya, by Kajiado, Nairobi and Narok, turning a 200-mile journey into one of 350 at the worst of the wet season. At Kajiado I had arranged for a meeting with my Kenya opposite number, for the Masai moved regardless of the frontier and we always had plenty to talk about in consequence. Here there was a message for me to wait for Ted Pike, the Deputy PC, who was following me from Arusha. Ted, later Sir Theodore as Governor of Somaliland,[3] was newly posted to the province and had decided this was a good opportunity to get out of the office and see the most northerly part of it. He duly arrived in a large American car, which looked much less suited to the conditions than my sturdy Bedford. Ted was brother to Andy Pike, who had taken me under his wing when I first arrived in the territory and had taken me out to Bagamoyo one day where Ted was then DC. This was the first time of re-meeting him, and a very genial and witty Irishman he turned out to be when we got to Nairobi and settled into our hotel. Next day we set off for Narok in appalling conditions, with Ted's Chevrolet sticking so often that he abandoned it in disgust in the hands of the DC who was putting us up for the night and announced that he would travel with me.

In fact the weather took a turn for the better and we bowled along quite happily over grassy plains with plenty of small game about. Presently Ted suggested that we ought to take some meat to Stevenson and his wife, and I dutifully stopped and shot a Grant's gazelle. A thought occurred to me. 'Do you realise, Sir, that we are in Kenya and have no permit to shoot; that we are probably in a game reserve; and that there is a police post at the border? Can you picture the headlines when we are convicted?' We set to in a reflective mood to carve up the carcass and stuff the meat into a sort of cupboard built into my box-body over the petrol tank. After a mile or two one of the boys called to us to look back. We were pursued by creatures, like seagulls after a fishing boat, and a trail of blood in the dust told us why. Fortunately it was siesta time at the frontier post and I took it at a rush while the *askari* were still frantically buckling on their gear.

At Loliondo we duly found some formula which released the police sergeant while saving Stevenson's face, and we passed a couple of days on the station before returning by the way we had come to retrieve Ted Pike's car. On my next visit to Stevenson a couple of months later I took him with me to visit the Sonjo, a tiny tribe who lived by agriculture near the shores of Lake Natron in the heart of pastoral Masailand. I was motoring down a stony track on my way towards the Sonjo, but miles from any habitation, when I saw a strange procession coming towards us. It was led by a wizened old man with an army-webbing haversack over his shoulder. He looked familiar, but I could not place him. Behind him and towering over him was a strapping Masai youth with a spear in his hand. At the rear was a burly man swinging a sizeable club. I stopped. 'Hello, what are you up to?'

'Doing what you told me, Bwana. You must remember me – the messenger from Endulen whom you told to go and catch that Masai *moran* [young man] who murdered his father.' Now Endulen was a hundred miles away and it was at least a month since I had been there.

'Now, *mzee*, I didn't expect…but never mind! You couldn't get him and you have spent far too long on the search and now you really must go home. You have already gone beyond the call of duty.'

'Not got him? Why do you think I am going home? Who do you think this is?'

'But he is armed and it is not safe for you even though you have got this chap with the club to look after him.'

'Look after him, Bwana? This is the cattle thief I have been looking for these past five years.'

'*Mzee*, this will not do, this really will not do. Arrested men should be under restraint, especially when you believe one is a murderer.'

At this point the old man looked a trifle sly. 'Bwana *mkubwa*, I had them under restraint, both of them.' Here he fumbled in his haversack and fished out a Tate and Lyle's Golden Syrup tin of antique look and from the tin produced a pair of handcuffs. 'I had them chained together with these, Bwana, but they got so upset with the lions roaring at night that I unlocked them when they promised not to escape. And now, Bwana, I must get along if I am to have them in Loliondo prison tonight.' And sure enough that was where the dauntless old man had delivered them when I got back there a couple of days later.

It should not be thought that nothing ever happened in Monduli and that I was therefore never there. There were a few white farmers below the forest at the base of the mountain. In particular any DC Masailand had to cope with Anderson on the one side of Monduli and Bennett on the other, both violently hostile to the Government and anxious to make their feelings clear to any new incumbent. Fortunately they disliked each other even more, and a little manipulation of this sentiment enabled me to rub along happily enough. In due course Frank Anderson was indebted to me for the survival of his home, though he was away at the time and it was his son-in-law who sent me an urgent message to say that there was a fire in the forest above him. I sent for the police and messengers to turn out all the station's labour, while I jumped into the Bedford and motored over to the Andersons', a mile away.

I have a confused recollection of the next few hours. Perhaps we had three hundred men, two thirds of them brought over by me, but we only had hand tools for them, axes, hoes, *pangas*, although there were disciplined policemen and messengers to help organise the men. The forest came down to the Anderson house and the farm labour lines, and the general drift of the fire was southwards towards the farm. The forest was heavy, but there were old fire-breaks established by the Forestry Department. These were much overgrown with the passage of time, and the light bush that covered them was a fuse for the passage of the blaze. And what a blaze! We were trying to clear the fire-breaks, with great trees going up in a twinkling and crashing down in unpredictable directions, while brief changes in the wind had us at times running for our lives. But the men never lost heart and, when we emerged, blackened and exhausted, at nightfall, the fire was checked and would in fact smoulder to extinction. I got a promise of suitable pay for my men from Frank Anderson's obnoxious son-in-law without any difficulty, but it took some anger to get him to do the decent thing and slaughter some cattle for them. Frank himself, much as I quarrelled with him, would always have been open-handed.

There was an elderly German farming a few miles from Monduli, he having been sufficiently anti-Nazi to be allowed to keep his land. He died in Arusha hospital when I happened to be in town, and his distracted widow begged me to make arrangements to have him buried on the farm. In the circumstances my Bedford was the most suitable hearse available, and I had the coffin loaded aboard. On the way we had a puncture. Changing a wheel on my big truck was always quite a job, and the messenger and I were sweating and covered in dust when the widow herself swept past. It was not, I felt, very seemly, and nor was what followed, for when some hours later I went to see how the grave-diggers were getting on I found them on strike. They had half-dug the grave when they decided the soil was harder than they had expected and they wanted more pay. Less seemly still, I lost my temper and hit the spokesman, knocking him flat on his back in the grave. This at least the widow did not see, and I got the grave dug and the old man buried.

In 1949 we got Sir Edward Twining[4] as the country's new Governor. Quite soon he came to Arusha, and the four DCs of the Northern Province were summoned to meet him. With him came at last an invigorating draught of fresh air for Tanganyika as a whole. Since the war things had been good or bad according to local circumstances, but always against a seedy run-down background. First there was no money and then there were too few staff, and above all there was no vision and no direction. Suddenly all the things that had been lacking came together. There was money for development and the ranks had filled up with people who knew how it should be used. The grey, sad figure of Sir William Battershill,[5] bedevilled by ill-health, was replaced by a great Governor in the imperial tradition. The country needed basic development, better ports, tarmac roads, clean water, hospitals, education, improved agriculture, consumer goods to move the people into a cash economy. Twining could provide the energy to drive forward a programme the people to some extent felt they now needed and which we British administrators knew they ought to need. (It was years before I wondered sceptically whether they were not more fundamentally happy with a simple subsistence economy.) We were in a mood for leadership, and the country was soon on the move.

Twining was a very showy man in a most endearing kind of way. In his extensive travels within the territory he liked to take the police band with him, and when he was entertaining he enjoyed conducting it himself, doing so not at all badly. He was large and stout, and he enjoyed being decked out in full uniform. Indeed my first sight of him was in uniform and with his band as he led it in procession along Arusha's main street. It was comic, but it was not a bad way of impressing on the people that they had a man in charge who wanted to be known to them. He was also very congenial company, a great generator of fun, with a famous capacity for alcohol. But on this first meeting, what we DCs had from him was a lively, stimulating talk about his intentions for himself and for us. I went back to Monduli wondering whether any other governor anywhere would have put himself on display quite so robustly.

Soon my stand-in time in Masailand came to an end with Jack Clarke's return from leave. I sneaked a few days leave and bagged what turned out to be my last elephant on the Tarangiri River, where the tstse fly made walking home pretty painful. I believe that the area later became a national park, but I doubt if those voracious flies have allowed it to be popular with the average tourist. Although I had not really taken to the Masai, I admired their manliness, and it was impossible not to respect the way such independent people co-operated with each other when their whole way of life depended on it. The wells at Ngasumet, for example, were so deep that they required seven *moran*, precariously balanced one above another on poles fixed across the wells, to throw leather buckets up from hand to hand to water their cattle. Now this took some organising, for the day-to-day contacts between families were limited as they scattered over the pastures, yet every day, morning and evening, each man knew his place and settled into it with no apparent direction.

My feelings about the people might be mixed, but the land I loved. Space and quietness, even the dust, the gleaming snow of Kilimanjaro seen at dawn from Naberera across a hundred miles of plain, elephant in huge numbers blundering in the light of my headlamps across the road near Kibaya: I carried these vignettes away with many others. Fortunately I had many years ahead of constant return to the Serengeti and Ngorongoro at least.

8

MBULU

We left Monduli for Mbulu, thus to complete a full round of the Northern Province in a tour of just under three years, but we had no great complaint at being shuttled around the most beautiful part of Tanganyika. And I was now promised some stability, not that I really believed the promise. The intention, I was told, was that I should be stationed in Mbulu for the next six months and then return there after leave and take over from Peter Bell, the current DC, when he went on leave, and that after my following leave I should come back once again for a full tour. Now that was looking seven years ahead in a service where we all were used to being moved around much too often and at the shortest of notice – just as I had been transferred from Arusha, where Donald Troup and I had been led to believe we were to stay as a team. To add to my scepticism, no administrative officer had ever been in one station for anything like seven years at a stretch. Yet, against all the odds, this was exactly what happened. Continuity, even from the point of view of those administered of 'better the devil you know', was vital to good administration, and here Mbulu did better than any other district in the territory. As DCs, Jim Rowe, Peter Bell and I spanned 15 years between us. Jim Rowe started that long spell in the most severe circumstances of wartime deprivation and shortage, but before he left he had been able to frame the first application for funds for a district development plan under the Colonial Development and Welfare Acts. Peter Bell, blessed with common sense to the point of genius, fleshed the plan out with practical schemes. I carried on the good work. One thing the four tribes of Mbulu District never lacked in this period was consistency and steadiness from the Boma in our approaches to their many problems.

The district was divided by the Rift Valley wall into steamy lowland and black highlands which were often bitingly cold. The station itself, no more than a small village, and a rugged drive of 140 miles from provincial headquarters at Arusha, was in high country where altitude was popularly supposed to send administrators crazy. The largest tribe by far were the Iraqw, who all lived in the uplands above the Rift. The Barabaig nomads roamed the south of the district, both above and below the great fissure which in their area began to tail away. In the low country to the east, on either side of the Great North Road between Dodoma and Arusha, lived the two small tribes of the Gorowa, closely related to the Iraqw, and the Mbugwe, the district's only Bantu. In addition there were white settlers. There was a powerful group of coffee farmers in the north on the slopes of Oldeani Mountain, which runs up to the lip of the Ngorongoro Crater. There was a colony of Greek farmers at Magara below the Rift, where Prince Bernhard of the Netherlands later bought land, and finally there was a notably eccentric little bunch on the uplands between Ndareda and Babati. There had been another large group at Kiru, also below the Rift, but that whole area had been closed to habitation by Government during the forties because of the onset of virulent sleeping sickness.

I have mentioned the Mbulu development plan and its funding direct from the British Government. The figures seem derisory these days, indeed they were derisory if compared with the millions being cast away at that very time on the Groundnut Scheme. But in those days £90,000 over five years, in addition to the normal expenditure by Government and Native Treasury, would go a long way, particularly if it were supplemented by a generous measure of self-help by the people themselves. The central issue at which the plan was aimed was one with which I was not unfamiliar from Sukuma days. It was to reduce the intense congestion of people and stock in the Iraqw Central Highlands, which was eroding the soil and degrading the grazing. To do that we would need not only to clear the tsetse bush and provide watering points on a grand scale, as in Sukumaland, but also to introduce a scheme of stock reduction such as had never been attempted anywhere in the territory. Matters were much simpler with the three smaller tribes in the district. They needed more land, but cleared bush could provide enough of it and there was no need to think about compulsory stock reduction with them.

If this was the central problem of the day, there was plenty else to think about. First, the European farmers, with their relatively sophisticated economics and markets, always took plenty of administrative time, and there were three groups of them. Then the Barabaig, who were infamous for the casual murder of wayfarers. Since the crimes were, as perceived by us, without motive, they were hardly ever solved. There was, too, incipient warfare between them and the neighbouring agricultural tribe, the Wanyaturu, in Singida District, while the Masai were equally likely to raid the Iraqw in the far north for their cattle. And there was of course all the normal business of improving farming practice and encouraging new methods at a time of good marketing opportunities. High forests, bare crowded uplands, hot plains, a great variety of often surprising colours made a curious setting in which to tackle a fair sample of Africa's many perplexities.

We had a strong team throughout my seven years in Mbulu. There were always four of us in the Boma, one usually a cadet.[1] Agriculture, veterinary, forestry, medical, police, all had an officer on a station, and the PWD supplied an admirably energetic South African as district foreman. There was a manager for the experimental farms and there was Greek Cypriot employed by the Native Treasury to build for them, while Development Fund money paid for four field officers scattered over the district. The station was very isolated; we were on no main line of communication, so there were no passers-by, and our highlands and steep scarps made us difficult to get at in the rains. So we were left pretty much to our own devices and we managed pretty well. There were enough of us for a lot of informal eating and drinking together and a great deal of bridge. The station was a pretty enough place and we were all well housed; we built to PWD plans, as we were required to, but we managed more cheaply than they did and could usually finish a house with an extra bedroom over and above the official plan. We had a tennis court and a squash court, the latter illicitly built from balances left one year in the vote of moneys for Grade B roads. When Governor Twining paid us a memorably enjoyable visit, I was instructed to take him on an evening walk. I sought to lead him anywhere but past the squash court, but that was the road he took. I had to confess. 'Quite right, my boy. People must make entertainment for themselves!'

Our time in Mbulu got off to a shaky start. As soon as we were settled into our thatched house across the valley from the Boma, Nona set off back to Arusha to stay with the Troups until our second child was due. I went off on safari to the north with Peter Bell to start to get to know the district, but we no sooner got back from this trip than down I went with a high fever. This turned out to be pneumonia, with pleurisy coming along later, and by the time I was transported to the Bells' house I was in no good state. We had no doctor on the station at the time, nor was there any penicillin, which was still in short supply. So the radio telephone was used and there was a considerable commotion and the provincial MO came rushing up from Arusha with supplies. All this stole Nona's thunder when our daughter Sheena was being born, and indeed I eventually found myself convalescing with her in the Troups' guest house in Arusha.

Once recovered and back on station, I resumed after a gap of a good many weeks the safari programme that had been so brusquely interrupted. By the time we went on leave at the end of April 1950 I had had six months to acquaint myself with the district's geography, its leading personalities and the general thrust of its development programme.

'Wewe ni baba na mama' ('You are father and mother') were words which were constantly on African lips, and they were justified, for the authority wielded by an effective DC was truly immense. The PC was remote from the African people. The DC was the man. That being so, as I look through the rather scanty papers surviving from my 16 years in the field, I am frequently surprised at the tremendous pains we took to carry the people with us. Sometimes the objective dictated the scale of consultation. Whereas the Germans could impose a form of local government, Hans Cory and I could not have brought about a system which the Wa'arusha themselves would believe in without discussions which at the time seemed likely to last forever. In that case there was an obvious aim, but why, I wondered, did I spend a whole day under a blazing sun trying to persuade the Sub-chief and elders of Bashanet to agree to the total closure to grazing of a small area of eroded pasture so that we could learn how the grass would regenerate? An outside observer might have thought the scene an encouraging example of the democratic spirit at work. In truth it was a demonstration of bloody-minded obstinacy on both sides. The elders did not want to tell me why they objected, and settled down happily to prevaricate. I was determined to have the truth, and when they were hot enough and hungry enough and thirsty enough I got it. It turned out to be nothing more substantial than that the plot was traversed by a path used by a handful of children on their way to school, and all that was necessary to keep everybody happy was an adjustment of the boundary.

Every colonial administrator had his own examples of this kind of mutual incomprehension over trivia, but there was little of that kind of thing where larger policies were concerned in Mbulu. Twining once wrote to me that our development plan was 'a model both in planning and execution', but he also said to me 'Keep it up, Meek – no bloody democracy!' In fact we could never have done what was done without the people's support. The central problem in Mbulu, constantly identified in concerned reports throughout the 1940s, was the steady degradation of essentially fertile land by overgrazing by cattle, sheep and goats. It was first and foremost an Iraqw problem, and slowly over the years the tribesmen came to accept that without extensive destocking their children would inherit only a land eroded to destruction. Not only did they face up to the need, but they went on to acknowledge that there could never be adequate stock reduction without compulsion, although, as far as we could discover, the law had never been successfully used for such a purpose in Africa and I doubt that it has been so used since. Peter Bell's powers of persuasion brought this about, but he never believed he could have done so if the Iraqw had not been first and foremost cultivators.

Not that cattle were unimportant, for they meant riches and prestige; and since no tribesman wanted to keep by him more stock than he could herd into his *tembe*, built into a hillside and fortified against the Masai, there were highly complicated systems of lending animals which were the source of endless litigation in the native courts. So livestock had a great social importance, but there was no mystique about them such as one found in the truly pastoral tribes, nor were they an essential part of bride-price, as among the Sukuma.

But making people sell stock was never going to be enough, for the soil was being too rapidly impoverished. In Central Iraqw, to take the worst case, we needed to get rid of just over half of their beasts to leave a not-too-generous three and a half acres of grazing for each remaining animal, which was far too difficult a target to think of hitting by using the law. We thought that at the best we might get numbers down by a third over a three-year period of compulsory sales. Any reduction beyond that must be by the dispersal of stock to new land. Here we were well placed.

A lot of Mbulu District was under bush infested by tsetse fly where cattle could not live. There was also a well-established practice of free service to clear it on a scale which made even the diligent Sukuma seem laggard by comparison. Every fit man was liable to 30 days unpaid labour a year, and he had to provide his own food as well. The Native Authority would mill the grain, transport it, provide all the tools and pay the wages of the few supervisory staff we employed. Life in the bush was fairly stark and the men were cut off from their families, and yet in my last full year I see that not far short of half a million man days were worked out of a total population, men and women, young and old, of 175,000. It was an astonishing example of self-help, and in seven years I never heard the system called in question. All the argument, of which there was plenty, always centred on where the main effort was required for that dry season, or how much should be shifted from the actual clearing work to water supplies or roads for the new country.

All of this, along with the improved agricultural practices our team sought to induce, amounted to a small revolution, and people who had known Mbulu in the forties would be astonished when they returned in the mid-fifties at the good heart the land was in, even after three years of poor rainfall. But we had some things going for us. For one thing the people appreciated that what was being asked of them was only one facet of a development plan which Government was paying for and which was bringing them tangible benefits. They also had before them an example of what we aimed to do for the whole district. A couple of miles from the Boma we had taken over 600 acres of the most bare and eroded land in Iraqw and turned it into a demonstration farm. Grazed at exactly the density which our culling programme aimed at for the tribesmen, the grassland had recovered in an astonishing way and stood out against the meagre surrounding pasture for all to see. Finally, cattle prices happened to be rising throughout the three years of compulsory sales. Forced sales in a falling market would not have been practical politics.

Peter's clinching coup in securing the tribesmen's support came when he got the backing of Nade Bea.[2] The Iraqw Native Authority had the usual structure of Chief, Sub-chiefs and headmen, and pretty good they were. Nade Bea, by contrast, had no official position, and was often referred to as the chief witch-doctor of the Iraqw, but it is nearer the mark to describe him as their spiritual father. He was a very old man by this time, born before any white man had been seen in these parts, or even heard of, though he lived for me to send him by air to see the sea and the sights of Dar es Salaam. He lived in the Iraqw heartland of Kainam, the small plateau a few miles from the Boma where the tribe had subsisted huddled away from the Masai and other raiders in the generations before the Germans came. There, before peace and security allowed the Iraqw to debouche all over the surrounding plains, a very stable agriculture had developed and, when the white-bearded old man compared Kainam with the ruined grazing elsewhere, he saw what we were driving at. So, despite being the largest cattle-owner of all, he put his weight behind us and swung the balance in favour of our plan.

The culling of cattle, sheep and goats was a backdrop to all my time in Mbulu; but, although stock culling was a revolutionary innovation, it was only one of the steps to save or improve the land which were a constant administrative preoccupation. Tsetse clearing went hand in hand with stock reduction, and the excellent custom of free tribal labour opened up great areas of bush for the people's cattle each dry season. But if the new pasture were to be used there had to be water, so a proportion of the labour force would be directed to the building of dams, the digging of canals and the laying of pipelines; so then, at minimal cost, the basics were provided, and courthouses, schools and dispensaries would follow.

In agriculture we pursued a single, simple theme, though not a popular one. In their hilly homelands both the Iraqw and the Gorowa cultivated steep plantations where the run-off of rainwater wasted its properties and eroded land lower down. The conventional cure was to terrace the land to retain the water. Now terracing the field was very tiresome for the farmer. On each terrace all the topsoil at the back would have to be pulled forward to level off the downward slope at the front. Short of even more laborious re-distribution of topsoil, this meant that the exposed topsoil at the back of the terrace would give a pitifully meagre yield for the first few years. Eventually, of course, the hard work would pay off, as the soil at the rear of a terrace improved and each step of the farmer's *shamba* retained the rainfall. But the fact remained that men would not put up with the work involved and the reduced early yields for the sake of much better harvests at some uncertain time in the future.

Our solution was what we called 'trash-bunding', cribbed from Kigale in Rwanda, where we had seen the success of the system. This is how it worked. After harvest on a steep-pitched field the farmer would lay the trash left behind along a series of contour lines. When the rains came, some topsoil would wash down as it always had; but now, instead of running away to waste it would be checked at a barrier of maize or millet stalks which was permeable enough for the rainwater to pass through. The repetition of this work from year to year led to a slow build-up of soil along each selected contour. In the end the farmer would be left with a series of terraces, but the process itself was so gradual that there was none of the severe loss of productivity at the rear of each terrace that there would have been from digging out terraces straight away.

All this sounds a painless enough way of avoiding soil erosion, raising productivity and eventually doing away with the hard labour of cultivating very steep slopes. At all events it was not too difficult to persuade the Native Authority to order that trash-bunding should be required practice on hilly land, which meant most of the district's plantations. Yet to our surprise there was more difficulty in enforcing this law than ever we had over the potentially far more unpopular compulsory cattle culling. The reason was that the trash was fodder for cattle, and any source of fodder was important where grazing was so inadequate for farmers' stock. But here again we were up against a bad habit, for the farmers' practice was simply to let their stock onto the land after harvest to feed on the stover. This meant that hooves turned the soil to powder, and that spelt loss of fertility. So we stuck to our guns, and so did the Native Authority; and, although many prosecutions were necessary to enforce the practice, trash-bunding became the order of the day. Without question it was a beneficial measure, but I never knew whether my successors maintained the pressure, still less whether terraces were created to be maintained into independence. I have my doubts.

I have sketched in those major themes because they related to problems of land use and were the backdrop to everything else during my years in Mbulu, just as the political tussles with the two tribes on Mount Meru had coloured all that I did in Arusha. It may be thought that what I have described were matters for the vet or the agriculturalist or a water engineer, but this was not the case. Subsistence agriculture means that any change in the use of the land from which a farmer scrapes his living is a change to the farmer's way of life, and that is the stuff of politics. Only the Administration could deal with the politics. Huge *barazas* to inform the people, long meetings to guide the Native Authorities, supervision of any subsequent support or lack of it in the native courts, all those were the lot of the DC and his DOs. And indeed sometimes restraint of one's expert advisers was required, for the ideal course of action was often not practical politics.

Having said that, in Mbulu the idea of the district team was well-rooted. I used to hold a formal meeting with all the senior staff once a month or so, but it was more to the point that we lived in each other's pockets. All our offices were housed in the imposing old German fort at Mbulu. One always knew where and when the agricultural or the veterinary officer was off on safari; and they and any others of the technical departments would make a point of dropping in to discuss problems or describe progress. People came and went over the years, and they naturally varied in their quality, but each of them was always a member of a closely bonded team, to the district's great gain.

Teams and team spirit were in vogue. We were, thank goodness, a long way from being governed by focus-groups, but I did pay heed to a variety of boards and committees and councils. At the beginning of the fifties, heavy agricultural machinery was still short. The allocation of what was available was controlled, for European farms, by a production committee of the farmers, chaired, like all these bodies, by the DC. In due course African farmers too needed to mechanise production, both to open new land on the fertile, volcanic slopes in the north of the district, and in cultivating land which had reverted to them as European short-term leases expired. Again, I chaired an African committee which made Government loans for buying machinery and oversaw the distribution of new farmland in economic packages. Obviously these controls led on to fairly close supervision of production programmes in relation to market demand. A progressive and sympathetic British farmer, Jack Ellis, also saw his chance to co-operate with Africans, unused to large-scale farming, in opening and developing land to the benefit of both sides. I was glad to see this last scheme work on trust, with nothing set down on paper.

Water was as crucial to modern farming in the north as it was for the simple grazing and cultivation we were opening by clearing tsetse bush for the Iraqw and Barabaig in the east. Coffee production in particular needed plentiful water, and here the big estates at Oldeani depended on pipelines from the mountain forest. Each main line supplied a number of farms, and fair shares for all were obviously a fruitful source of dispute. The system was run by a water board, and our meetings were lively affairs, as neighbours accused each other of malpractice. There were indeed plenty of opportunities for dirty work at the junction boxes, where small adjustments could increase the flow of water on one side and diminish it on the other. There were one or two cases of armed confrontation by night, and we had the odd criminal prosecution. I always thought that defeat in a water dispute led to one of our farmers shooting himself in a drunken depression.

Then we had our local councils. In each sub-chiefdom the *gausmo*, to use the local title, was accustomed to confer regularly with his elders on all matters of local concern. Towards the end of my time in Mbulu I sought to strengthen these useful groups by persuading them to co-opt educated younger men, priests, clerks, dispensers or shopkeepers. That was well enough, but I was much more doubtful about the black, brown and white groupings which were now being keenly promoted from the Secretariat. Multi-racial district councils were all the thing. It was easy enough to foster a good African core, though difficult to see how the highland majority could contribute help for local problems below the Rift, or vice versa. I could also prevail on one or two good candidates among the white farmers to join ship. But there were no Indians of consequence, such as were to be found in Arusha or Moshi, only small shopkeepers of narrow outlook. I could see no prospect of forming an effective district council on the lines enjoined by our masters in Dar es Salaam, and, with a little deft manipulation, I left this project hanging in the wind for my successor.

The province too boasted its committee system, with the PC always in the chair, instead of the DC at the lower level. There was one, whose title I forget, dealing with natural resources. I appeared before it to argue the case for re-opening the alienated farmland at Kiru, which had been closed to human habitation a decade earlier following a virulent outbreak of sleeping sickness. My brief on this occasion was not an easy one. Its essence was that my reconnaissance party and I had crisscrossed the whole area, had been eaten alive by tsetse and had emerged with some discomfort but without having contracted sleeping sickness. However, this was enough for my hearers, and in due course I was able to advertise a parcel of large farms for clearance and fresh settlement.

There was a provincial advisory council, which for us administrators was a useful sounding-board for the advice and opinions of the provincial departmental heads. I recall it devoting much time to the need for separating the African from hard-won savings. This was neither as brutal nor as mean as might appear. There was plenty of cash around, particularly among the prosperous coffee growers on Kilimanjaro and Mount Meru. The trouble was that useful consumer goods were hard to come by in the shops, and money stowed under mattresses did little for the local economy. I doubt if our deliberations did more than air a problem which the market would shortly have spotted for itself. At all events, supplies of small wirelesses, cheap watches and so on proliferated.

Among regular gatherings, the DC's six-monthly conference held pride of place. For a start, we were such a team of close friends. I had set one territory record as the youngest cadet to join the service, another for the period I had avoided even setting foot in the capital, and yet a third in due course for the longest service in a single district. But with my colleagues in the Northern Province I found myself part of a record-breaking relay team. Over four years we had Mike Molohan, as our very distinguished PC, John Shaw as his Deputy, Basil Stubbings as DC Moshi, Mickey Davies DC Arusha, Pip Fraser-Smith in charge of the Masai, and myself at Mbulu.[3] Such continuity had never been heard of, and we made the most of it by becoming fast friends. We were a highly experienced team, so plenty of good ideas, often aimed at what we required of the Secretariat rather than what we could do for them, were aired at our formal discussions. Off duty we partied or danced or played cards, and once Arusha put on a remarkably good variety show.

Since the territory was subject to a UN mandate, we were subjected to visiting missions at three-yearly intervals. I vividly recall that of 1948 when I was DO in Arusha, because during the visit I was having a man beaten in my office for the sort of offence that was best dealt with out of hand, even though that was quite improper. Meeting Tim Revington, our excellent PC and himself a well-known advocate of summary justice, that evening I remarked to him that I hoped nothing untoward had been heard from my office. He turned white, and I knew the times of youthful indiscretion were past. Probably the 1951 mission did not visit Mbulu, for I do not recall it. But in 1954 we were given a close look, and I had a hard time countering the deeply inbuilt prejudices of the American chairman, Mason Sears. Fortunately, both Nona and I had much happier memories of Arthur Gaitskell, who visited us about the same time as the UN mission. He was a member of the Royal Commission on East Africa. Whether or not he learnt much that was germane to the commissioner's task, he showed a sympathetic understanding of what we were up to, and was himself a mine of information on the great Gezira cotton scheme in the Sudan.

Let us now get away from our committee network. Some of these groups had a useful influence on one's thoughts about general directions, but few had much to do with the day-do-day running of a complex society in a district about the size of Wales.

Court work was one of the basics, on which I have barely touched in earlier chapters. Civil proceedings were very few in our lower courts, which was just as well, for the field was an obscure one for me; and if a case loomed I was successful in passing the buck to someone else. In criminal cases we were governed by the Indian Penal Code. Here I was effective, for I cannot remember having a judgment or sentence revised, as a cadet, when I was subject to constant High Court supervision; nor, when I was fully qualified, was any judgment of mine overturned on appeal. The most serious cases, such as murder or manslaughter, were of course reserved to the High Court. The job of the magistrate in his district was to hold, with two local assessors to help him, a preliminary inquiry. Apart from hearing the evidence in the case, the preliminary inquiry leant heavy weight to local custom, which was obviously helpful to the

High Court judge to whom the case was eventually committed. Here again, my findings over the years provided pointers to the eventual outcome of cases. At Mbulu, with three DOs to support me, my magisterial work declined. I took only the more serious cases and left the others to them.

When there were convictions for murder, it was the practice to seek the DC's advice, because of his knowledge of local attitudes to the particular crime and because of what he could find out about the convicted man's family and social circumstances, as to whether or not the death penalty should be applied. This was a heavy responsibility.

Along with the courts, the police and the prison were there to support law and order. I had a police officer in post for most of my time in Mbulu, but there were considerable periods when I had to take charge with a sub-inspector looking after the day-to-day running of our little force. As ever, this was a cause of a difficult balancing act from time to time between one's duties as a magistrate and as an officer in charge of the police. Supervision of the prison and its inmates sat lightly on the DC's shoulders. Hard cases among the prisoners were packed off to the more secure prison in Arusha, and the remainder were useful contributors to Mbulu society. A trap door in the rear of the official houses gave the daily access to empty the thunderboxes. When cattle put their hooves through the pipeline which supplied the settlement from a dam a mile way, prisoners did the repairs. They patched up the station's roads. They built the squash court. And when routine work dried up they could always water the DC's lawn and weed his garden. There were plenty of tales to illustrate their own appreciation of their standing. One was of the working party filing up to the DC's house one evening to complain that the chief warder was drunk and would not let them back in. Another was of the fellow who made a break for it one day. 'After him, boys!' cried the warder in charge, and all scattered in pursuit, to return an hour later with the delinquent.

Between us all we saw a great number of the people. The four field officers had their houses in the sticks and rarely came into headquarters. The most able, Roger Austin, was the only one who was married. His wife had a lonely time, but all passers-by from the Boma made a point of calling for a chat and she bore her lot pretty well. Tsetse-bush clearings provided the high spot of the field officer's year. The lead-in to three months of frantic activity took weeks of preparation. Crucially, the areas of operation had to be defined and marked out in consultation with the local Sub-chiefs. Water supplies had to be assured so that campsites could be marked out and stocks of food and tools laid down.

Austin had no problem with the rest of the year. Ingenious and substantial water schemes were his forte. They were always intelligibly set out on paper for consideration, and over the years many of them were brilliant successes. None of the field officers had any powers to enforce cattle culling, but they were admirable monitors and sources of information about the progress of this all-important scheme. And all expected a wide variety of odd jobs from the Boma. Altogether they were a handy bunch of practical performers.

The agricultural and veterinary officers, in the nature of their jobs, were much on safari. With the views I had always held on the importance of safari for good administration, even when things in the field were comparatively quiet, I made sure that my team were not behindhand. My three DOs were each assigned a major area to take under their wings, namely North Iraqw, South Iraqw and Below Rift. Each was expected to spend ten days a month in his parish, and I did at least as much myself, supplemented by some necessary contacts with neighbouring DCs and of course visits to the PC in Arusha. This steady contact between Boma and people did not preclude controversy and disagreement, but it did spell trust and confidence. The variety of Mbulu's tribes and landscape made it a delight to run, but we had a well-knit district nonetheless.

All this sounds very much a 'get up and go' sort of life, but control of a major district also means a great deal of paperwork. The provincial level had to be handled with care. The DC knew that his was the job that counted, but the PC did not share this view. So the PC had to be made aware of difficult or potentially troublesome issues; and he had to be persuaded of the need for significant changes of policy. The appointment of a new Chief needed his endorsement, a question which arose when I persuaded the incumbent rascal to resign from the leadership of the Barabaig. One used to correspond direct with the provincial departmental heads, and here differences of opinion would need reference to the PC. Financial estimates for the year's revenues and spending by Government and the Native Treasury estimates were immensely time-consuming in proportion.

Not only were there many conflicting pressures for various schemes, but there was also the knowledge of meticulous scrutiny higher up. And there were endless reports. The Secretariat needed to know how compulsory cattle culling was faring, anything that bore on white-settler interests was still at this time politically touchy and needed a report. So did security matters, even when there were none of significance. Lastly, the annual report was a labour, but one of some love, for one felt, however mistakenly, that it was for the archives as well as for immediate higher authority. This would show what we did and how we did it.

I was lucky enough – for it was a rare blessing in a district office – to have a good young African stenographer on my staff. He was an enormous help with all my English correspondence. Alas, Pitman's shorthand does not cope with Swahili, so all my letters to Chiefs, Sub-chiefs, sometimes individuals, had to be done by hand. There were a few where I could tell my head clerk 'Tell him so-and-so,' and sign the result, but usually I preferred to draft myself for nuances of meaning, and this took much time.

What of the Boma itself, where most of us had our being while we were on the station? It was a splendidly picturesque old German fort, with a handsome tower at one corner. At the top of it was my own spacious, airy office. It had a fine view on one side up to the wooded hill where the prison was concealed, and on another to my own tree-framed house, with the valley which divided the station stretching away beyond it. It had too many working memories for me to touch upon, but two unconnected with business stick in my mind.

The first concerned our wire-haired terrier, Sally. She was Nona's constant companion, but for some reason on this particular morning she was in my charge in the office. Suddenly through the open window came Nona's clear tones from down below. Instantly, without a downward glance, Sally leapt through the window. The drop must have been the best part of 20 feet but, miraculously, she landed safely on all fours and jumped into her mistress's arms. Sadly, she was less lucky when we came to Dar es Salaam. We had left her with friends while we were on leave. By arrangement with us, they boxed her up and put her on a lorry for Dodoma to catch the train. On the way a kindly African opened the box to water her, but she was too quick for him. She was out and into the bush, where doubtless a leopard got her. It gave us a gloomy moment when we met the train at Dar es Salaam.

Mbulu, perched above the fault line of the Rift, was unsurprisingly subject to earthquakes. Here was my second incident, for I was in my office for a quite severe shock which shook my tower considerably. Having made sure the Boma was still in one piece and nobody injured, I ran to see how Nona and the young ones had got on. All turned out well, but they had nearly been pinned by the refrigerator sliding at them across the floor.

The account I have given of the bare bones of administration may appear to reflect a routine job in exotic surroundings. Nothing could be more misleading, for routine in Africa was always interrupted. Interruptions might be dramatic and prolonged and of great moment in the lives of many people; or they could be adventurous or funny, and perhaps significant only to oneself. Let us look at some that occurred over our years in Mbulu.

First, here is a deadly tale. In the upland grazing of the Barabaig nomads I was well used to seeing streams of field voles crossing my road on safari. I believe I was half-aware that plague was enzootic among them, but I attached no special importance to them, since there had not been a plague case among humans there. At some point in the early fifties I noted that the columns of these little beasts were more numerous and much denser than usual. I thought nothing of it, little thinking that the enzootic was about to become epizootic, killing them off in great numbers and leaving their parasite fleas looking for new hosts – people. I was in Arusha on business when the PC had a telegram to report an outbreak of plague at Basutu, a pretty little lakeside headquarters in the Barabaig uplands. We were without a doctor at Mbulu at that time, but two were ordered from the Arusha hospital to join me at Mbulu and go on with me to the site of the epidemic. Mike Molohan, the PC, advised me to go and get myself a prophylactic jab against plague before I left, but I said I would go at once and the doctors could bring along a shot for me. It was the dry season, and my Bedford box-body made good time over the 140 miles to Mbulu, though dust and rough roads and our two steep and long escarpments on the way never let one improve much on four hours. The doctors were not far behind me, but when I asked for my protective injection I was disconcerted to hear that there had only been two doses available in Arusha, and my medical friends had absorbed them.

I did one or two things at Mbulu that had to be done, and we then made the 60 or 70 miles to Basutu that evening. Our rest-house was a small *rondavel*, and the first sight to greet our eyes was a dead rat, paws stiff in the air, lying right in the middle of the cement floor. As we sprayed DDT prodigally around floor, walls and grass roof I tried unsuccessfully to feel glad that my two friends were prophylactically protected, even though our servants and I were not. I might add that I must have developed quite a kink in my back over the following week as I kept an eye out for fleas on the khaki stockings I wore beneath my regulation shorts.

But it is time to turn to the real sufferers, soon to be dead men or women. There was a grove of trees by our rest-camp, and here, with the minimum shelter necessary for the dry season, the local medical auxiliary had lain out the sick, for whom he could do so little. Most of them were bedded on blankets on the ground, but we were at least able to organise the very modest comfort of string beds for them. We all offered what human consolation we could, while more to the point the doctors used whatever they had to alleviate the ghastly, panting end of those in the last throes of pneumonic plague. But we had no sovereign remedies, and the disease proved entirely lethal. Before the then wonder-drug streptomycin came on the scene all the way from Dar es Salaam we had 50 cases precisely, and 50 deaths. Thereafter, mercifully, all recovered, save one old man who was at his last gasp as the needle was inserted. I recall no children in that ghastly camp of the dying. I have always supposed they died quickly in their *kraals* and nobody thought to bring them in. The same was doubtless true of many adults.

We had passed the catastrophic time in a week, and I could head back home. There I was met by the always-practical Nona with pumps lined up to spray me, my cook and boy and Boma messenger, the car and every bit of our belongings. Wise enough in any event, but I think she mainly had our children in mind.

In the same area we had another major diversion from our so-called routine in the shape of a small war between my Barabaig and their neighbours the Wanyaturu. The latter tribe lived in a different district, Singida, in the Central Province. They were largely agriculturists, but possessed enough cattle to tempt my pastoralists. Furthermore, the border ran through light forest and was not visibly defined. Almost inevitably there came a time when run-of-the-road cattle raiding and a drought leading to fierce disputes over rights to borderline grazing between the tribes produced some broken heads;

and worse violence then followed, with some dead Wanyaturu as a consequence. Bruce Ronaldson, the capable DC Singida, and I arranged a hurried border meeting, with a few armed *askari* in attendance.

There was no question that the Barabaig were the aggressors. It was equally clear that guilt would never be brought home to individuals. I promised the tribesmen severe justice rapidly to come, but the immediate job was to get the disputed border clearly defined. This entailed blazed trees and stretches of trench along a compass line through the forest, and there was clearly going to be plenty of hard work to do. 'I can turn out five hundred men in a week's time,' said Bruce. 'How many can you manage?' 'Oh, about fifty.' The Barabaig were few in number, nomadic and averse to manual labour unless they were fighting or engaged in tsetse-bush clearing for their own obvious benefit. So I made no large claims.

A week later I was back on the border scene to find Bruce and his men all ready for business. 'Here we are. Where are your lot?' 'Oh, somewhere around, I expect.' Off I went to search, and sure enough I found rather better than the promised number sitting in a patch of shade. I was glad to see they had their *jembes* (mattocks) with them, but they also had their full complement of spears and shields. 'Bring them along,' I said to the Chief. 'There's work to do.' I led them, singing, back to the meeting place, but as we came into view round a corner of the bush the sight of armed Barabaig was too much for the Wanyaturu. They were up and away in panic over the neighbouring hill. 'Here are my men at last, Bruce. But where are yours?'

Needless to say, we eventually had the arms stocked under guard, recovered Singida's tribesmen and got on with the task of delineation, keeping the two sides at a prudent distance from each other. Marking the boundary took two or three days, and proved rather enjoyable. Admittedly, the two warring sides had to be kept well apart, so one was on one's toes; and the Barabaig needed plenty of drive to keep at work, for digging trenches was for women in their philosophy. But there was plenty to joke about, particularly the recollection of the fleeing Wanyaturu, and things passed off in good temper. But I was also preoccupied with getting the borderline exactly right through the long stretch of woodland. We had started with a back-bearing on one trigonometrical point. Thereafter it was a matter of innumerable compass bearings from one tree to the next prominently visible one.

To emerge after a couple of days exactly on a line for the next hill-top trig point gave me extraordinary satisfaction.

But punishment was still to be meted out, as I had promised it would be. Young Barabaig men had been responsible for aggressive cattle raiding, from which theft and some bloodshed had resulted. Individual culprits would never be identified. The perpetrators were relatively few, but this sort of thing was sport for the whole tribe; and, unlike the Masai, the Barabaig were a compact group despite their nomadic way of life. If ever there was a case for communal punishment, this was it, and this was what I resolved upon.

There was provision in the Native Authority Ordinance for communal punishments, but any such penalty required the Governor's sanction, no less. True, with a robust character like Sir Edward Twining the prospect of eventual approval was good, but I shuddered to think of the time it would take. The PC would have to be convinced first, but the Chief Secretary would have to advise. Above all, legal advice would be necessary, and I could envisage endless quibbles about the definition of the tribe itself, let alone the propriety and size of a fine. One way and another, months would elapse rather than weeks. If at the end approval were not forthcoming, I would lose all confidence among the tribesmen, to the detriment of the future administration, as well as my own, of these difficult people. If, on the other hand, approval were forthcoming, it would be too remote from the offence to have the salutary effect I wanted.

So I decided to bypass the system and rely upon my relationship with the elders of the tribe to impose my authority. Accordingly, I called them together in *baraza*, and told them this whole episode was so bad that it should be referred to the Governor himself. 'But this, I know, would hurt your pride, so you must accept my punishment instead.' I went on to fine them 500 head of female stock, to be collected in any way agreed between Chief, headmen, elders and people, and sold on the market, with the proceeds going to the Singida Native Treasury. The stock were to be healthy, and I set a time limit for payment. No one demurred. This was a very sharp penalty on people to whom cattle were almost life itself, and I felt some unease as to whether I had presumed too far. But over the next couple of months those 500 head were duly brought to market. A few were unacceptably broken down and were rejected in favour of something healthier; but in the end all was smartly and quickly accomplished. My opposite number in Singida was well content, and so were the Wanyaturu. Above all, for the remainder of my time at least, there was no further trouble between the two tribes.

These goings on after a major border fracas could not be kept from my superiors, but I was not too stretched to put a good gloss on them. 'How did you manage it, Meek?' from Mike Molohan. 'Not too difficult, Sir. I told them to volunteer these cattle, or I would have to refer to the Bwana PC and the Bwana Governor, when much worse things might be expected.' My masters seemed satisfied. The Barabaig themselves were unresentful, for it was not much later, as my long spell in Mbulu finally came to an end, that I was presented with a shield and spear and declared a blood brother.

The chiefly office had no traditional standing among the Barabaig, but the incumbent at the time, Gidornyau, was in the Native Authority and his power was useful. He was indebted to me, for I had promoted his candidature after easing out his drunken predecessor, who was convinced that his tenure of office had led to evil spells being put upon him. Gidornyau was a capable man, but I also dealt more and more with the clan heads who, as with other pastoralists, were the real repositories of traditional authority. It was through them that I attempted to attack the great Barabaig problem of casual murder of strangers, with as little success as my predecessors or successors.

To the best of my recollection Barabaig murders were always of strangers on their way through their countryside. They were often hideously barbaric, throats being cut slowly with a rusty spear, for example, and the bodies were usually sexually mutilated. Lengthy anthropological studies had from time to time produced theories as to why these apparently motiveless killings took place. I held to the old belief among DCs before me that a man could demonstrate his virility to his sweetheart by bringing her a trophy to demonstrate the killing of any human being, so that an infant's penis, an old woman's breast or a young man's spearhead were all as valid as one another.

Cases were relatively rare in my time. In the absence of apparent motive and with the lack of skilled investigators we got nowhere with them, and I was not surprised to hear of fresh cases in later years. I took my own last shy at this practice through the lips of Governor Twining, when he paid the district a happy visit in 1954. I greeted him and his wife in the north, where we met the Oldeani farmers, who were all in good heart, and had a buffet lunch. Then we motored back to Mbulu to my considerable enjoyment as I savoured the Government House car in contrast to my accustomed box-body truck. According to practice, Nona and I gave up our house to the Twinings and stayed with the doctor, while the children were parked out with their friends. Much fun followed, for it had to be a serious topic indeed to check Sir Edward's jollity and sense of fun. A meeting with the district team in my office dealt with serious matters in a thoroughly perceptive way but was never solemn. Nor was a full uniformed *baraza* at Endagikot, a couple of miles from the Boma, for this was the headquarters of Wewutmo Elias, Chief of the Iraqw. And the Iraqw could with justice be praised for adhering staunchly to the compulsory stock-reduction programme which carried lessons for all East Africa, and for persevering with the other extensive programmes of self-help in bush clearing and soil improvement.

A drinks party on our lawn lit by fairy lights, on the second evening, had its amusing moments. With an appearance of high occasion I introduced the Bishop of Dareda, from the south of the district, to the Governor. I had forborne to warn the latter that the Bishop and his minions were a good-hearted, hard-drinking bunch of Irish peasants. The Bishop's scruffy robes and steady chewing and expectoration of tobacco provided rapid enlightenment, though neither got in the way of much Christian good work. Then the police band had come along with Sir Edward and in no time he was enjoying himself conducting them. I was beginning to wonder how long the party would continue when the matter was decided by well-dressed guests hopping up and down, hoicking up skirts and trouser legs and generally showing signs of distress. A large column of safari ants were upon us, and adieux to the Governor were swiftly made. Fortunately Nona and I, with Mike Molohan, were dining with the Twinings, so at least we did not have far to run.

The next day the Governor was to take his departure, but travelling south through Barabaig country, where he was at my request to lecture the tribesmen on their bad habits. On the way, still among the Iraqw at Dongobesh, I took him off the main road to see the spectacular canal at Muchlur. This we were digging under Austin's supervision with free tribal labour to fill a large new dam site and so provide water for people and stock in the area cleared the previous year of tsetse bush. The deep cleft of the canal disappearing into the distance and the work going into it were indeed something to see, and were admired by Twining, who promised to come and open it when the water was ready to flow. Mike Molohan was equally impressed, and one way and another there was a degree of self-satisfaction touching me and my team. It was not to last long.

I had forgotten the delicacy of town-bred cars. We had two Government House Chevrolets in our party. Lady Twining was in one, outbound for a tour of missions and schools. The other carried Twining, Molohan and myself, with the rest of the party aboard less comfortable vehicles like my own box-body. The Chevrolets had done well enough on the rough track from Dongobesh to Muchlur, but on the return a sickening sound in the Governor's car told us that the rear axle had gone. Various options were considered and discounted, in particular any interference with his wife's arrangements; I fancy he thought that any disruption in that direction might interfere with his lunchtime gin. In the end the Governor, Molohan and I filed into the Reuters correspondent's tiny little A40. I was tall but slim, but the other two were very large men indeed, and the discomfort in the heat was considerable. It did not stop Sir Edward from keeping us amused with reminiscences of nefarious goings-on in his early days as a Governor in the Caribbean.

When we got to Katesh, the Barabaig headquarters, I knew we would find the tribesmen lining the route, and under strict orders to stand up and cheer their heads off as soon as they saw a large black limousine flying a large union flag. Now here we all were arriving in a very squalid little car, but Twining was well up to it. We stopped well back and marched forward, and there was no mistaking the imposing presence of the Governor, with his various minions marching in support.

Lunch was first item on the agenda, and there was a minor fumble to begin with when the aide de camp, Twining's nephew Sam, appeared to have gone a little light on the gin supply. But with others holding back, the Governor was well supplied, and in due course we strode out to the *baraza*. After the Chief's welcoming speech, it was the Governor's turn. He spoke in English, which I translated into Swahili, and – Twining's Swahili being rough and ready at best – I took a pretty free hand. After the usual complimentary pieces – self-help in the tsetse clearings, better relations with the Wanyaturu, and so on – came the nub of the matter. 'But,' quoth the Governor, 'there remains the foulest blot on your escutcheon,' and he gave me the most hideous leer as he mouthed the word 'escutcheon'. I was quite unabashed. Nothing was going to lead me into prattle about stains on heraldic shields as I launched my attack on the disgrace their murders brought on the otherwise brave traditions of their nomad tribe. At the end the right things had been said, a measure of remorse had been expressed, if not felt, and the customary presents were produced. The Governor was given the metal headdress of a successful lion-killer, snatched indeed from the head of the young hero who had earned it. A sheep was produced for the PC. By now Lady Twining had re-joined with the other Government House car, and so in due course the party went on its way.

1. Mount Kilimanjaro in the early 1950s. The snow covering was more extensive than it is now.

2. (left) CIM hunting for elephant in Masailand, 1949.

3. (above) 'It was a hardgame.' Relaxing after a day prospecting for elephant in Masailand on the same trip. His thumb is bandaged as a result of a scorpion sting.

4. Setting out on safari, 1949.

5. Washing in a collapsible canvas basin on safari, c.1955.

6. The box-body Bedford.

7. Meeting with the Masai in the Ngorongoro Crater.

8. A Barabaig *baraza*. CIM (obscured) and the elders are on the right.

9. Sitting with the Barabaig and the Wanyaturu to delineate the boundary between the two tribes.

10. CIM and Sir Edward Twining at a *baraza* with the Barabaig, 1954.

11. The Boma at Mbulu.

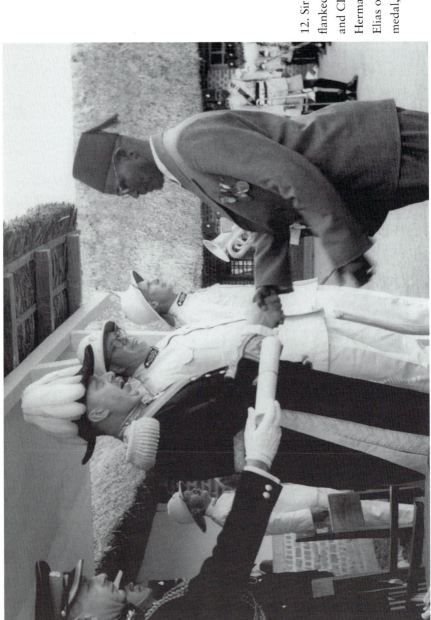

12. Sir Edward Twining, flanked by Mike Molohan and CIM, investing Herman, the son of Chief Elias of the Iraqw, with a medal, 1954.

13. Nade Bea, 1956.

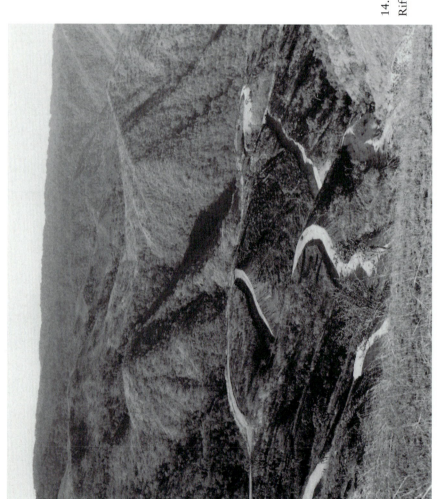

14. The road down the Rift to Magara, 1956.

15. CIM and Nona Meek outside the Hunter's log-built house in Oldeani in 1961.

16. Julius Nyerere's Cabinet in 1961. Paul Bomani is on his right and Sir Ernest Vasey, Minister of Finance, on his left. Oscar Kambona, subsequently Nyerere's bitter enemy, stands immediately behind him. Rashidi Kawawa is standing second from the left. CIM is included in the photograph as Cabinet Secretary.

9

DOMESTIC MATTERS

No picture of life in a district posting is complete without a chapter on how we lived and how we diverted ourselves in our periods of release. Through all the Mbulu years Nona and I were raising a family, which in the African bush is an exacting test of wisdom, common sense and pertinacity.

Our eldest child, Innes, was still only 18 months old when we came to Mbulu in 1949, and our daughter, Sheena, was born soon after we got there. Then, after a long gap Kip came along in 1955. We were, mercifully, free from malaria in our highlands, but even that healthy place provided its fair share of childhood ailments. These were a constant worry to my wife with, for the most part, no doctor to hand; and she became an expert on a book of family medicine which saw us through those years. Indeed, she became so good with sick young that she set up a baby clinic which was much appreciated by the local African families. She took great pride in the work, but it was often far from pleasant. Infants often suffered the most horrific burns from the open fires in windowless *tembes*, and the mothers were very glad to have the *memsahib* to run to.

Schooling the children was a hard chore. An organisation in Dar es Salaam helped with guidance and materials, but the age gap added a dimension of difficulty in keeping childish attention, a hindrance which teachers in infant schools are usually spared. Innes's mind tended to wander towards the chances of more fun outside and Nona always found it hard to keep his attention. It was quite a relief when he was of an age to be packed off to board at Arusha School. It did him no harm then to make friends among the Afrikaner children from a different background and culture.

Wildlife was always present. On most nights we would hear the haunting cries of hyenas, and on one occasion they chewed up the cushions which we had left out on the chairs on our verandah. Snakes were also a feature. I remember coming on a small Innes one day standing stock still in the middle of the road outside our house, picking nervously at his cardigan. He was staring at a huge puff-adder. The snake had been run over the day before and was dead, but it could still generate fear in a child who at that time knew nothing of snakes and certainly had not seen one. The fear of snakes is a deep instinct in us.

We had snakes around the house a good deal. There was one cheerful occasion at a poker party, where a good deal of drink had been taken. Our wire-haired terrier, Sally, kept barking at something just behind the open front door. 'I'm sure there is something there,' said Nona, who was playing cards. 'Just a toad,' said I. But the barking persisted until I had to go and look, and of course found a snake, poised and ready to strike. A much more alarming instance occurred when we had Mary Younie, wife of one of my DOs, staying with us. Her husband was away, and we were putting her up with her latest-born baby. Our drawing-room led off at one end to a little lobby, with our bedroom on the right and a guest bedroom to the left, where Mary and the infant were sleeping, with a bathroom between the two. Mary went off early to bed, and we followed a good while later. As I led the way, Dietz lamp in hand, into the lobby, so a three-foot snake glided out from under our bedroom door and headed swiftly for Mary's. There was no time to stop and think. I jumped at it and came down on it with the snake's head just forward of the heel of my shoe, so that it was trapped but otherwise unharmed. I stood there with my lamp, unable to move and with the snake's body lashing up most unpleasantly around my leg. Mary appeared, white with alarm and baby in arms, but Nona by now was yelling for the boy, and Laisiak quickly appeared with his *panga* in his hand. Africans share my view that all snakes are dangerous, and this one was quickly dispatched. Alas, I never identified it.

In Mbulu itself leopards were troublesome. They had no natural prey there and dogs were an obvious alternative. Our police officer on one occasion was putting his dog out at night and had his pet snatched from him right alongside the lamp he was carrying. Once when I was away on safari villagers surrounded a leopard in a bush and two or three guns came from the Boma to have a go at it. But it was the leopard that had a go, and had torn half the scalp off our Sikh sub-inspector of police before it was shot. Fortunately we had a doctor on station who was able to repair Singh's tonsure.

Our *ayahs* were locally recruited from the settlement. We had a succession of unsatisfactory girls. One was a young woman of vivacity and intelligence who dearly loved her charges. But she also dearly loved the bottle. When my wife found her one evening swaying perilously with the precious infant in her arms, ways parted. Next came a young flibbertigibbet, suffering from the Victorian complaint of too many followers. So we were delighted when we found Maria. She was a respectable elderly widow. Indeed she was a grandmother, but still vigorous. She drove, however, a hard bargain. We were swiftly in agreement about wages and hours of work, but she refused to live in. She preferred her own home in a village half a mile away, and no money would induce her to change her mind. I knew what the next demand would be. On nights when we were out after dark, I would have to drive her home. It was not proper to let an elderly woman walk back home alone when the rains came and conditions might be unpleasant. I could see this, and was irrationally irritated when Maria gave a different reason, which was that she might meet a leopard. Leopards, as I have said, could be troublesome, but they were wary and not generally a threat in the villages, where there were people walking around at every hour of the night. Leopards indeed, I said to myself as I drove Maria home one evening in a sulky and oppressive silence. On this occasion the hour was early, it was scarcely dark and the night was fine. Who has seen a leopard at large in the village before eight o'clock? I set Maria down at her door, the headlights gleaming on the earth road, the thatched huts, the primitive shops, and drove back up the main street. We had a 'You are here' map painted onto a board at the entrance to the settlement. There in my headlights squatted a large, handsome leopard looking at the board, for all the world as though he were reading the legend and planning a trip for the night. He was off in a flash, but foolishly I told my wife – and she told Maria. There was no further argument about the lift home.

Our biggest alarm concerned a leopard that never was. We used to spend many happy weekends with our friends John and Jane Hunter, who owned a coffee farm at Oldeani. They had a large and wonderfully comfortable log-built house high up the mountain at the very top of the farm. There were superb views southward over the plains below, but at the back of the house the rainforest pressed upon us. It was full of game and, of an evening, we often walked into it to watch elephant playing in the dam, which was the farm's main water supply. But there were leopards, rarely mentioned but much in our minds when our children were around. But there came a time up there with our children, including Kip, when our vigilance slipped. 'Where's Kip then?' 'I thought...' 'Well, I thought...' At once we and our hosts and their African staff were whistling and shouting all over the property, even, with growing apprehension, examining the forest edges. I will not try to describe my feelings when I found him hiding behind our guest-house door with a happy grin on his face.

And once there was a lion. I was just breaking off at the Boma one day to go home for lunch when I was told that a lion was loose on the demonstration farm we ran a couple of miles away. Lions were a great rarity in the thickly populated area, for, as with the leopards, there was no natural prey to feed them, and this one could only spell danger to livestock and perhaps people. So I collected my rifle from home, picked up the children with a boy to make sure they were kept well out of harm's way, and set off to the farm. This was run by Paddy Joly, an engaging young Irishman.[1] He had no experience with big game, but he was a wild fellow and was not going to let that stop him. He was already in a patch of thick bush as I arrived, with a tracker behind him who clearly could not hope to see anything. Almost as I got to him, he fired, and there indeed was a very dead lion. We dragged it out and photographed the excited children with it. Then I took them home, had a bite to eat, and was back in my office smartly on time. The whole affair had taken exactly an hour, which prompted me to write it up for *The Times* as a turn-out article, a popular feature of the newspaper in those days, under the title 'A Lion at Lunchtime'.

I had given up elephant-hunting at Nona's urgent plea, but I did shoot a couple of rhino. This was a loveless affair. There was none of the empathy that I felt for elephant, nor, in my limited experience, the same hardship of the hunt, even though it was a rhino which had killed my friend Victor Findlay. Frankly, I needed the money for my young family – not that the horns fetched more than a modest price in those days.

John Hunter learnt to fly, and had a little Cessna at the bottom of his farm. He was a very careful airman, but there was nowhere really safe for his airstrip. Effectively, one landed on one little, flat hilltop, bounced on to another and hoped the brakes held before one went down the facing ravine. I flew with him a lot, for a light aircraft made a perfect platform for overseeing general progress in the annual clearings. Even Nona mastered her dislike of flying in general and small aeroplanes in particular in the face of crises. Notably, Kip was born when the rains had made Arusha almost inaccessible, and she let John fly her and the precious infant to Oldeani, where I could pick them both up.

Robin Johnston farmed on the slopes of Kilimanjaro. He had been in the Administration, and we had met when I was DC Masai and he had a difficult assignment in charge of Kongwa, where the disastrous post-war Groundnut Scheme had its headquarters. The men who ran the scheme were threatening to take over some of southern Masailand, and I had to go and fend off this possibility, which was how I met Robin. He had had a brilliant war with the RAF, and inevitably he too had his own aircraft.[2] I made a number of trips with him, which I mention now because I was so consistently amused by the contrast in flying styles. John in the ordinary way was a natural taker of risks. As a flier, however, he had just been through the hard grind of flying school in Nairobi, and before take-off he went exactly by the book, meticulously observing every required check. With Robin, the old warrior, one shared a couple of drinks, walked out to the plane, a quick look at the petrol gauge, turned the switch and off we went. They both seemed to get there.

My district was so absorbing that we never felt much urge to get away. We saw in any case a fair amount of Arusha's modestly bright lights, there were duty trips to neighbouring districts, there were our weekends with the Hunters. There loomed ahead of us, too, the enormous expense of a boarding-school education in England for the children, so we were not inclined to squander money on local leave. The exception we made was a fortnight in Zanzibar, where our friend John Murphy was now installed as Attorney General, and offered us open house in return for his many stays with us in Mbulu and elsewhere. Tradition hung around Zanzibar as closely as the pervasive smell of cloves, and we enjoyed the island. There were the marks of respect for the Sultan, paid by the Administration as much as by the citizens. We admired the intricate Arab carving on the front doors of houses, and enjoyed the police band at the English Club of a Sunday evening. More prosaically, we loved the swimming in the sea, of which we had been starved. We never saw Zanzibar again until we paid a short visit in 1971 and had rather more than a glimpse of the sad horrors of the Karume dictatorship.

We had become acquainted with John Murphy on the sea voyage home on one of our long leaves, and this is perhaps the time to say a little on this feature of a colonial-service career. When the job itself was so enthralling, it may seem odd that leaves should rate as highly as they did. But most of us had strong ties of family and friendships at home, and these needed renewing after absences of two and a half or three years. Equally, working life is hard sweat until retirement comes; and it was worth the effort on our part to make the most of the glorious months when, within our means, we had nothing to do but enjoy ourselves. So, despite the draw of the job, many an evening was spent in planning leave, and we threw ourselves into the pleasures and contrasts of Europe when the time came.

The Colonial Service had many compensations, but pay was mean. So it was always something of a surprise to me how generously we were treated over our sea passages home and back. Here, for a month each way, Government was paying all our expenses, while we loved the voyage and made the most of cheap drink and cigarettes. British India, with its superb uniformed stewards, was our preferred line, but we often had to take what we could get. In 1956 we travelled by the SS *Africa* of the Lloyd Triestino line. The passengers were mostly Italian, much given to bursting into spontaneous song. They delighted us on the whole, for there were splendid voices among them. She was a well-run ship by and large, though things tended to give in a crisis, such as a very severe storm off the Horn of Africa. And at the end of the voyage, for no obvious reason, all passengers were thrown off in Venice instead of going on, as booked, to Trieste. But what a lucky chance! We ended up in a fine hotel in Europe's most splendid city, with beautiful cool white rooms and a cot already erected for Kip. And, in due course, I was able to persuade Lloyd Triestino to pay for it in lieu of the balance of our voyage. Six years later I insisted on our final departure from Tanganyika being by sea. Once again the voyage was not on a par with those early passages by the British India line, for Messageries Maritimes were losing money and it showed in the facilities. But at least there was a delightful and authentic French atmosphere to accompany us to Marseilles, and after time spent in the fascinating but deeply provincial life of a British colony, this was a refreshing change.

A return to humdrum English life had a lot going for it for a family fresh from the excitements of bush life in Africa. But it worked better with a bit of glitter. There was a perfect example of this on our very first home leave in 1950, even though good luck intervened to magnify the effect and bad luck cast a later blight. From an advertisement picked out of a magazine in Tanganyika we had hired a simple cottage in South Devon. Here in due course we felt able to leave our children to give ourselves a good break in the South of France. Talk of a 'good break' sounded strange to our friends at the time, for 1950 marked the peak of post-war austerity in Britain and the travel allowance was a wretched £25 a head each year. But we, working abroad, were allowed to accumulate our allowance for the three years of our absence, so that we had between us the handsome sum of £150 for our holiday. That sum, now the price of a good dinner, represented several weeks of modest living, and we took our little Austin Minor across the channel in high spirits.

Motorways were yet to come, the scars of war were all about, but we armed ourselves with a detailed, personal route from the AA and enjoyed a sunny journey south. We found ourselves a splendid little inn at Le Treyes, a few miles west of Cannes. It had half a dozen bedrooms, with a single shower and lavatory to serve the lot. It was built on rocks sticking straight out into the clearest sea and offering the swimming of a lifetime. The food was simple and very good. So here we were for a quiet time of sea and rocks and food, pleasures we missed in Africa. But we did have in mind two extravagances. We had set aside a fiver for Cannes Casino and no less than a tenner for a really good dinner. I lost our fiver in the Casino in twenty minutes and, with great strength of will, walked straight out.

There remained our dinner. We spent many days discussing it and thumbing through the Michelin Guide to find the right place. We settled finally for a restaurant at Les Mougins, some hundreds of feet up above Cannes, where Picasso eventually made his last home.

There we arrived one night to dine on the terrace, with the lights of Cannes and a moonlit Mediterranean shining below us, and I set about ordering our meal. The speciality of the house was hors-d'oeuvres, and this of course I asked for before going on to more substantial courses. Our kindly waiter said, in effect, 'Don't be silly. If you're having our hors-d'oeuvres you won't want anything else.' How right he was! One trolley followed another, fresh plates were substituted for used ones, and we ate till we could eat no more. Plenty of good wine went with it all, and then at the end we sat over coffee in a state of happy surfeit. And we thought of the Casino. We had budgeted on a tenner, but our one-course meal had only cost us half that. Our way down went right past the Casino. 'What about another go?' And so it turned out, but with different fortunes this time.

It was not long before my number, 27, came up. I was about to scoop up my winnings when Nona, who normally has little interest in gambling, said over my shoulder 'Leave it on.' I left a good whack on and, sure enough, up again came 27. We paused to consider. We had won about £70, and in 1950 that went a long way. So – here come the joys of contrast – we moved for three days to the most expensive hotel we could find. It will give the measure of change to say that instead of sharing a shower with other people, each of us had a bath and lavatory on either side of our immense bedroom. Food and service and swimming from our own rocky garden were of the same pattern, and life was blissful.

Bliss was not forever, as things turned out. We set off after three days, intending to take in Italy's north-west corner, going on to Nona's brother and his wife at Aix-les-Bains, and so home. We took the long, damp, pot-holed tunnel through the mountains. We enjoyed our night in industrial Turin. There was much singing in the streets, we fed decently, we went to see the film *Bicycle Thieves*.

It was hot next day as we cleared the city. In the distance on the straight road ahead we could see the entrance to a sort of elementary autostrada, a long farm gate at which, presumably, one paid a toll (we never found out). Astonishingly to a modern traveller, the road was empty in the sun, save for a small car just clearing the autostrada gate. He accelerated, as we slowed down, so the combined speed was about 80 mph as the head-on collision took place. I had seen him swerve towards me on the wide road, but had assumed he was avoiding broken glass or something else I could not see; and by the time I realised he would just come on, it was too late to avoid him. It was early in the day, but he had driven a long way, and he must have either slept or had some sort of fit.

Both cars were crushed on impact, our Austin making quite a sight on the front page of Turin's newspaper next day. Jammed behind the steering wheel, I could not turn my head to see Nona, and was terrified when she did not answer to my voice. But soon there were helping Italian hands and it was clear that, despite being knocked out, her injuries were going to spell trouble but nothing worse. I was cut from head to toe by broken glass, but, when pulled from the car, I could stand. So stand I did, in a spreading pool of blood, in the middle of the road, disregarding the growing line of furiously honking cars in each direction.

An open-backed vegetable van was going, it transpired, past Turin's special crash hospital. Nona was put in the front alongside the driver. I was dumped in the back with the driver of the other vehicle, only semi-conscious, lying among the swedes and turnips, with our rescued luggage alongside. In the hospital's casualty clearing station I was laid on an operating table and stripped, while a charming doctor proceeded to try his hand at both his English and at sewing me up. He had a lighted cigarette stuck to his lip, as he went about me rather haphazardly – an eyebrow here, a stomach gash there, back to the scalp and down to a leg. 'What you think of the Korean War, eh?' and we launched into discussion, animated on his side at least, until I spotted Nona sitting forlornly in a corner. She, with a broken arm and collar-bone, needed attention more than me, and I was rolled off and she was laid out in my place. Eventually, though still unwashed, we were patched after a fashion and wheeled off in search of a room.

The nuns who administered the hospital were very kind, but did not believe in anaesthetics. Their notion of a soothing drink for the night was a flask of delicious, cold black coffee. But that was a small thing. It was decreed that Nona's collar-bone be re-set. This was done with no anaesthetic, a knee in the small of the back and soothing words. A huge bunch of flowers from our crash-mate did not dispel the miasma of pain.

Back in London, there was much haggling before the insurance companies came to a settlement satisfactory to us. It was clear from the start that in Italian eyes our ruined leave, the pain and grief, the time without a car, the continued employment of a nursemaid, all this was of no great consequence. But Nona's legacy was a jutting collar-bone, and it was this damage to the *signora*'s beauty which shocked them and was worth huge quantities of lire to us. In the end the balance was about right.

I have stressed the need for contrast as the essence of a good leave, although I would also say that it plays its part in enjoyment throughout life. We had one such happy contrast in Paris, a matter of choice on this occasion and not of luck at roulette. We were there primarily to see the sights, and living most humbly on café meals. On our last afternoon we went to the cinema and were sitting over a drink afterwards. 'Look, we can't tell the future. We may never be here again. We might be dead tomorrow. Let's have the best dinner Paris can provide!' So we went to Maxim's. Cocktails to begin with. 'Bring us a half bottle of champagne while we look at the menu.' And then an unforgettable dinner, with a partridge dish as the centrepiece, and a long time dancing among the wealthiest Parisians and their bejewelled mistresses. The reflected glow later brightened our spartan lodgings.

10

MBULU AND THE ROAD OUT

The Mau-Mau rebellion in 1955 had direct impact on all the white settler plantations in northern Tanganyika. Accounts of mutilated cattle, of atrocities against fellow Kikuyu and white families, tales of malignant oath-taking had been general throughout East Africa before a state of emergency was declared. Kenya was effectively engulfed by the struggle with Mau-Mau.

Nona and I happened to be in Nairobi when these events struck. The Nandi tribe in Kericho were nomads who had been successfully introduced to the cultivation of tea as a peasant crop, rather than grown on large plantations. The people had welcomed this stable element in their wandering tradition, and I decided that the Barabaig might find that this little revelation might bear lessons for them too. Accordingly, I took a charabanc-load of elders to Kericho; and Nona and I decided to have a few days holiday afterwards, so we parked the two children with friends and she came with me.

If the cultivation of a valuable cash crop like tea was worth the adoption of a more sedentary form of life to the Barabaig, the tribesmen kept the thought well concealed, but in other ways their visit was an enormous success. Clan names and a certain amount of language in common with the Nandi revealed that they had been closely related, at the very least, in the distant past; and my lop-eared scoundrels found themselves most honoured guests. As the crow flies, there were only some two hundred and fifty miles between the two tribes, and Africans are great travellers, so it was curious to discover how totally unaware of each other's very existence each was, leave alone of the roots in common.

The time came to send the tribesmen home, while Nona and I went on from the Kericho highlands to spend a weekend with Tom Watts and his wife at Kisumu on Lake Victoria, where Tom was DC. He and I had known each other at school and at Oxford, and had in due course made together that long wartime voyage to East Africa. So we had a happy weekend by the great lake, with many reminiscences from which Nona, as sister to my best friend at school, was far from excluded.

But Mau-Mau was in everybody's thoughts. Indeed it was in all too many people's words. In our short Kenya stay we had been much disturbed at the clacking of tongues on sensitive matters around too many dinner-tables, as though the attendant servants had no word of English between them. Too much was known of the gathering of Kikuyu servants and gross breaches of security at home to excuse this folly. At all events, Mau-Mau was at the front of our minds, so it came as no surprise when Tom, on bidding us goodbye that Monday morning, whispered to me not to delay on the long drive to Nairobi. 'The balloon is going up.'

Nothing was said between us, but my wife told me later that she knew from the intensity of my driving that there was urgency in the wind. If not then, she would have guessed later that things might be amiss when, as dusk was falling on the sleazy outskirts of Nairobi, we had a puncture. Time and place could not have been worse, and changing a wheel on the Bedford was always a bit of a job, but Kassum, our boy, and I did it in record time. I forget if the state of emergency had already been declared as we got to the city centre, but there was at the least a general sense of crisis as we settled into the comfort of the Norfolk Hotel.

On the next day the Lancashire Fusiliers were making their presence felt. Any Kikuyu seemed to be a target for questioning. They all seemed to own bicycles, and vast piles of these machines showed where the owners were being gathered for examination. I wondered vaguely how an innocent ever got his bicycle back from a stack ten feet deep. We saw something of the less agreeable side of Kenya's white settlers in the shape of two or three drunks jeering at the tribesmen as they were rounded up. However, our immediate concern was to rescue Kassum, who had been with us since Arusha days. He was a relatively unsophisticated man from the Tanganyika coast, had never seen Nairobi before, and had probably never thought of a town so big. We found him eventually wandering innocently around, and presumably concluding that British soldiers arresting Kikuyu in their hundreds and stacking bicycles in piles was all a part of city life. We brought him firmly to safety in the hotel grounds.

The next day we headed back to Mbulu, stopping at Arusha on the way to report to Mike Molohan and to consider with him the likely consequences for us of Kenya's emergency. These turned out to be not too troublesome. Rumours grew of oathing among our Kikuyu plantation labour and we took some domestic precautions. I got Nona a small automatic pistol and taught her to use it. But when I was on safari, she was required to separate any firearms into their component parts and hide them around the house to avert the risk of theft of a usable weapon; and I could never persuade myself or her that she would have put anything together in time to take a shot at an intruder. However, it was not an issue for long. Tales from the plantations in the Northern Province and down to the coast in Tanga Province, though never substantial, grew more threatening. In the end we were not prepared to risk trouble in what was fundamentally no affair of ours, and we rounded up our large numbers of Kikuyu workmen throughout the territory's plantations and put them in what was effectively a large open prison in an isolated area under the charge of a DO and a police force. There they dwelt until the end of Kenya's emergency let us return them. Had we at once sent them back, unemployed, to the hands of the evil oath administrators in their tribal land, I suspect they would have given plenty of trouble in Kenya. We never compensated the settlers. The Kikuyu were doubtless better workers than could be found locally. Yet the settlers would have served the local economy by employing and training Tanganyikans, but they chose to serve their own interests instead. A bit of rough justice, we thought, would do no harm.

The Mau-Mau emergency was of course a full-scale rebellion of a very nasty kind, something very much of its own. But in Tanganyika, to come right down the scale of villainy, we bred gangsters of our own. Our very long sojourn in Mbulu produced many friendships, but it necessarily led to personal enmity with one or two who knew full well that I would be on the watch for the least offence as soon as they were out of prison. In these cases the animosity was never pleasant, but I could be pretty sure of eventual mastery. They did not resemble a far more complex case which came to take my time and trouble my conscience half-way through my last tour of duty.

The men concerned were a gang of Chagga from Moshi. From their home base they had rapid access through Arusha and southward along the Great North Road[1] to my settlements of Magugu and Babati, which were bases for groups of quite prosperous Indian traders serving estates in the neighbourhood and the Gorowa and Magugi tribes. There was a small police post in each place, but the Chagga came by car at night, armed with *pangas*, and they would target one store at a time with such brutality and speed that they would beat up or otherwise terrorise the Indian family concerned and be off with their loot before my police could intervene. The only successful defence came when the Native Authority tax boxes were the target of the gang. The boxes were hastily pushed into the cell of a remand prisoner in the local lock-up by the clerk in charge, the prisoner was armed with a cudgel and told to defend them, and the door was locked on him. Defend them he did, for long enough that help arrived and the villains left empty-handed. I do not know what the Controller of Audit would have made of the incident, but I made sure the hero was suitably rewarded.

However, this little reign of terror was a serious matter. The traders were cowardly, even when windows were barred and with shot-guns in hand. There were brutalities to women and children as well as men, stores stripped of every last thing of value. Confidence disappeared, as to a large extent did trade, and the villains prospered. To catch the gang became a major preoccupation, and in the end we did so. Awkwardly placed as were above the Rift, the raids were frequent enough to bring down police reinforcements to lay traps, and I was helped by first-class police support from Moshi. The gang too became over-confident, notably in stealing a highly distinctive American pick-up truck from a missionary at Babati – currency difficulties made American vehicles hard to get well into the fifties. We had our quarry behind bars. How now to proceed?

The issue was troubling. I had a competent sub-inspector at Mbulu, but by chance I had been without a police officer throughout this episode and I had controlled the police work myself. We often had to reconcile political responsibilities with our impartiality as magistrates, but this was a case so serious as to require it to be obvious that the two duties were clearly kept apart. It was equally plain that the offences were too serious for the powers of the district court and should accordingly go to the High Court. However, I knew full well something that I could never openly plead, and this was that there would be no convictions, if the men were indeed guilty, before a High Court judge in Dar es Salaam. Far too much local knowledge was needed. Terrain, personal characteristics, questions of timing along the Great North Road, even weather conditions, were involved. This knowledge was built into me.

My conscience was not really too far stretched. I knew I could keep my policing duties out of mind and divorced from magisterial impartiality. The mere knowledge of local circumstances would not prejudice the case, or at least it was a lesser evil than the certainty that without it there would be no possibility of convictions however guilty the accused might be. The case was too important to leave to subordinates. I would take it myself.

My inspector proved a sensible prosecutor, and all the four gangsters were convicted by me. I squeezed every last bit out of my powers of punishment and put them away for four and a half years apiece. A few weeks later the High Court pronounced. I took severe criticism for hearing a case which was plainly beyond my powers and should have gone to the High Court. This was qualified by comment on the care, patience and impartiality with which I had heard the case, to such an extent that there was no disposition to quash the proceedings and remit it to one of their lordships. I was happy with this.

One year there was a major diversion of some of our tribal labour for the normal tsetse clearing and settlement expansion. Mbulu stood only a few miles from the Rift at a particularly steep part of it. Yet to visit the Mbugwe people at its foot involved a long diversion through the southern Iraqw highlands, the fringes of Barabaig country, past Dareda with its bishop and white settlers, before reaching the relatively all-weather Great North Road and turning northwards at Babati in Gorowa country. Likewise, to get to Arusha one had to go north over a difficult Aitcho escarpment and onwards before turning east at Karatu in the Oldeani foothills, descending the Rift to the lush settlement of Mto wa Mbu (Mosquito

River) and then pursuing a track across flood-prone places to join the Great North Road at Essimingor.

So it was no wonder that generations of my predecessors had sought to build a road a few miles east from Mbulu, down the Rift, via Magara and a few miles on again past flamingo-covered Lake Manyara to the Great North Road at Magugu. It would be good for the district's economy, give easy access to the Mbugwe and Gorowa tribes and to the white settlers below the Rift, and a much quicker journey to Arusha. One DC in the late twenties had indeed built a road, but it was so impracticably steep that he had to move a whole village to the foot of it, where the men found that their main job in life was to push the *bwanas'* cars up the Rift. Even in those days that did not do! My heart became very set on this undertaking. It was not a job I could ever persuade the PWD to take on. Building to their standards would put the cost out of all proportion to the return. But if I could persuade the tribesmen, which I could and did, of the road's utility, my labour costs would be negligible. And, above all, I had what had not been available to those who went before me, Austin's great surveying skills. So we built the Magara road one dry season, and an amazing sight it was. It was a twined mass of hairpin bends, and, standing at the top, you could never tell in which direction a vehicle would be pointing even when it was known to be going up or down. But the gradients were easy, we had it well gravelled, and it survived the first rainy season in good shape. Does it survive today?[2]

Austin and I took Chief Elias down on the first full descent. Almost the first person I met, surrounded by a group of aides, was Prince Bernhard of the Netherlands, who had just bought a farm in the area. He was in company with the leading farmer in these parts, a Greek called Matsis, who had been there for many years. He was a friend of mine who had been a valued adviser when we opened up the Kiru farms after they were declared free of sleeping sickness. He stared at me in astonishment. He had never believed the road could be built, and he took some convincing that we had breakfasted in Mbulu and would be back there for lunch.

Another demanding break out of the ordinary was an invasion from Kenya of the Sudan dioch, more properly known as the red-billed quelea, less properly as the locust bird. Our wheatlands were all in the far north of the district, and, when it comes to wheat, flocks of dioch are wholly destructive. These birds were quite suddenly on us in enormous numbers, and in no time we could see our whole wheat crop at risk. This was a new plague in Tanganyika, and we were short of information from Kenya or elsewhere as to how best to deal with it. It was a time to improvise.

A labour force gave no problem. We turned out every appropriate officer from Mbulu and picked some extra supervisors from among the affected farmers, white and black; and we took all the men we needed from those whose crops were at risk. The birds were nested over a great area of dense thorn bush on the edge of the growing wheat. The bushes were close together, and each one had some fifty round dioch nests hanging from it. The dioch is related to the weaver-bird and builds a similar nest. I always marvelled at a bird's instinct for home, as it looked down upon a sea of apparently identical nests and, unerringly, plummeted straight into its own. How could they possibly tell?

But this was no time to stand and admire the dioch's instincts or abilities. We tried various means of attack, and found to our dismay that much the most effective were flame-throwers, improvised from oil-drums and pumps, which we got in numbers from Arusha. Burning them out was no pleasant substitute for a scarecrow or a few warning shots, and we detested doing it, but we had found no other way to be rid of them. These devices were also most unpleasant to use. The heat in the airless bush was in any case severe in daylight hours, and it was blistering near our flame-throwers when they were in use. But they worked. In a few days' time we were left with a damaged wheat crop and acres of smouldering bush, but the remnants of the Sudan dioch had moved on to pester farmers elsewhere.

In Mbulu itself social life was very agreeable. There was a lot of bridge, some high-risk poker whenever our brick-building contractor, Charles Kypris, and I got together, and there were many good parties. But I was increasingly concerned that all this jollification was for whites only. The Capricorn Society was preaching multi-racialism, all over the territory the dominance of the whites was being played down in discussion in favour of partnership of the races, yet simple mixed entertaining at home did not occur to people as natural or likely to be pleasurable. I may say that this was not simply a Tanganyikan problem. In Kenya at the time the idea would have met active hostility. More than six years later I was staying with a mine manager on the copperbelt in what was still Northern Rhodesia.

That evening he had Kenneth Kaunda in for a drink. Considering how soon Kaunda was to be President, it is hard to believe that that was the very first such social occasion on which they had met.

Now we had had Chief Elias to lunch on several occasions, but, enjoy it though we did, that was in the straight course of duty. I had arranged a visit to Britain for him, and a 'knife-and-fork course' was needed. It provided some hilarious moments, with an agitated Akonnae, our boy, whispering instructions on how to handle, for example, the consumption of a jelly; but it worked, and his UK visit passed off well.

But I was looking at an altogether different challenge. I had by the end of 1955 an African DO, Othman, who may have been still a cadet but was unquestionably one of our own service. Herman Elias, the Chief's son, with a personable English-speaking wife, was secretary to the Native Treasury and very much part of the establishment. He was, incidentally, a few years later, the only non-TANU African member of the Legislative Council, a job his personality was not strong enough to support with any distinction. The same consideration applied to two of the Boma clerks, one African, one Goan, and to Ali Lasseko, who administered the all-important cattle-culling scheme. I talked things over with Nona. The Meeks must break the mould and set blacks and whites actually enjoying themselves together instead of chattering about it. Picking the occasion was easy. Every year since I took over we had given a grand party for the whole station, meaning whites only, to celebrate Christmas or New Year. Once it had been a grand curry lunch, more often an evening affair with music and dancing or party games. This time we decided to go for New Year's Eve dinner. We considered a dance to follow, but our excellent agricultural officer was South African and we felt that mixed dancing might push his principles too far. So party games it was to be.

It was getting on towards nine p.m., when the guests were due, on the last day of 1955. Our drawing-room was cleared, the boys were in their best rig, buffet supper was set out in the dining-room and looked splendid, drinks and ice were ready. Nona and I and our house-guest John Murphy sat around the periphery of the drawing-room. John was a man of strong prejudices and much intolerance, but had taken a surprisingly easy view of this venture of ours, possibly in reaction to the respectful treatment always given to the Sultan of

Zanzibar and his entourage. However, Nona and I were sitting, glass in hand, in a mood of deep depression. Previous New Year's parties had always been a success, and here we were willfully throwing away our pleasure and everybody else's at our last celebration. Setting an example? To whom? Nobody whose thinking we wanted to enlarge would even know what we were up to.

Guests arrived on time, the gramophone was playing old favourites, drinks were pressed into hands, and the party never looked back. The silly games were well chosen, with one exception. This is the game where a matchbox is passed from nose to nose. It had not occurred to us that the African nose is less well adapted to this exercise than the Caucasian one. Fortunately everyone saw the funny side, and the game was laughed off as another cunning European device for gaining advantage.

Many little incidents coloured the final few months before we finally left Mbulu at the end of June 1956. There was the night when the doctor and I had to disarm the violent vet before he did an injury to the beautiful wife of whom he was so jealous. We had a spate of tax robberies which, as always, caused trouble with the auditors in Dar es Salaam. A young white girl on the station was infected with VD by one of the house servants. But I always like to think of the party as our grand finale in Mbulu.

My field service was now over, after 16 years. Ahead loomed the intense interest and excitement and grinding hard work entailed by nationalist politics and the pursuit of independence for Tanganyika. Before coming onto that, a few words of review of my long and settled period in Mbulu. I had been on the station for almost seven years, first under Peter Bell and then in charge myself. In the normal way, the Administration did not make much of an impression on the mass of the people. Whatever we got up to, the farmer in the bush paid his taxes so that we would leave him alone, and got on with the job of wringing a hard living from his *shamba*. But in Mbulu, Peter Bell and I had a clear impact on this man. Cattle-culling and trash-bunding affected the whole way he lived, and the Administration was in no way remote.

So what sort of a stamp had I left? For all that I had built on the foundations laid by many predecessors, I had run a benevolent dictatorship for years and the stamp was mine. How much did it amount to?

At the time it amounted to plenty. The agriculturist and the cattle-owner were deeply affected, as I have just remarked. The Native Authority machinery for influencing him was strong, and its attitudes at all levels had been deeply affected by me and our discussions and our struggles over the years. I liked to think too that my authoritarian methods had been tempered by a proper respect for the individual and by fair play. Perhaps it was too much to suppose one could leave much of a mark on a quarter of a million people, particularly people who were not easily pushed around. I have already mentioned that in the first territory-wide elections they were the only Africans who refused to return a TANU candidate to the Legislative Council. So securing their co-operation, as I had done, meant more than might have been the case elsewhere. I would have to go back after nearly two generations to get my answers. This will not happen, so I can only hope that I would still find traces of a more careful comprehension of what the land required for its care, and a touch more of kindly manners than might otherwise have been.

11

POSTSCRIPT

During our last long leave, after our farewell to Mbulu, we embarked on the serious business of sending our eldest son, then aged eight, to boarding school in England in the autumn of 1956. There was no financial support from the Tanganyika Government for private education, despite the lack of choice available in Tanganyika itself, and our finances were so stretched that we knew we would not be able to fly him out to Dar es Salaam until the summer of 1958. Why did an 18-month separation seem so great a divide? It had been my fate and my brother's, and over the generations of tens of thousands like us. Indeed a hundred years earlier at the height of the Indian Empire partings between parents and children had lasted years. But I knew from experience that 18 months was bad enough, for I could well remember the great uncle who was headmaster at my own prep school telling me that I should be at Victoria Station the next day to meet my parents; and the sinking feeling with which I thought that I might not be able to recognise them.

We hired a house near Chipping Norton, a cheerless place, despite the winter beauty of the surrounding Cotswolds, and it was from here that Innes started the Christmas term at the Dragon School in Oxford, with occasional weekend visits from us, which we fancy he found rather a bore. Time rolled on, we managed to postpone the end of our leave until after the end of the Christmas holidays, and we duly put him back for his second term. So, with much grief, we left him at his school and flew to Dar es Salaam in January 1957.

We lived at first in a small house on Gillman Avenue, in Oyster Bay, some way from the centre of town. My posting was as Principal Assistant Secretary in the Ministry of Local Government and Administration. We were very short of cash, and money for our son's and later our daughter's school fees was a perennial anxiety. I had to borrow from the bank to pay for flights and to cover leave expenses. We missed the freedom of our up-country posting, and the pressure of Secretariat work was relentless. Fortunately, I turned out to have an aptitude for it and received a series of exceptionally rapid promotions, culminating in my appointment as Permanent Secretary in the office of the Chief Secretary, Sir John Fletcher-Cooke, in July 1959.[1] This promotion eased the financial pressure and allowed us to move with the two younger children into a larger house within walking distance of the Secretariat in the centre of Dar es Salaam. It also gave me a deep involvement in the heady process leading up to Tanganyika's independence and paved the way for me to become Permanent Secretary in Nyerere's office when he took over as Chief Minister in September 1960. I shall devote the remainder of this memoir to a brief survey of this period as it appeared to me, and some reflections on my friendship and collaboration with Nyerere in the short period between September 1960 and the achievement of independence in December 1961.

Nyerere was born in Butiama, a small town to the east of Lake Victoria. He was the son of a Chief of the Zanaki tribe, which sounds grand, but since he was one of the numerous sons of a very insignificant Chief he enjoyed in childhood a full measure of the grinding poverty which was the lot of any peasant community wresting a living from poor soil in a hostile climate. He tended the family goats like any other little boy. I have never asked him how he happened to go to school. There are conflicting accounts. Lady Listowel[2] writes of the persuasion exercised by another minor Chief whose son had gone to school and wanted his friend Julius to join him. I was always led to believe that it was pressure from the local DC that sent him there. The Administration was never engaged, as is sometimes averred, in restraining African children from achieving the education for which they thirsted. They may indeed have thirsted, and certainly there were not enough schools to accommodate them all if they had all been forced to attend, but nevertheless our problem was to fill the schools that did exist. An eight-year-old looking after goats, such as Julius

Nyerere, was at this time contributing usefully to the family economy, and parents usually resisted in every way the loss of that contribution from their children. Every administrative officer had experience of the struggle to ensure that school places were fully taken up, and we all preached and cajoled and cozened and bullied to that end. I should be surprised if Chief Nyerere was not pushed by arguments of duty into sacrificing Kambarage, as Julius was named before his later baptism, in the cause of education.

At all events, to school he went, and a brilliant pupil he turned out to be; and after the local village school and then Tabora School, with its British-public-school aura and preference for the sons of Chiefs, and Makerere College, he became a teacher in 1945. In due course, the White Fathers' Mission, for whom he worked, sponsored him for a scholarship, and in 1952 he returned from Edinburgh University as Tanganyika's first young man with a master's degree. In the years that followed he increasingly loomed in our eyes as the Enemy. He moved steadily into nationalist politics, first breathing life into the moribund Tanganyika African Association and then, on 7 July 1954 (the seventh day of the seventh month, hence Saba Saba Day), he and a small group of associates founded TANU. He had decided to abandon the teaching profession for politics – not, I am sure without deep heart-searching – although to this day he is known to his people as Mwalim, 'the Teacher'.

The span of time over which TANU was strong enough to make any impression on the colonial Government was very short. At the point when he founded the party, Nyerere himself was looking twenty-five years ahead for independence, and so indeed was the UN visiting mission of that year, as I mentioned at the outset. It is true that by the mid-fifties the movement had captured a substantial following in Dar es Salaam and in a handful of other urban centres, but Tanganyika was primarily a country of peasants, and the mass of the agrarian community was not touched at all. At the end of my posting as DC Mbulu, TANU meant no more to me than two weak and poorly organised branches on the periphery of the district. They had a certain nuisance value, tending to obstruct measures for improved agriculture and cattle-raising on which my heart was set. That, though, was the sum total of my knowledge of the movement that was to take the country to independence within five years.

If rural Tanganyika was untouched by the nationalist surge, it was very different in the capital. We were in the last stages of Sir Edward Twining's governorship, and relations between him and Nyerere were bad and deteriorating. Twining had made various efforts to counterbalance TANU's influence, including the promotion of the multi-racial United Tanganyika Party and the calling of a Chief's convention as an embryonic upper house. It was a hectic and dangerous time, with TANU branches being closed by the Government in the provinces and with the constant worry that there would be bloodshed and that we would have to declare a state of emergency. There was serious trouble in Sukumaland, Iringa and Singida.

The tussle between the British and the nationalists was always about timing. The nationalists did not believe us, but we administrators were brought up in the credo that it was our mission to bring the country to independence. But, as I said at the start, not in our own lifetimes. This misconception coloured our thinking and vitiated our planning. If a man does not expect something to happen within the span of his own career, he tends not to think too hard about precisely how many trained men and what development of resources are required for independence. This was our failing.

Government servants were not supposed to fraternise with TANU at all, but on a couple of occasions I went out to mass meetings at the old Dar es Salaam airport and sat on the ground among thousands of African supporters and found myself deeply impressed by the skilled stage management of the proceedings and by the good humour of my neighbours whenever points were made against the colonial Government. But most of all I was forcefully struck by Nyerere's oratorical powers, and by the reason and moderation of his arguments.

I and a small number of younger officials were soon convinced that changes should be made faster than in fact they were and that the prospect of violence would not disappear if we were seen to be constantly endeavouring to stem the nationalist tide. The burden of our advice was that the next step was best taken twice as quickly as first envisaged. And as it turned out our expectations were overtaken by events: we moved from ministerial government to semi-responsible government, full internal self-government and then independence within the amazingly short period of three and a half years. We seemed to shed constitutions every six months, like a kind of political striptease.

My views were quite out of harmony with those of my superiors, until the departure in 1958 of Twining, with his worthy but doomed commitment to multi-racialism, and the advent of Sir Richard Turnbull. Turnbull was a very different character from Twining, shy and awkward where Twining had been bluff and ebullient. He was, though, highly intelligent and attuned to the seismic shifts taking place in Tanganyika's political climate. His previous experience had been in Kenya, mainly in the Northern Frontier District, where his toughness and sardonic wit had earned him legendary status, and latterly in Nairobi dealing with the Mau-Mau emergency. At the outset his tenure seemed most unlikely to run smoothly. Nyerere had just been convicted of libel against a DC in Geita, and had he elected to go to prison rather than pay his fines, the country would have been in turmoil. Fortunately he rejected the course of martyrdom, quite possibly because of the relationship of trust that was set up from the beginning with Turnbull, who showed that he was prepared to work with Nyerere and not against him. 'You and I have important work to do together, Mr Nyerere,' was Turnbull's greeting, and this set the pattern.

The change of attitude from repression to co-operation required considerable adaptability and was not easy for either side. TANU in 1958 was ill-organised, and outlying branches tended to do much as they pleased. In consequence there were many areas where law and order had largely broken down and the Administration was disregarded. The likelihood of a state of emergency loomed from time to time, an anathema to Turnbull after his Kenya experience. It can be imagined that the TANU rank and file entertained no high hopes from the 'Hammer of the Mau-Mau'. It was Turnbull's first task to persuade Nyerere and his lieutenants that it was in the future interests of TANU as well as the present interests of the Administration that the law be obeyed. Nyerere flung himself into the task of ensuring that this should be the case.

There were plenty of disagreements along the road as constitutional advance proceeded at daunting pace. How many ministers could the nationalists claim at the stage of semi-responsible self-government? They were offered four, but when the Council of Ministers was formed in May 1959, they secured five. The five were the portfolios of no weight – co-operative development and so on – while all the commanding ones, law and order and the control of the economy, remained in the hands of officials from the *ancien régime*. This was a reflection of a mistaken view that power is divisible and can be handed out in slices. Give them a bit, then when they have demonstrated that they can use it properly, let them have some more. It was not a shameful strategy, but it did not work. This was perfectly demonstrated in the Council of Ministers. In the event it only subsisted for 16 months, but in that time I could see power passing visibly across the Council table from us to them.

In this way, the next stage came sooner than had at first been expected. On 1 September 1960 Nyerere, 'the agitator' as he later described himself with humorous irony, took office as Chief Minister of a cabinet of 12, which included only two members from the Colonial Service. He inherited me as Permanent Secretary to the Chief Minister and Secretary to the Cabinet and, in due course, as Head of the Civil Service. These were positions of power, giving a degree of control of the country's administrative machinery, together with the influence that came from constant access to its dominant political figure and from the part that I had necessarily to play in the organisation of his affairs from day to day. In prospect my position was an uncomfortable one: not only did Nyerere not know me, but he had reason to be suspicious of me. I was an object of mistrust to some of those earlier members of the Council of Ministers with whom I had had dealings, and well before Nyerere had taken office they had solicited the Governor to appoint somebody else. Happily for me, the Governor did not agree, and in the event any suspicion or mistrust between Nyerere and me disappeared at our first meeting.

Work was an immediate bond. We had to compress into months the preparations which in our earlier imagination would have been spread over years. Crash programmes of Africanisation of the Civil Service had to be conducted at a time when the service had to undertake more tasks than ever before. The provincial Administration had to be maintained while its old authority was slipping away and while DCs were having to get used to political appointees working alongside them. We had barely got used to the innovation of a ministerial system of government in place of the old Secretariat-dominated one when we found that ministries we had just established had to be reshuffled and adapted for new tasks. Preparations had to be made for the decisive constitutional conference in London in the summer of 1961. The size and nature of the armed forces had to be determined. The common services with Kenya and Uganda had to be preserved in an odd relationship in which only one of the three was independent. An embryo diplomatic service had to be trained and preparations made for opening offices overseas, at the same time as the harbingers of embassies of other countries descended upon us in growing numbers. Safeguards had to be agreed for British civil servants who elected to continue under the independent government. And finally, the extent of future British financial aid had to be negotiated in the face of an initial low-ball offer. Turnbull flew to London to argue the case with a sympathetic Iain Macleod, Colonial Secretary, and a less sympathetic Treasury, and returned in triumph with a satisfactory deal. Almost as time-consuming were the more minor trappings of independence – the national anthem, the flag, the coat of arms. Nyerere upset the College of Arms by insisting that Tanganyika's coat of arms be flanked by a man and a woman rather than representatives of the animal kingdom, as the College deemed the rules required.

Nyerere needed no lessons in how to cope with endless work. His political campaigns had taught him all he needed to know about that. But all the nuts and bolts of the business of government were new to him, and one might well have expected him to find himself at sea, all the more so because he would never have claimed to be an administrator. In fact he was never at a loss: he absorbed advice, sorted out the political issues from the administrative, and was a constant spur to faster action. Despite the endless grind, he continued to maintain the intimate relationship with the common people on which his whole movement was founded. However hectic his pace, he always found time to be out and about.

The anomalous constitutional position could have been a complication. I was Nyerere's Permanent Secretary, but I was also a servant of the Crown. I had to keep links open with the Crown's representative, the Governor, as did Nyerere, but our relationship with him was different, for I was a civil servant and he was a politician. I was responsible to Nyerere for pushing Africanisation forward with all speed, but I also had responsibilities to my British colleagues in the Civil Service, on whom the administration of the country still depended, and many of whom were at the difficult point of making choices about their future careers. Some of his cabinet were not only uneasy about working alongside members of the colonial regime, but were actively hostile. One of them even suggested to me that I was putting Nyerere at risk by failing to ensure that the Government aircraft were properly serviced. Since I used them frequently myself, this struck me a bit far-fetched, but illustrates how difficult some of the party leaders found it to throw off the spirit of struggle against the colonialists. Not so Nyerere, for he had entire confidence that the system was now working for him. He toured the country, rubbing in to cheering crowds that TANU would need money to govern just as much as the white men had, that taxes would still have to be paid and the law obeyed, whoever was in control. His grasp of the subtleties of the position was instinctive, and such was the rapport we established that divided loyalties never caused us serious problems. His only lapse in this respect was an article he wrote for the *Observer* in March 1961, carefully timed for the Prime Minister's conference in London, where the central issue was whether South Africa should remain in the Commonwealth. The article set out with his customary persuasiveness the case against South Africa and its apartheid policies, and made it clear that if South Africa were a member, Tanganyika would not be. The article was influential in leading South Africa to withdraw its application, but this foray into foreign policy was a breach of convention, since, although he was Chief Minister, external affairs were at this stage the prerogative of the Governor on behalf of the British Government. Nyerere was at the time spending a few days at the hill station in Lushoto, and it fell to me to fly up there at short notice to point out the constitutional position and the incorrectness of what he was doing. My arguments had not the least effect on him.

My wife and I lived at this time at 10 Park Road, not far from the Secretariat, as I have said, and across the way from the arabesques of Government House, now State House. Our house was an old German one, raised above the ground for coolness, nicely positioned so that the verandah caught the breezes from the sea. Nyerere's house was the Deputy Governor's former house, and just down the road. In those early days he was apt to be beset in the evenings by his political associates, and when he wanted peace he would drop round for a drink or an informal meal. Inevitably we would talk over the problems of the day, but we were just as likely to discuss *Julius Caesar*, which at the time it was his diversion to be translating into the mellifluous Swahili of which he was a master. I recall a long discussion about how best to render Shakespeare's pun about 'Rome and room enough', a challenge which in the end he wisely dodged. Often enough we just amused ourselves, for he had a highly developed sense of fun, an aspect of his personality that is often overlooked by those who did not know him personally.

He could, though, be moved to anger. His readiness to work through the established machinery of government always exposed him to extremist attack, and on one occasion he almost came to blows when his political opponent Zuberi Mtemvu compared him, in his own office, to the Western apologist from Katanga, Moise Tshombe. On another occasion he spoke with passionate fury in the debate on the Tanganyikan Citizenship Bill in the National Assembly a few weeks before independence. The bill, which allowed for white and brown citizens as well as black, had been viciously attacked by nationalist parliamentarians. This was an assault on Nyerere's principles. His ideology he could change, his religion he could change, the one thing he couldn't change was his colour, and he rubbed his skin as he spoke. No man should be treated differently because of the one thing he could not change. He would resign rather than accept a racially defined citizenship.

Looking back, I am impressed by the consistency of his political thinking. Indifferent to material riches himself, he held that conspicuous wealth in a poor country was an affront, and that the capitalism which tended to produce it was alien to the egalitarianism of African tradition. From the early 1960s he was drawing the analogy between the extended family and the Tanganyika he wanted to see, where all those with the ability do their share of work, where the safety net of the family is there for those whose working days are over, and where there are no gross differentials of wealth. *Ujamaa*, which translates roughly as 'familyhood' was the word for his thrifty, austere and communalist vision. *Umoja*, or 'unity' was another of his themes, out of which grew his conversion to a one-party state. It was not what we had envisaged, committed as we were to the Westminster model, but in African conditions the rationale was clear. Africans seek consensus, and the concept of a loyal opposition was not easily grasped. He was right to seek a political structure which was adapted to the dispositions of an African electorate. This view was not then, and still is not, fashionable, but his reasoning was cogent, and though his experiment did not long survive his departure it is not clear that multi-party politics has brought benefit to Tanzania. CCM,[3] which succeeded TANU, continues to win all elections, and Tanzania carries the burden of single-party rule without the internal checks and balances that Nyerere envisaged.

Nyerere and I had our differences. Ceaseless work, vital issues, contrasting standpoints all ensured that from time to time we would be at odds. Not often, but it happened. On reflection he was probably more often in the right than I was. I recall one instance three months or so before independence, not for the issue over which we were arguing but for what seemed a chance remark with which he concluded our discussion. 'Alright, it's an administrative matter. I don't belong with administrative matters. I should resign and get back to the people where I do belong and make sure that the grass roots are healthy.' Disagreement forgotten, I piled in with conventional advice. Did he not know how much the country depended on him? He replied with his usual trenchant good sense that no country ought to depend on one man, and that it was not going to be much of a country if it did. We passed on to other topics. But I thought of it again when I was back in London on leave in what I had hoped would be a quiet period after independence. I had seen a newspaper report that he was about to resign. I telephoned Turnbull in Dar es Salaam, and found that he had in fact already resigned to devote himself to the affairs of TANU, and had been succeeded by Rashidi Kawawa,[4] a former trade-union official with whom I could not have worked in the same way. I knew immediately that this was the end of my African career.

APPENDIX 1

Annual Report for 1945 for Maswa District submitted by the District Commissioner, Maswa to the Government in Dar es Salaam

Introduction

The end of the war inevitably dominates any consideration of the year 1945. The successive defeats of our two great enemies brought an immense thankfulness and relief to those members of the community who were able to appreciate the scale of the death and destruction that had been wrought in the past six years. But for those whose war work has been so far from the great scenes of action this spiritual relief was matched by little alteration in physical and material strain; the war and its aftermath were indistinguishable in the efforts that they demanded. Indeed the latter half of the year was in many ways the harder. The increasing tiredness of staff and the removal of the powerful stimulus of the war coincided with the increase of work involved by the sudden posing of the manifold problems of reconversion. Yet the strain has been well met and it is reasonable to hope that the foundations have been laid for a return to a more normal life in 1946; but, as in every other part of the world, it will be a normality never known before.

1. The War Effort and its Aftermath

The Basukuma continued to give loyal support to our cause to the end, as they did from the beginning, little though they have been able to comprehend the tremendous issues involved and the direct bearing that those issues have had upon their own fate. At the beginning of the year 559 tribesmen were conscripted for sisal labour. It is a source of great concern that of labour conscripted for a year two years ago 118 are not yet accounted for; their return has not been notified, nor is it known whether they have volunteered for further work.

The machinery ran smoothly and no difficulty was experienced, but it is a cause for rejoicing that this necessary but unpleasant measure of compulsion will not have to be enforced again.

The drive for cattle for the troops went on despite obstruction and the intense unpopularity of what the Basukuma have always seen as an assault upon one of the bases of their social structure. The district's quota was 35,000 head to be produced in the course of the year. In the first half of the year monthly production on the markets was steadily below that which was required, but in August and September a great and successful drive brought to the markets cattle in such numbers that, had its continuance been allowed to the end of the year, the quota would have been easily passed. But in October Messrs Liebigs[1] were forced by shortage of grazing beyond this District to give up buying for the rest of the year; in consequence the actual number of cattle produced in 1945 was slightly under 28,000.

Money contributions continued to come in from the Africans for the various war funds, with Sengerema under Chief Mataba's direction as usual in the lead.

The secondment of a British NCO and an African NCO to the District throughout most of the year was of the greatest assistance in the payment of family remittances, the rounding up of deserters, and the handling of leave personnel. They were equally invaluable towards the end of the year as demobilisation began to get into its stride and at the end of September the Army provided the most efficient help by the detachment of two lorries from a transport platoon to the District. Without the latter aid the problem of returning large batches of demobilised *askari* to their homes could not have been carried out efficiently in Maswa District, with its large area and dearth of porters in the neighbourhood of the District Office. Some 160 soldiers were demobilised in the last three months of the year and it is pleasant to record that the machinery has hitherto worked with the greatest efficiency both on the part of the Army and at the receiving end in Maswa District itself. Great care has been taken that every man should be properly interviewed on his arrival with a view to assessing his capabilities for future employment, should he wish for it, and the foundations were laid for the employment of as many men as possible in the service both of Government and of the Native Administration, as an important part of the reintegration of returning soldiers into civilian society. But among the Basukuma it remains clear that a great many have no other desire than to return to their villages and stay there.

2. Agriculture and Economic Position

The total rainfall for the year was 24.47 inches. Fortunately this very small fall was well distributed and the District was self-supporting in food throughout the year, save for some comparatively small importation of foodstuffs through normal trade channels. Cotton brought much money into circulation for the export of 6307 bales of cotton lint registered a great improvement on the two previous years, although it did not approach the record year of 1939 when over 10,000 bales were exported. Fifteen tons of groundnuts were exported, but figures for chick-pea, rice and gum were negligible.

In the improvement of farming methods it is wise not to confuse the African mind by a multiplicity of instructions. It was therefore decided to concentrate upon the introduction of tie-ridging, which has shown such remarkable results at the experimental stations of Ukiriguru and Lubaga, and upon an assault on the pest of 'striga helmonthica'. This dual campaign was inaugurated at a full Chiefs' meeting at the end of August. The importance of the uprooting of striga is now recognised by the people themselves and it may be expected that there will be full cooperation from the Native Authorities, the Chiefs themselves suggesting that every Monday be a day for a full turn-out of all tribal officials to enforce up-rooting; heavy penalties were also to be exacted from Chiefs who fail to carry out this order, on the good grounds that a defaulting Chief would vitiate the efforts of his neighbours if he gave shelter to this self-broadcasting weed in his own Chiefdom. The tie-ridging campaign will, however, prove much more difficult, for towards the end of the year it became clear that, although Chiefs paid lip-service to the idea, they were not really convinced that the extra work involved on a smaller area more than made up for the decrease in total area of cultivation. Nevertheless, tie-ridging is to be enforced as thoroughly as possible and the recent appointment of a Crop Supervisor to Maswa District should greatly help the campaign.

The grave shortage of hoes caused, and still causes, concern about the prospects of cultivation for the 1946 season. Despite efforts which began in January, 1945 to ensure an adequate supply when the planting rains came, importations never allowed of the supply even approaching the requirements.

A food store was constructed in the course of the year to hold 100 tons of grain. It is proposed that annual sale and re-purchase of fresh grain shall keep the store always filled with this reserve against potential famine. The idea is a welcome one to Chiefs and people, who undertook to initiate the scheme by making use of the Sukuma custom of 'sororo' to present 100 tons of food free. This was duly done.

3. Soil Erosion

Soil erosion and conservation of water are two facets of the same problem and it is intended to continue elsewhere the practice followed at Ng'wanampalala. What was there an experiment may now be said to have proved a success. Water was put there and people with their stock have moved in, clearing the land with the exception of those forest reserves which are an integral part of the scheme. It may be hoped that this is the best method of all to relieve pressure on exhausted areas, although, as a natural corollary, the proper use of new areas must in the future be subject to a degree of supervision which has not been feasible in wartime.

Efforts on these lines were severely limited in 1945 by the pressure of other work and only in Sanga Meatu was it possible to start the progressive, annual digging of tanks, the spoil from which can in due course be consolidated into a single dam. The District's other dams were maintained in good condition.

4. Markets

The produce markets functioned smoothly; 45 booths were leased, an increase of 12 on 1944 which reflected the better season. The only important production figures have already been quoted and the brake on the cattle markets caused by the cessation of purchases by Messrs

Liebigs has also been mentioned. The total value of the 27,776 cattle sold was £63,765. 13s.00d.[2]

5. Native Administration

During the year under review the Native Administration has been as heavily burdened as at any time in the war, during which such vastly increased responsibilities have devolved upon it. Few people would have thought in 1939 that the comparatively flimsy structure of tribal organisation would have proved fit to undertake the tasks which fell to its lot in 1945. That it has done so is a matter for congratulation on the past and for the highest hopes of the future, for it is fair to believe that the indigenous system of Government has shown itself sufficiently resilient to develop and sufficiently sound to endure.

Chief Majebere of Mwagala has, as ever, been a tower of strength both in Council with his fellow Chiefs and in his own most efficiently administered area. He remains a dominating personality in all aspects of Native Administration. Chiefs Mataba and Ndaturu also deserve mention for outstandingly good work in the course of the year, the former having been voted an increase of salary as recognition of the extension of his population and the new duties which have come upon him in connection with the work on the new Federation Headquarters at Malya.

In Dutwa in the extreme north of the District four years of maladministration by Chief Mushuda resulted in the withdrawal of recognition from him for chronic drunkenness and dishonesty. He was succeeded, with rejoicing among the people of Dutwa, by Kasiri s/o Ileme, a young man of 17 who is at school at Tossamaganga. Until he comes of age the Chiefdom of Dutwa is being administered by a Regent, Gregory s/o Nkuba, who was seconded there by the Binza Federation Central Agency after many years of faithful service. Dutwa and Kanadi continue to be a source of concern to the Administration, for their remoteness from the District Office makes supervision difficult, particularly in times like these when opportunity for touring is so restricted.

The Dutwa affair was the only blot on the escutcheon of the Binza Chiefs during 1945. Their intelligent and progressive attitude was well illustrated throughout the year by the promptness with which almost all instructions were carried out, even to the vastly unpopular measure of compulsory sale of cattle. The Chiefs showed themselves at their very best at the end of August when they met the District Commissioner and Assistant District Officer, and, during two days of reasoned and intelligent discussion with them, thrashed out almost every aspect of Administration.

At the end of the year the Central Agency staff was strengthened by the appointment of Mr Alexander Tobias, a Sukuma graduate of Makerere College, Uganda, to be Secretary and Treasurer. The incumbent of this important office needs to know English really well, if only to handle the Central Agency's surprising amount of correspondence in that language.

In August the Assistant District Officer visited the Masai settlements at Subeti, only the third visit to this very remote area by an Administrative Officer in the course of 15 years. The Masai and Wanderobo there number only about 300, but there is no doubt that they are well within the Maswa District. At the time of writing their future remains unsettled and it is open to question whether they should be returned to Masailand or accepted in this District. Maswa was comparatively free from raids by the Masai in 1945, only two small herds of cattle being lifted. This might have been due to sentences imposed for theft, when some of the raiders who did such damage in 1944 were captured. It might also be ascribed to the deterrent effect of two Police patrols which made extensive, roundabout tours between the Kimali and Kanadi Police posts.

However, although the Masai border remained quiet, there were ravages from another direction. A party of 60 or 70 Wanyiramba from Singida District crossed the border with two Policemen in September in search of a noted cattle thief, from whose activities they had suffered and who was alleged to be sheltering in this District. To begin with, their search was to some extent legitimate, but the Wanyiramba tribesmen got out of hand and ended by committing rape and arson among the Wataturu in the south of the District and lifted some 800 head of stock. However, a saner spirit prevailed when they re-crossed the Singida border, and a Veterinary Guard was allowed to quarantine the stock. The Police from Kimali post were fairly close on the trail and were able to recover all the stolen beasts from quarantine. The culprits in this affair were brought to book and incurred severe sentences.

Two of the Chiefs' activities deserve mention. Chief Majebere decided on his own initiative to build a museum for those relics which are in danger of being forgotten by the young men of today. This commendable idea received the blessing of the Provincial Commissioner when he performed the opening ceremony in the presence of a large gathering in October. Four Chiefs also visited Busmao at the end of the same month in order to study the co-operative system there for the production and sale of clarified butter. As a result, it is hoped to organise a co-operative system here in 1946. It is good to record a great improvement during the year in social and welfare activities. The gift of a Strip Projector and a Wireless were good examples and at the end of the year a start was made with the building of a Welfare Centre and library at Nyalikungu.

6. Native Treasury and Tax Collection

The Binza Native Treasury remains as sound and resilient as ever. A balance of £11,102. 01s. 06cts. was carried forward to 1946, exceeding the estimate by nearly £200. Tax collection was also very satisfactory, the total sum received being £26,974. 10s., which was very close to the estimate.

7. Native Courts

The Native Courts as usual discharged the vast bulk of the District's legal work with commendable efficiency. Five hundred and forty-seven civil cases and 593 criminal cases were tried. There was a total of 35 appeals to the Chiefs' Court, which sat for eight Sessions in the course of the year. Only four appeals came forward to the District Commissioner, which is a good illustration of the confidence of the people in their own Courts. As in the past, stock theft was the most serious and recurrent offence. A new complication in this year was the tremendous effort to enforce the sale of cattle for the war on an unwilling populace. This oppressive, but necessary, measure Junfortunately involved some 300 people in heavy fines from the Native Courts. The Court of the Chief's Deputy in Dutwa was abolished during the year as the Regent is now hearing all cases in his own Court.

8. Native Health

The year saw a considerable extension of the facilities provided by the Native Administration at the District's one hospital, and progress in measures for the protection of health in Nyalikungu and its environs; in the latter connection African Assistant Medical Officer Pim Ibreck is to be congratulated on his anti-malarial work. A series of 14 small, inexpensive cottages were built at the Hospital for the accommodation, with their families, of out-patients who live too far from the Hospital to attend for daily treatment. This may be regarded as a highly successful experiment, which has gained the approval of the Medical Authorities. There was also built a Maternity Ward with money presented by Chief Majebere in the previous year. Nor has building been confined entirely to district headquarters, for a good start was made with a programme aimed at providing in-patients' wards at all dispensaries. Malampaka dispensary also benefited by the installation of a large water tank.

An effort was made during the year to improve the diet at the Hospital and on the station of Nyalikungu by the provision of vegetables. These are grown in a garden irrigated from the Nyalikungu Dam, which has now passed from the experimental stage and is maintained by subscriptions from European and African consumers. More larvicidal fish were introduced into the Dams in an effort to keep down malaria, and the same waters have also supplied a considerable number of fish for human consumption.

The African Medical Assistant (A.M.A.) system continues to work as satisfactorily as possible under the present lack of supervision. One A.M.A. was dismissed in the course of the year after a conviction for having *moshi* in his possession.

As regards disease, there has been the usual trickle of cases of cerebro-spinal meningitis, which this year amounted to 241 and caused 46 deaths. In the latter half of the year there was a widespread outbreak of smallpox mostly in a mild form, but severe in places, Lalago in particular suffering a considerable number of deaths. A vaccination campaign run in conjunction with the rinderpest campaign brought the disease almost under control by the end of the year. African Assistant Medical Officer, Joseph M'tahangarwaq, continued his investigation into treatment of tuberculosis by local African practitioners with the help of a grant of £25 from the

Sukumaland Central Medical Store. His results are interesting, but as yet inconclusive.

9. Native Administration Roads

The roads were early put in condition in 1945, only to suffer heavy damage from a cloud-burst after the rains were supposed to be over. A supplementary estimate of £100 was necessary to put this to rights, and the total amount spent on roads by the Native Treasury amounted to £350.

10. Native Livestock and Veterinary Activities

The number of cattle sold and their value have already been mentioned in connection with the political aspects of the forced sale of stock. A great deal of propaganda has also been directed to convincing the people of the economic value of their cattle markets. That this wordy campaign has not been without effect was shown towards the end of the year when compulsory sales stopped in consequence of the cessation of buying by Messrs Liebigs Ltd. As might have been expected, there was a heavy initial slump, but this was followed by a marked recovery in the markets, voluntary though they were.

Grazing was desperately short from July until the November rains and the condition of cattle was correspondingly poor. In July and August, in order to mitigate the severities of the trek to Arusha, the Veterinary Department cleared a cattle track from Kimali through Subeti and up to the border shops of Kakesyo. It is this Stock Route which is now passable to motor traffic; if it can be maintained, besides benefiting the cattle it provides the Lake Province with an outlet to Ngorongoro, which might well be exploited for Local Leave when petrol and tyres are plentiful once more.

A big rinderpest campaign from September to the end of the year was carried out and showed a count of 568,279 head of cattle, 178,738 sheep and 331,557 goats. This represents an increase by almost a third over the 1942 count, and is an alarming emphasis on the need for measures of redistribution of people and stock and for the utmost encouragement of voluntary marketing.

26,756 kilos of ghee of all grades were exported. In the past a number of Chiefs have had a hand in the ghee industry, owning their own separators, but the Council of Chiefs has now very rightly decided that Chiefs should not take part in industry and those concerned are therefore selling their machines to the village co-operative societies which, as previously mentioned, should be organised in 1946.

11. Education

The need for educational advance is a constant subject of concern to the Chiefs and the people, who take every opportunity of asking for schools. It was not possible during 1945 to launch out on any extended policy, but at least the ground work was laid for big steps forward in 1946. A long discussion with Missionary representatives in September and consultation with the Chiefs paved the way of the setting up of a District Education Committee, the building of four Day Schools to be interposed between the Boarding School at Nyalikungu and the low standard Village Schools, and finally for a degree of supervision of the Village Schools which they have never had in the past. These measures will take effect in 1946 and it is proposed, as soon as a suitable man comes forward, to appoint an Educational Inspector whose sole duty will be to tour the locally supported Village Schools. These institutions received some encouragements to their efforts to teach the three 'R's by a gift of slates from the Education Department.

12. Missions

An effort is being made to secure the co-operation of all the Missions in the field of education, and it is earnestly hoped that this will be forthcoming, in order to avoid an absurd duplication of effort as between the Native Administration and the Missions in the vast programme needed. But of course this co-operation implies willingness by the Missions to admit to their schools pagans or children of other denominations, and it remains to be seen whether they are all prepared to take a step which for some of them will be a revolutionary one.

The Africa Inland Mission was permitted during the year to establish a Community Village School in the Chiefdom of Badi.

13. Native Administration Forestry

Forestry efforts have been mainly devoted to planting at Malya. Elsewhere in the District there have been prosecutions for infringement of the regulations reserving hill-tops and for cutting timber in the reserves at Ng'wanampalala. There has also been a certain amount of experiment in tree planting in the irrigated garden below the Nyalikungu Dam. A large fuel plantation at Kilolele in the 'Dust bowl' was also established.

14. Tsetse Reclamations

Nothing to note.

15. Political and Economic Development

When the British took over the Administration of Sukumaland in 1916, there were a large number of independent Chiefdoms. Rivalry and boundary disputes were common and it took several years to settle down.

In 1926 the position had so far altered that the majority of Chiefs of the Shinyanga District formed a federation, to which the remaining chiefdoms adhered at later dates. The Chiefs of Maswa District followed suit and the Binza Federation came into being in 1927 followed by similar federations in both Mwanza and Kwimba Districts.

This process of federation into larger units, for the purposes of co-operation in all spheres of local government, has continued to develop steadily, if unobtrusively.

In 1932, the first meeting of all the Chiefs of Sukumaland was held in Mwanza. This was the first step towards a unified Sukumaland Native Administration but the meetings, begun in 1932, were not continued as a regular practice, perhaps largely because no standing organisation was created.

In 1942, after the opening ceremony of the Sola Dam by the Provincial Commissioner, the Chiefs, who were present on that occasion from the Sukumaland districts, revived the request to form a single Sukumaland Federation. Owing to war conditions it was not possible to make progress at once but in 1944 progress became possible and, as a result of careful investigations, Government was satisfied of the spontaneity of the Sukumal-and Chiefs' desire for federation and of the concurrence of the people and elders in this wish.

Careful consideration was therefore given to the selection of a site for the Federal Headquarters. All the Chiefs of Sukumaland agreed that a rocky hill, known as Malya Luguru, in the centre of Malya village in the North of Sengerema Chiefdom, Maswa District, would be the most suitable locality for their new Federation Headquarters as being, not only the most central suitable point on the railway but also adequately removed from the distractions of urban centres. Further investigations were made into the adequacy of the potential water supply at Malya as it was decided that this new Federation Headquarters would be most suitably linked with the headquarters of the inter-departmental development team which is to become responsible for the rehabilitation and development of Sukumaland in relation to the complex problems arising from the mal-distribution of both people and stock.

In the event, the potential water supply was found to be adequate for any scale of development that might conceivably take place and preliminary work on layout and on raising the existing dam began on the 15 November, following a survey made earlier in the year of some 60 square miles of country surrounding the rocky hill at Malya.

This great federation of Sukumaland is perhaps one of the most important federal developments of local government in Africa, embracing as it does a population of over three quarters of a million in an area of about the same size as Switzerland. Progress cannot be spectacular, as it is, of course, essential that the greatest care and forethought must be exercised in laying the foundations of what may well become an African nation of no small importance.

Appendix A: Labour Agent's permits issued during 1945

Name	District	Number of Labourers
No. 9/45 Tanganyika Sisal Growers Association	Maswa	86
No. 16/45 Geita Gold Mining Co. Ltd	Maswa	Nil
No. 23/45 Tanganyika Sisal Growers Association for Nderema Tea Estate	Maswa	Nil
No. 42/45 Alamasi Ltd, Mwadui	Maswa	Nil

Appendix B: Statistics relating to the recruitment of labourers in the District during 1945

559 Sisal labour conscripted under compulsory ordinance No. 23/1940.

86 Sisal labour recruited by the Tanganyika Sisal Growers Association. No labour was attested locally.

Appendix C: Statistics showing the prevailing rates of wages

Skilled	Semi-skilled	Unskilled	Porter rate	Posho rate
Shs.	Shs.	Shs.	Cts.	Cts.
30.80	15.30	9.15	–/35	–/15

Appendix D: Annual return of requisitioned labour

	No. employed	Total no. of man-days worked	Nature of work	No. of convictions		No. of deaths	No. of sick	Average no. of hours worked per day	Rate of wages	Reference to authority for requisition	Remarks
				Fined	Imprisoned						
A. Labour requistioned on behalf of government departments											
(i) Porters	58	–	Tax etc.	–	–				–/50 cts	Cap. 47 section 8(i)	
(ii) Others	559	–								The Compulsory Service Ordinance 1940 no. 23 of 1940	

	No. employed	Total no. of man-days worked	Nature of work	No. of convictions		No. of deaths	No. of sick	Average no. of hours worked per day	Rate of wages	Reference to authority for requisition	Remarks
				Fined	Imprisoned						
A. Labour requistioned on behalf of native authorities											
(i) Porters	Nil.										
(ii) Others	Nil.										

Note: Labour rendered as a communal undertaking should not be included, but details should be given in a separate memorandum attached to this return.

Appendix E: Number of convictions obtained in respect of requisitioned labour during 1945

Number of Convictions	Sentences	
	Fines	Imprisonment
–	–	–

Appendix F: Statistics related to the working of Section 29 of the Master and Native Services Ordinance during 1945

a) Number of accidents to labourers: Nil.

b) Compensation awarded in each case: Nil.

c) Extent of contributory negligence: Nil.

Appendix G: Population statistics for 1945

Asiatics		Natives		Total	
Male	Female	Male	Female	Male	Female
230	176	93,671	83,918	93,901	84,094

Appendix H: Formal orders and rules made under Native Authority Ordinance Section 8 (c) during 1945

Nil.

Appendix I: Statistics relating to the collection of Native Tax during 1945

a) Number of taxes due (according to Revised Estimate):

@ Shs. 10/–	51,513
@ Shs. 5/–	5340

b) Total amount of tax collected:

@ Shs. 10/–	Shs. 518,990
@ Shs. 5/–	Shs. 29,580
	Total Shs. 548,570

c) Number of taxes remaining unpaid

@ Shs. 10/–	Nil
@ Shs. 5/–	Nil

d) Number of tax defaulters employed: Nil

Appendix J: Return of number of days and nights spent by administrative officers on tour during 1945

Name	Days	Nights	Means of Transport
D.W. Malcolm, District Officer	33	45	Car and lorry
H. Corry, Temp. Asst. District Officer	5	3	Lorry
R.J.G. Dewar, Asst. District Officer	8	6	Lorry
C.I. Meek, Asst. District Officer	12	37	Lorry and District Commissioner's car

Labour Report 1945

The only industrial concerns are the two cotton ginneries at Malampaka and Luguru. It has been difficult for these ginneries to get labour but not so much so that they have had to curtail their activities. One conviction was obtained for the employment of child labour and a fine of Shs.700/– imposed.

In spite of the numerous recruiting permits issued only 86 Natives have volunteered and been sent forward by the Tanganyika Sisal Growers' Association. It seems that the Tanganyika Sisal Growers' Association Labour Bureau are confining their recruiting efforts to the other Sukumaland Districts.

559 Basukuma were conscripted for sisal labour at the beginning of this year. There was no tax defaulter labour.

Maintenance of village roads was as usual performed by communal labour and so was the repair and maintenance of dams.

Donald Malcolm

APPENDIX 2

Annual Report for 1955 for Mbulu District submitted by the District Commissioner, Mbulu to the Government in Dar es Salaam

1. General Observations

Nineteen fifty-five was a quiet year of considerable, solid progress. This was so, despite no help from nature, for the weather was unkind to food production for the fourth successive year, and the cash economy of Northern Iraqw was equally hard hit when disease almost wiped out the wheat crop. Severe though this double set-back was, record cattle sales from the District did much to repair them both, while communal self-help on the same massive scale as 1954 bore witness to good morale in the District and ensured that there was no check in the general progress and advance of recent years. The good sense of the people continues to make them a difficult target for self-seeking politicians, and the chief political difficulty of the year was a renewed necessity for disciplining the troublesome Barabaig.

The appointment of Chief Amri as Member of Legislative Council gave the District its first representative there, and this distinction for him has not been unappreciated.

Last year's conferences between the District Teams of Mbulu, Kondoa and Singida led in February to the largest visit that the District has yet had, when 70 Africans from the other two Districts came to study progress in land use in Mbulu. There was a further conference at Kondoa in October. It was as interesting as its two predecessors, though it remains difficult to see how the three Districts can be more closely tied together than by liaison of this nature for some years to come.

The posting of a District Officer at Babati for most of the year secured closer supervision of the area below the Rift. However, it was considered more appropriate to post there a Settlement Officer, when one became available at the end of the year, for his special qualifications are of the highest value in this endemic Sleeping Sickness area, and arrangements have been made for more touring of the area by a District Officer from Mbulu than used to be the case in the past.

His Excellency the Officer Administering the Government[1] paid his first visit to the District in July. He fulfilled a very hard programme, which included an exhausting day in the tsetse clearings and a visit to the Iraqw Expansion Area in the Yaida Depression. His Excellency made a descent of the new Magara road, and at a luncheon party at Magara met some of the leaders of the District's Greek community. Other distinguished visitors during the year were the Members for Agriculture and Natural Resources and for Communications, Works and Development Planning, the Director of Water Development and Mr D.K. Makwaia, OBE. The District has also acquired a new parishioner of the highest distinction in Prince Bernhard of the Netherlands, who has leased one of the new farms at Magara.

2. Development Plans

Details of development in the District can be found under the various subject heads in this Report. The development of the District, and indeed its whole life are entirely bound up in the preservation and improvement of its land, which was so gravely imperilled a few years back. To these ends the people have been guided during 1955 by the same few simple ideas which have lain behind all the policies of the past decade.

What was said in the 1954 Report about the problem of stock densities in the Iraqw Chiefdom has been borne out in 1955. This is the most crucial and the most stubborn of the District's problems. The Iraqw again responded well to the pressures for high sales from each area, albeit the percentage of their stock of which they disposed was not so high as in the preceding year. From the slightly incomplete figures available at the end of the year, it appeared that the total numbers of Iraqw stock had risen only by some 5000 units; this was a smaller rise than in 1954 and represents a less dense stock population than previously, since the land made available by the season's bush clearing was more than enough to take up the increase. It was gratifying to note a slight decrease in numbers in Central Iraqw, which is the area of greatest potential danger. Thus the general picture of stock numbers in the Iraqw highlands remains as it has done in the past year or two – first there was a welcome, although insufficient, initial decline in numbers under the impact of compulsory destocking, followed by a breathing space in which heavy sales have kept increases down to the numbers which can be absorbed by land expansion.

The other major aspect of development is this land expansion, which has gone ahead in 1955 on the same great scale as in 1954. The people of the District put 440,000 man days into schemes of communal self-help. Some of this work was on water works and roads of general benefit to the areas concerned, but by far the greatest proportion, 384,000 man days, was expended in bush clearing. Despite a good deal of effort which might have been saved, owing to the impossibility of carrying out selective clearing without adequate technical supervision, the results were magnificent. The Western Expansion Area, which is divided between the Iraqw and Barabaig, is now, apart from some small pockets, a firm base for further advance against the tsetse fly. Indeed the first step in this new advance was taken in 1955 when operations were commenced in the Yaida Depression. It should not be long before a whole section of the Western fly front rests securely on the natural, fly-free barrier of the Yaida Mbuga system. That day will mark the achievement of one of the great objects of the Development Scheme.

Of course, an expansion area would not be of much use if people and stock were not expanding into it; in the West they are doing so, and Sub-Chief Simeon now has well over 800 taxpayers and nearly 15,000 stock units, a big advance on 1954. It has been this District's experience that settlement in a new area starts slowly and hesitantly and the people hang back from pioneering – and then, when a few have ventured in and survived, suddenly everything goes forward with confidence and growing speed. That has been the case with the big Gallapo Expansion Area in Gorowa. It got off to a slow start, but there has been much movement in during the last two years and settlement seems now sufficiently secure for consideration of the next move towards the well-watered area of Madege.

In the agricultural expansion area of Mbulumbulu the same air of energy prevails as was reported last year for the first time after years of stagnation. This remains true, despite the set-back to the African farmers there by the destruction of their wheat crop by rust. As an example of the new popularity of Mbulumbulu, the 300 acres which reverted to Native Authority use at the end of the year, on the expiry of the share-cropping scheme with Mr Ellis of Oldeani, were divided into 10-acre holdings, and there were no fewer than 435 applicants for these 30 small farms. Indeed once the Ellis lands are completely re-allocated by the end of 1956, it is probable that the Mbulumbulu Sub-Chiefdom will be as intensively farmed as is possible until water can be brought into the area between Rotian and Simba.

Another big advance in North Iraqw has been the formation of a Co-operative to handle the people's crops. It is another example of the growing tendency of the farmers up there to think of their crops in terms of cash; the Co-operative should give scope to the small man in this direction, while the wealthier are illustrating the same trend by fresh investments in machinery. This new mental outlook has spread to Mangola, which is a low-lying, malarial place where the Iraqw used to fear to settle; but in 1955 there were many Iraqw among the people who have not only taken up the land irrigated by the former Native Authority furrow there, but have greatly extended the irrigation works.

Major water works have been carried out in the District during 1955 in furtherance of plans made some years ago. They included two major dams undertaken by the Water Development Department and Irrigation, while improvements to the Muchlur furrow, mentioned elsewhere, had resulted at the very end of the year in raising the level of the Lake by 3½ feet. Thus it may yet be that the coming long rains will fill Muchlur so that the water may be piped into the dry areas to the West; much preparatory work was done in the West during 1955 in readiness for the time when the Muchlur water becomes available, and this included an excellent contour map prepared by the Field Officer of the whole of the Western Expansion Area.

Development cannot be bought for nothing, although it comes more cheaply in Mbulu than in many other places because of the admirable willingness of the people to devote their own labour free to work of importance to their tribes. But finance must also be forthcoming and expenditure has continued to rise, so that the Six Year Development Plan (1952–57) which, under the aegis of the Native Authority alone, followed by the Colonial Development and Welfare Scheme, is now scheduled to cost £125,000. Fortunately revenues too have been rising, and there is no reason to think that the District is undertaking tasks beyond the people's strength. If they continue to retain the common sense and trust in those who guide them which they have displayed in the past few years, they should have a future of reasonable prosperity.

3. African Affairs

a) Local Government

An attempt to set up a District Advisory Council in 1955 proved premature, in face of a lack of homogeneity in the District – the areas above and below Rift have very different problems, and the four tribes of the District show little interest in each other's doings. The result was public apathy to the project, and it has been decided instead to form two Natural Resources Committees for the areas above and below the Rift. Joint meetings of these Committees in due course should lead to the natural growth of a Council for the District instead of the imposition of such a body.

In the District's largest and most important Chiefdom of Iraqw Chief Elias has enjoyed better health and has continued to give good leadership to his people. His caution and conservatism are more than offset by his high moral character and spotless honesty. His extreme good nature does not prevent him from being outspokenly severe in *baraza* with his people when severity is necessary. In 1955 he has had good support from his Sub-Chiefs in most directions. Two of these, Hau and Qamara, retired on account of old age after very many years of service; each was succeeded by his son, with the approbation of the people. The Headman of Oldeani resigned and a more energetic young man was installed in his place, but the administration of this difficult area, surrounded as it is by alienated land, remains unsatisfactory.

The District's only branch of TANU was established in Iraqw at Dareda. But the branch has not yet applied for registration and appears to have excited little interest.

Gorowa, under the leadership of Chief Amri, MLC,[2] assisted by his able half-brother Zuberi, has had a year of competent administration. The Sub-Chiefs, more closely supervised than in the past, have improved. There has been a welcome interest shewn in the use of land, with record cattle sales and an outstandingly successful campaign of trash-bunding and manuring. The Gallapo re-settlement area has filled up apace and it must shortly be hived off from Gendi as a separate Sub-Chiefdom.

Mbugwe also has had much more supervision than used to be possible, both from the District Officer, Babati and from Mbulu, which the Magara road has made so easily accessible. Chief Michael has shewn energy and intelligence in his conduct of his small Chiefdom, and has provided a useful spur to his lethargic people in many ways. The Native Authority structure has been made better balanced by a reduction in the number of headmen, and Magugu has been brought more closely under control. Magugu used to be an entirely alien settlement, but the high rate of Mbugwe immigration has completely altered the balance of population.

Barabaig has presented a slightly less peaceful picture. When the Native Authority was reorganised in 1952, so that the Chief-in-Council took the place of the Chief, the original intention had been to dispense with a Chief altogether, since the institution is not an indigenous one in this tribe. It was considered more appropriate that a Council of clan heads should be the Native Authority, working through the three educated Sub-Chiefs as Executive Officers. The people at that time were unwilling to take this step, the clan heads being nervous of their unaccustomed political responsibilities. However, in 1955 the proven ineptitude of Chief Gitamuka led to his resignation. He has not so far been replaced, and, for the time being at least, the Tribal Council under an elected Chairman functions as Native Authority. It may well be that this temporary arrangement will become permanent and that the people will thus after all adopt the constitution which was suggested to them in 1952.

The Barabaig Tribal Council and Sub-Chiefs, as distinct from the Chief, functioned satisfactorily in many ways during 1955 and there was a great improvement in their control and grip within the Chiefdom itself. Where they failed lamentably was in checking warlike cattle raids upon their Nyaturu neighbours. The Mbulu authorities had not been aware of the degree of provocation to which the Wanyaturu were being subjected; but matters were brought very clearly to their notice in early October when the Wanyaturu indulged in demonstrations and threats of retaliation which necessitated the despatch of a platoon of the Mobile Company and other Police reinforcements to the area. Intense investigation subsequently shewed that, although Barabaig living within the Singida District had been responsible for much raiding and Wanyaturu 'quislings' had frequently given wholehearted assistance, the fact remains that Barabaig from Mbulu District had been raiding repeatedly. The Barabaig were not, in turn, without complaints against the Wanyaturu, but they were unable to disclaim an accusation that their young men had taken to cattle raiding as a deliberate act of policy, in place of the murderous habits which they have notoriously displayed in the past and which for the time being they appear to have abandoned. The clan heads, in acknowledgement of the tribe's penitence, agreed to a levy of 500 head of cattle to be produced by clans, so that £3000 in compensation could be paid to the Wanyaturu. This obligation was discharged before the year's end. The Barabaig also entered into a reciprocal arrangement with the Wanyaturu for compensation for future cattle thefts and by the end of the year a healthier sense of confidence seemed to prevail along the border than for some time past.

In 1955 there was a substantial increase in the wages of Native Authority employees. It must be recorded with regret that this led to no reduction in the number of clerks convicted of peculation. Four of them went to gaol, the same number as in 1954. It remains clear that integrity is not to be bought.

b) Native Treasuries

In 1955 the Barabaig Native Authority at length agreed to amalgamate their Native Treasury with that of the Iraqw, Gorowa and Mbugwe. In a District where there are no deep political breaches between the tribes there appears to be everything to be said in favour of a single, strong and united Treasury. The Barabaig have refused to acknowledge this in the past, and it has been for a number of years an object of policy to persuade them to do so. Consequently their decision was very welcome and at the end of the year the Estimates for the two Treasuries for 1956 were combined. The revenues of the two Native Treasuries for the past five years compare as follows:

Iraqw, Gorowa and Mbugwe Native Treasury

Revenue	1951 £	1952 £	1953 £	1954 £	1955 £
Share of native hut and poll tax	5042	7647	15,092	15,645	16,643
Graduated local rate	7176	7145	6614	6647	7455
Other revenue	19,132	20,775	24,849	22,172	29,683
Total	31,350	35,567	46,555	44,464	53,781

Barabaig Native Treasury

Revenue	1951 £	1952 £	1953 £	1954 £	1955 £
Share of native hut and poll tax	781	1082	2511	2152	2326
Graduated local rate	1265	1162	1153	1047	1121
Other revenue	2264	3394	5403	5058	6498
Total	4310	5638	9067	8257	9945

These revenue collections in a difficult year give great cause for satisfaction. In particular, tax and local rate collection, at their record levels, reflect great credit on the Native Authorities. It should be noted that the larger Treasury benefited by some non-recurrent items, particularly the £2000 of profit which accrued from the successful 1954 harvest on the share-cropping scheme at Mbulumbulu. In both Treasuries intense drives to collect outstanding fines yielded higher Court Revenue than ever before, although at the end of the year there still remained arrears of £1000 to be mopped up.

Expenditure in the two Treasuries has been as follows in the past five years:

Iraqw, Gorowa and Mbugwe Native Treasury

1951 £	1952 £	1953 £	1954 £	1955 £
19,788	32,327	52,559	47,547	58,717

Barabaig Native Treasury

1951 £	1952 £	1953 £	1954 £	1955 £
4000	6336	5909	6721	9886

It will be noted that in both Treasuries expenditure, like revenue, easily surpassed all previous records.

In the major Treasury it was satisfactory to find that the number of outstanding ledger accounts had been much reduced by the end of the year. In particular, the famine debt of over £10,000, referred to last year, had been practically discharged.

c) Local Courts
Statistics of hearings in Local Courts were as follows:

Cases of First Instance

Year	Civil Cases	Criminal Cases	Total Cases
1951	779	1397	2176
1952	700	1492	2192
1953	777	1295	2072
1954	796	1249	2045
1955	764	1645	2409

Appeals

Year	Chiefs' Appeal Courts		DC's Appeal Courts	
	Heard	Allowed	Heard	Allowed
1951	181	63	81	16
1952	137	57	69	17
1953	159	59	70	14
1954	243	77	88	27
1955	242	94	124	36

It will be noted that the high figure of hearings before the Chiefs' Appeal Courts in 1954 was maintained this year. There was also a very high proportionate increase in Appeals to the District Commissioner. This was probably a delayed result of the large number of hearings before the Iraqw Appeal Court.

There has been a very slight improvement during 1955 in the standard of work in the Iraqw Courts, though this does not apply to the Chief's Court, while the collection of outstanding fines has remained generally inefficient. Arrangements have been made for the appointment of a Magistrate in Iraqw in 1956. The Below Rift Courts, on the other hand, have much improved the standard of their work.

4. Townships, Minor Settlements and Government Stations

There are no townships in the District.

The Sanitary Authorities at Mbulu and Babati have continued to do good work. They have done much to improve the appearance of both places and have certainly secured healthier living conditions for the inhabitants. Both Minor Settlements have had good butcheries built during the year, and these buildings should ensure the sale of meat in a more sanitary condition than in the past.

Application has been made to Government for the Trading Centres of Magugu and Karatu to be promoted to Minor Settlements. These two places, as well as Mbulu and Babati, have all been re-surveyed in 1955, and this makes possible better planning of their future development.

The Government Station at Mbulu has been improved in numerous ways, notably by the provision of a broad concrete bridge across the Endamaksin River and of a dual carriageway from the village to the District Office.

5. Social Development

While the Social Development Officer from Arusha was unable to repeat in 1955 the visits that he has paid in the past, he did again provide the tsetse clearing gangs with the benefit of film exhibitions by the Mobile Cinema. These shows are extremely popular, and the Native Authorities have welcomed the news that the District is to share its own Mobile Cinema with Kondoa District in 1956.

Sport has continued to flourish more than in the past, the keen enthusiast mentioned last year having, in association with an Indian devotee of the game, added cricket to the list of sports in which the Mbulu community indulge. Association Football has also been much better organised than in the past; there is the makings of an effective District league, while a local Indian merchant has presented a cup for annual competition between Mbulu and Singida.

The admirable little baby clinic, run by women of all communities, has continued to provide a popular service for local mothers.

The Indian community at Mbulu deserve credit for an excellent little school which they started on their own initiative and which caters for all races.

6. Finance, Trade and Industry

There is nothing of note to report. With the exception of the wheat farmers of North Iraqw, the big onion growers of the Centre and a few large African farmers below the Rift, the African economy in this District remains primarily a subsistence economy.

7. Judicial

The number of cases heard in the District Court was the highest ever recorded, at 368. Among these, eight were committals for murder. After the very high figure of 42 cases of cattle theft in 1954, a decline to a mere 16 cases was very welcome; it is, however, perhaps a fair deduction from the troubles with the Wanyaturu, recorded elsewhere in the Report, that the bulk of the thefts of cattle committed by citizens of this District actually takes place in the Singida District – and cases, if brought to Court, are eventually heard there.

Once again four Local Court clerks received heavy sentences for peculation or allied offences.

8. Police

In April a Gazetted Officer again took charge of the Mbulu Police, providing welcome relief to the District Commissioner.

The total number of cases reported to the Mbulu Police was 571, and from these there was a total of 374 convictions, a very creditable proportion.

The troubles between the Barabaig and the Wanyaturu involved the Police in much extra work. In August a Police party from Singida, following up a cattle raid, shot and killed a Barabaig tribesman at Haidom; this was the result of an affray, following successful investigations by the Police party. At the subsequent Inquest the Coroner recorded a finding of justifiable homicide. When the differences between the two tribes came to a head in early October, Police action was intense and effective, the operation being controlled from the Central Province. Apart from the activities of the Mobile Company and other Police reinforcements, the Stock Theft Preventive Officer operating in the area achieved striking results, which did much to restore confidence.

9. Agriculture

Rainfall in 1955 was 22.04 at Mbulu, or about two-thirds of the normal. This was the third successive year of drought and the fourth year of poor crops. Food crops failed badly in the District as a whole, particularly in Mbugwe and Central Iraqw. Fortunately Karatu and Mbulumbulu had an exceptional maize crop, and many people from the worse effected parts of the District obtained relief there; there was also a substantial export to Arusha of some 500 tons from this area, the new Co-operative handling the crop.

It must be remarked at this point that officials in the District feel increasingly that less attention need be paid to food shortage than has been customary for a long time past. With ample supplies of food available in the Territory as a whole and with great improvements to the system of transport and communications in recent years, it should be unnecessary to extend any special help to a District which is a large producer of cattle, and should be larger still, except in the most extraordinary circumstances of disaster or for the relief of individual cases. When food crops are poor, the people should sell more cattle and buy their food in the shops.

Just as drought smote the food crops, so was the important wheat crop in the North of the District wiped out by rust. It was a new form of rust that did the damage and about 80 per cent of the total crop was destroyed. The Europeans at Oldeani were fortunate that this occurred in the last year of the GMR[3] system, and nearly £16,000 were paid out. The large African cultivators were unprotected by this form of insurance and the setback to them was very severe. Also involved in the debacle was the share-cropping scheme between the Native Authority and Mr Ellis. The fine crop of the preceding year had brought a profit of £2000 to the Native Treasury. In 1955, the one year when Mr Ellis was able to cultivate the whole area of 670 acres, there was nothing for the Native Treasury and precious little for Mr Ellis – he must be counted very unfortunate after engaging himself in a scheme which at the very best was not likely to bring him great profit, but has been of incalculable benefit to African progress in the area.

Towards the end of the year arrangements were made for the Africans who will move on to the first 300 acres of the land in question, now that Mr Ellis has completed the agreed two years of cultivation. After much discussion as to whether the big cultivator or the small man would do better in this area, the decision was made in favour of the latter, and the land was apportioned in 10-acre holdings. It may well be that 10 acres of this rich and heavy soil is more than a small cultivator can manage efficiently, but the Native Authorities were very insistent that this should be the minimum figure and respect was paid to their wishes. The new tenants, who received their land from the Development Committee for the area, were told that their customary tenure would be limited by the right of the Committee to sub-divide these holdings if they did in fact prove too large.

A fact worthy of note, while considering African agriculture in North Iraqw, is that Sub-Chief Stephano paid the Soil Conservation Service Shs. 40/- an acre to put in broad-based terraces on a 30-acre field of his. This is a great advance in African opinion and must be ascribed to the good example of neighbouring European farmers. Apart from this excellent effort, it was found in 1955 that certain modifications had to be made for soil conservation on other large wheat areas in North Iraqw. The District's standard method of trash-bunding is admirable on small fields throughout most of the District, and has achieved in places a spectacular build-up of natural terraces; but the size of the fields in parts of Mbulumbulu and Karatu and the lack of sufficient stubble from the wheat has led to the encouragement of narrow-based terraces, which are surveyed by trained African Instructors, and can then be made by the land owners either by tractor or by hand. A further modification to standard practice took place in Bonga in the Gorowa Chiefdom. Here many of the fields are so flat that the people were rightly able to complain that trash bunds served little purpose and indeed caused water-logging. In consequence it was arranged that cattle should be permitted to graze the fields, provided that all crop residues and all manure were returned to the soil; the people have so far met their side of the bargain faithfully.

Some mention should be made of new crops. There was a revival in Mbugwe of interest in cotton under the inspiration of Chief Michael. Many attempts, particularly before the war, have been made to encourage cotton growing in Mbugwe without success. Some eight tons of Grade 'A' cotton were harvested this year and there are signs that the people will be keen to plant again. Seed beans were also more popular than in the past and the year was a good one for them. Several European farmers planted under contract, and five or six of the progressive Africans in the North also tried a few acres as an experiment. Preparations were also made for trials in numerous places of coffee for African production.

The Oldeani coffee farmers had a record year, almost 900 tons of parchment having been harvested by the end of December. Bigger crops can be expected in the future, for not only the Oldeani farmers have been increasing their acreage recently; farmers below the Rift have also now put 600 acres under coffee.

At Mangola the final crop from the Native Authority Irrigation Scheme was very disappointing, probably due to the salinity of the soil. The maize produced was used in the tsetse clearings, and the Scheme was then handed over to individual persons, on payment

the figure of 35,185 sold in 1951. This is the more remarkable because the 1951 figure was achieved during the first year of compulsory destocking in Iraqw, which enormously boosted sales. Sales this year reached so high a total because of the exceptional rate of disposal from Barabaig and Gorowa. The Barabaig for the first time sold over 8000 units, while the Gorowa, responding to instruction and advice about the danger of too many stock on the land, sold 5600. The last figure is really remarkable in that it represents 12 per cent of the total Gorowa stock. The Iraqw in 1955 sold or despatched for slaughter in the tsetse clearings 8.2 per cent of their stock. This is a decline on last year's percentage of disposal and to that extent is disappointing. It still represents a good response to the semi-voluntary system of area quotas which replaced individual compulsion at the beginning of 1954. Furthermore the nett effect on the numbers of cattle remaining on the ground – and this, after all, is the important figure – showed an improvement on the preceding year. The total increase in the Iraqw figures of stock on the land was 5000 units as against last year's increase of 7000. A bigger percentage of land was added to existing lands through bush clearing in 1955 than 5000 units represent as a percentage increase on existing stock numbers and the density of the stock population has therefore been relieved.

Figures, however, can be made to shew anything. The fact is that the Iraqw Chiefdom would be vastly better off with two-thirds of its present stock holding, but there seems no point in thinking of such reductions until a completely new mental outlook alters Iraqw farming practice; otherwise, all experience here and elsewhere in the Territory show that the heaviest reductions are rapidly replaced by the better conditions for cattle that those very reductions have brought about. In Mbulu the initial reductions and the breathing space that we have made for the land since 1951 have effected enormous improvements throughout the Iraqw highlands. Although it may be a modest hope, it is probably as much as can be done to hold the present position until a growing appreciation of cash slowly revolutionises local farming, but nevertheless the threat of a return to compulsion is constantly extended to the people.

Much interest has been created among the people's leaders in the District by proposals for ranching schemes to offer an additional market for immature stock and eventually a new economic outlet for progressive individuals. A party was taken to the Government ranch at Mkata during the year and were greatly impressed with some of the aspects of the work that they saw there. However, local schemes have so far aborted, through failure to find an area of sufficient size which can be developed at reasonable cost. The search continues.

No success can be reported with large schemes of controlled grazing. The most promising pointer in this direction remains the control exercised by the elders of Bashanet over certain wire-grass areas in the uplands there. A survey of the Waama Ridge, one of the devastated areas in Central Iraqw, showed how severely limited schemes in this area must at present be. It is not that the people are unwilling to improve matters or are obstructive: it is rather that the very small cattle holding per household and the great part that milk plays in Iraqw diet make schemes of controlled grazing and closure of cattle tracks within an area extraordinarily hard to carry out, while total closure of an area is too drastic to consider. Some progress has however been made in persuading certain of the Sub-Chiefs to close altogether the worst of their hillsides.

There was a considerable further increase in the spraying and dipping of stock. This method of removing parasites is popular with the people and large amounts of Gammetox-plus have been used. The annual rinderpest campaign went off well, with the exception of Barabaig where the people are customarily reluctant to have their beasts inoculated, and a special subsidiary campaign had to be arranged to deal with them. Altogether 116,000 head were immunised. There was no serious outbreak of disease during the year, except for foot and mouth, which was widespread early in the year, but mild.

The former Development Farm at Tango near Mbulu had its first year as an instrument of social service, producing milk. It is as yet too early to say if this will be an economic service for the Native Treasury to provide.

11. Forestry

In a year of almost unprecedented drought, following on two preceding seasons of exceptional dryness, it was not surprising that the year was a very bad one for forest fires. Despite a fireline programme which was punctually completed, every Reserve suffered seriously, except Bereko. Bereko Reserve had been subjected to controlled early burning and its immunity from fires this year obviously carried a lesson for the future. Hanang and Marang Reserves were the worst hit, and both suffered immense damage. The only cheerful comment that may be made on this record is that the turnout of local people to fight fires was very creditable.

Two new nurseries at Kaiti, in Mbugwe, and at Mbulumbulu were opened in February and March, making a total in the District of eight. Total plants issued numbered over 45,000, the same as in 1954. A useful enquiry has been set on foot into the survival rate of plants issued from the nurseries in the past. This has obvious importance to our knowledge of the suitability to local conditions of the species at present raised. It was encouraging to find that in the exceptionally adverse conditions that have prevailed this season the survival rate up to the coming of the short rains was between a third and a half. The same happy fate did not befall the plantation at Tango, which is designed to solve Mbulu's difficult fuel problem in a few years' time. The plantation was practically re-planted in March, but by the end of November, saving about four acres with an 80 per cent survival rate, only 5 per cent of the rest of the plants had pulled through. A new re-planting started at the end of the year.

12. *Water Supplies*

A mechanical unit of the Department of Water Development and Irrigation was working in the District for most of the year. The Setchet dam, on the borders of Iraqw and Barabaig, was completely rebuilt on a scale sufficient to retain water against a succession of dry years. A fine job of work was done and, in particular, the troublesome old spillway has been replaced by one which should serve its purpose without severe scouring. The work at Setchet took, however, an inordinately long time, owing to disagreement as to the height by which the dam should be raised. It was not until the Director visited the work in March that a decision was finally made to raise the spillway level by 10 feet in accordance with the original recommendation. On the completion of the work at Setchet the unit moved to Ghalosabit in Barabaig, where it completed a new dam. This was a very welcome piece of work, since supplies at Ghalosabit will offer a valuable alternative to the Endesh wells, where, in a very dry season, there has often been intense competition between the Barabaig and the Wanyaturu for the limited supplies available.

By the end of the year, after withdrawal to Arusha for mechanical overhaul, the unit had made a start with the Endalls dam in the Endabash Sub-Chiefdom of North Iraqw. This is a project which has been outstanding for a number of years and will complete the immediate programme for dam construction in the District.

Another project on which the Department has its eye for the future is the Mangola Irrigation Scheme. The small-scale development on the former Native Authority furrow which is now being carried out by individual cultivators may one day give way to a major scheme, since there are 20 cusecs of water available, and several thousand acres can be commanded.

The improvement of Muchlur furrow, an amateur job, conducted 'on the cheap', with the object of watering the dry Western Expansion Area, has continued in 1955. The furrow had been deepened by a foot over 3½ miles of its length before rain intervened and prevented the completion of the final mile and half. Within the Western Expansion Area itself there has been much development of minor water works.

13. Tsetse

It has already been mentioned that 440,000 man days were devoted to communal self-help in 1955, and of this total 384,000 were spent on bush clearing. The work proceeded exceptionally smoothly, since the very experienced Field Officer, Dongobesh, who had been on leave in 1954, was once again available to control the main operations in the West. The base at Mbulu was also efficiently organised and transport was exceedingly well maintained. There were no serious hitches, even though in August, at a time when the water table was at its lowest and water had often to be transported for many miles, six different camps were being maintained with a total of 5700 men between them.

A fourth bad crop year made particularly difficult the problem of feeding the tsetse gangs in 1955. It may be recalled that this difficulty had also to be faced in 1954. The solution then was that the food, which the people are meant to provide free, would be bought in 1954, and paid for by a cash levy of Shs. 4/– per head in 1955. It was not possible to demand a further levy in cash to feed the 1955 clearings, and it was accordingly arranged that stocks of famine food should be diverted to the clearings in 1955 and silo stocks of equivalent value be sold when the silos were filled by the 1955 harvest. Most fortunately it transpired that the Shs. 4/– levy per head for the 1954 clearings, together with payment by the Barabaig for food supplied to them by the Iraqw, proved adequate to cover also the obligations incurred for 1955 supplies. It therefore seems likely that despite the recent bad seasons next year's clearings may after all begin with the silos reasonably well stocked; this will make a pleasant change from recent experience.

One great improvement in the organisation of the clearings was made by the purchase of a hammer mill and engine for grinding flour. This job has previously been done by inefficient merchants, whose products are suspect both in quantity and quality and whose machines habitually break down at the most crucial moment. The new machine should comfortably cover the cost of its purchase, its installation and its running within three years.

It was remarked last year that there were differences of opinion about the extent to which discriminative methods could be used in the Mbulu clearings, where so little trained supervision can be provided for such very large bodies of men. A meeting of the Provincial Team was held at Mbulu to examine this matter; it was considered that under present circumstances much more work than was strictly necessary would have to continue to be done, although suggestions were made for preventing waste of work in the future. The needs of settlement of course often require more clearing than is technically necessary.

The year's work is detailed below.

Western Expansion Area
Over half the total effort, 238,136 man days, were expended here; of this figure the Barabaig contributed 72,747 and the Iraqw the remainder. The Barabaig were working for the first time under their own Sub-Chiefs, as the Iraqw do, instead of under a hired European supervisor; the experiment was a great success and the tribesmen worked very much better than in previous years. As a result 16.28 square miles were cleared by them in the dangerous Waredig area and little now remains to be done here.

The rest of the work was concentrated in the general areas of Dagaid (28,354 man days, 6.50 square miles), Dirim (57,436 and 17.36) and Yaida (63,418 and 11.59). At Dagaid a belt of bush which has been a serious deterrent to settlement in previous years was removed. At Dirim a great area was freed for settlement and grazing above the Yaida escarpment. There is good land here and, with the provision of minor water supplies, settlement should proceed rapidly. Three substantial blocks of bush were left uncleared for the provision of firewood and building poles in the future. In the Yaida Depression a 1000-yard barrier was established along the Singida District border and a broad defensive barrier was put in along the old cattle track from the top of the scarp to allow access to the Yaida mbuga[4] system for stock from up above. Unfortunately the depleted water supplies after the poor preceding rains made it impossible to maintain large gangs in the Yaida after July; consequently no more than a start was made with the clearing of a belt below the escarpment in order to break the fly contact between the Depression and the area above the escarpment. The completion of this barrier must be the first job in 1956.

Subsidiary Iraqw Clearings
A. Central Iraqw
At Endofa Sub-Chief Leo extended the 1948 Sinyaani clearings to free a new water supply (16,181 man days). Little time could be spared for supervision of this work, which suffered as a result; but the new water source is a valuable one and nearly five square miles of light bush were cleared for grazing around it.

Last year's Giyedamara clearings were extended by the people of Bargish (30,682). Work at this camp was slack and ill-controlled by Sub-Chief Hatsinay, while the grazing freed was indifferent. The people of this Sub-Chiefdom should return to the main South Iraqw clearings in 1956.

Sub-Chief Areray's people (17,915) started from a base on the Udahaya River some miles from Hatsinay's off the Aitcho–Mangola road and worked southwards to link up also with the 1955 clearings. The work done was quite excellent and so was the country freed. At some date in the future these clearings should be pushed north to provide a broad fly-free passage between Central Iraqw and Mangola.

B. North Iraqw
The people of Endabash cleared a large area of light bush around the Giyedamog waters, working towards the Rift Wall as far as the

Forest boundary (21,433). Game was very troublesome and several people were injured by buffalo.

Sub-Chief Bakari's gang (3810) continued 1954 operations on either side of the Oldeani–Mangola road.

Sub-Chief Qambash (8507) and Sub-Chief Stephano were both occupied with the Sisyphean task of clearing regeneration downwards into the ever-troublesome Marera Gorge.

C. Gorowa

Nearly half of the Gorowa communal self-help was used on work other than bush clearing. However, 47,250 man days were spent on clearing the environs of the main road from Babati to Dareda as far as the Singu estate boundary; protective clearing near Babati; settlement clearing at Nakwa; and regeneration in Gallapo.

D. Mbugwe

20,560 man days were expended on the re-slashing of regeneration in various parts of the Chiefdom.

14. Game

The fate of game in the Mbulu District has become more hazardous in 1955. Well-equipped hunting parties, with all the advantages that modern vehicles and firearms can give, have frequented every well-known hunting-ground in the District, while in the inhabited areas increasing population densities have meant the steady elimination of herds of animals from many areas where they used to be found. Then African poachers have been doing immense destruction in the area below the Rift between Madege and Mbugwe; Madege in particular is a maze of snares and deadfalls, though some successful prosecutions had checked illicit hunting there by the end of the year.

Fresh alienations of land below the Rift in the regions of Magara and Shauri Moyo and Sangaiwe are bound also to wipe out large numbers of game in places where they have hitherto been relatively secure and this process has indeed begun already. With equal inevitability one may forecast the eventual destruction of animal life in the Yaida Depression, which is required for Iraqw expansion and which was the scene of its first major bush-clearing operations in 1955.

The high price of rhinoceros horn and of the hide earlier in 1955 led to very large numbers of licences being taken out and there was great slaughter as a result. The reduction of the number of rhinoceros allowed on a licence annually to one only had been suggested from this Office and was welcomed when it occurred.

The issue of Local Game Licences has proved in this District at least to be valueless in checking illicit hunting. Far more supervision than the present staff of the Game Department can allow appears to be necessary to this end.

No lion has been seen in the vicinity of Mbulu for many years. During the year one lost its way and was shot within two miles of the Boma during the luncheon interval between 12.30 and 2 p.m.; the unfortunate animal thus showed a praiseworthy respect for office hours.

15. Co-operative Societies

The North Iraqw Farmers' Co-operative Society Ltd was formed and registered. Its foundation was made easier by the experience gained from the running of the Karatu African Farmers' Association who went into voluntary liquidation and merged themselves into the Society. Their store was bought by the Native Treasury and rented to the Society. Membership of the Society is confined to Africans with farms in the Karatu–Mbulumbulu–Oldeani area, and there are now 225 members. Maize and wheat were the only crops handled by the Society in 1955, as the Committee thought it wiser to deal only in products with a guaranteed price until the Society had more capital and experience. 4400 bags of maize and 900 bags of wheat were marketed before the end of December.

The Society is mainly a marketing organisation but it hopes to supply its members with farming equipment at wholesale prices, and is now feeling its way by dealing in fuel and oil.

16. Land

A number of new farms have been alienated in the area below the Rift in 1955. The areas concerned are heavily infested with tsetse fly carrying Sleeping Sickness, while there is no population pressure to encourage the clearing of bush. In these circumstances alienation is encouraged by the Native Authorities, as the only method of relieving the danger to their people from the disease.

A string of new farms were either taken up or advertised in the Magara–Shauri Moyo area, immediately below the Rift Wall east of Mbulu; the new Magara road connects Mbulu with these farms. The soil is rich and water supplies are good, but the land is very heavily forested and infested with game. The problem of communications across the Mbugwe flats to the Great North Road is a particularly difficult one, since the whole area is liable to heavy flooding in normal rains. Fortunately Government is spending money on a new road of access.

The first two new units in Kiru, adjacent to the Dudumera farms, were allocated to a single tenant who had an option on existing Rights of Occupancy there. Plans are well advanced for a steady re-opening of Kiru, which was a thriving farming area before it had to be closed when it became the scene of the original Sleeping Sickness outbreak in 1943.

To the east of the Great North Road the Sangaiwe units were advertised, but they have so far attracted little interest. Water will be a serious problem there and applicants have been deterred by this fact.

In the Western Expansion Area of Iraqw there were applications for short-term leases with the support of the Native Authority. The local people were anxious to get mechanized farmers on the spot to assist them with their own cultivation by tractor ploughing. The idea had its attractions, but was eventually abandoned owing to bad reports on the agricultural suitability of the area for the scheme envisaged.

17. Medical and Sanitation

The year saw the completion of the new Mbulu hospital, which now has a total of 94 beds in use in fine modern buildings. Most of the equipment is now available, though the X-ray unit has still to be brought into use. The Oldeani hospital too is a considerable place, with a rating of 65 beds. It dealt in 1955 with nearly as many in-patients as the Mbulu hospital, but the out-patient department at the latter is more than twice as busy, with a total of 30,000 re-attendances.

Although there were no serious epidemics, tuberculosis continues to be a source of great concern. Special efforts are being made at

Mbulu to deal with it, and when the total number of beds is brought to 108 at the beginning of 1956 one-third of these will be allotted to TB patients. Another chest disease of local significance is pneumonia, there being 274 in-patients at Mbulu hospital during the year. Malaria continues to be the most common disease; 389 patients were admitted at Mbulu and well over 2000 were treated as out-patients.

In addition to the excellent Catholic Mission Hospital at Dareda the Lutherans now operate a hospital at Haidom. To see the staff at work in this remote spot in the Western Expansion Area, with their large number of patients sprung from an apparently uninhabited countryside, and to observe their cheerfulness in difficult working conditions, must excite anyone's admiration. The existence of this hospital does much to encourage settlement there.

The Sanitary Authorities at Mbulu and Babati have continued to exercise a beneficial influence on the living conditions of the inhabitants of the two places.

The Native Authority dispensaries provide a valued public service. At the end of the year their direction and control was reorganised in order to bring them more firmly under the guidance of the District Medical Officer. During the year a new dispensary replaced the old one at Mangola, where, in accordance with practice in this District, social services were being improved in order to attract settlers to this expansion area. A new dispensary was also built at Muray and will open in 1956. Attendance figures at dispensaries were as follows:

1953	New cases	64,364
1954	New cases	89,599
1955	New cases	100,840
1953	Total attendances	108,124
1954	Total attendances	156,353
1955	Total attendances	149,013

18. *Education*

The Ten Year Plan continued to be operated satisfactorily by the Native Authority and the two major Missions. The 11 new schools built in 1954 were opened and the ten new ones of the 1955 construction programme were duly erected. The Education Committee agreed, however, that the policy for 1956, the last year of the Ten

Year Plan, should be modelled on the principles which it had earlier accepted for the new Five Year Plan beginning in 1957. That principle is the simple one of quality instead of quantity. Thus the emphasis will change from great numbers of Primary Schools to more Middle Schools and increased sessions in the Primary Schools. It was high time for such a change, for although the proportion of children receiving schooling is not as high as it should be, the lack of concentration of population in this District was making it extremely difficult to find new places for siting schools economically.

Barabaig, always an educational problem of its own, was at last served with a Mission school providing some boarding facilities, such as have long been found necessary by the Native Authority at Katesh and Basotu. This was the Pallottine Fathers' school at Basodesh, which had moderate success in its new guise, whereas it has been a total failure as a day school. The Native Authority at the same time took a further step ahead by providing a dormitory for girls at Katesh, and at that place the girls from the Basotu school will also be sent, so that all come under the care of a Barabaig female teacher, the first of her species.

The District Education Committee made a sensible decision in increasing Middle School fees to Shs. 200/–, with an undertaking to increase them again to Shs. 240/– in 1957. Nevertheless, the people of the District remain extremely reluctant to pay for Middle School education for their children.

19. *Labour*

There was no shortage of labour during the year. As customarily happens when food supplies in the District are short, the Iraqw turned out in adequate numbers to supplement their incomes and food supplies. Even the very large coffee crop at Oldeani did not produce any fiercely competitive struggle for available supplies of labour. It is noticeable that the farmers at Oldeani now have a much better appreciation of the qualities of the Iraqw as workers.

20. *Missions*

The District's two main Missions, the Pallottine Fathers and the Norwegian Lutherans, continued to play a full part in the education programme. The Augustana Lutherans from Singida proceeded with their application for land in Barabaig. They wish to work there, whatever part they may in due course be able to play in educational work in the District. It is already clear that they will in fact be very closely associated in their work with the Norwegian Lutherans.

21. Prisons

The number of committals to Prison has more than doubled in the past four years, the figure for 1955 being 641, as against 283 in 1952. The big increase in 1955 over the 1954 figure of 500 committals can be ascribed to a drive to clean up outstanding fines in Local Courts; this led to many offenders being committed to a prison in default of payment. It cannot be said that a prison sentence yet carries any stigma in the District. Deplorable as this fact may be from many points of view, it at least means that a released prisoner is absorbed back into tribal society instead of becoming the misfit which he might become in a more civilised society.

The average number of daily inmates was 63. Prison discipline was quite good, there being 22 offences by prisoners and seven by warders, mostly of a minor nature.

22. Communications

The District road network was greatly improved in 1955. The Public Works Department took over as a Local Main Road the link from Babati through Dareda and Katesh to the Singida border. This road is Singida's outlet to the Northern Province and the increasing weight of the traffic using it, together with its lack of local importance to the Mbulu District, has made it quite unsuitable for maintenance as a District road. At the end of the year the important Bubu bridge on this road, which had long been in a dangerous condition, was being rebuilt.

The main programme of maintenance work of the District roads was this year started earlier than ever on 1st May. The decision proved a well-judged one for no further heavy storms occurred after that date, while slight showers kept the soil easily workable. Big improvements were made at numerous dangerous corners, which were widened, while dual carriageways with 'Keep Left' signs were installed at those of them where the width of the road allowed. The programme of replacing wooden decking on bridges by cement was continued, and so was regular brushing of the road during the dry season, while much additional gravelling of stretches liable to flooding was carried out.

Two roads received special attention. The first was the Oldeani Circular Plantation road, where Government provided special funds for extensive improvement. The main work was the replacement of four small and troublesome wooden bridges by solid cement structures. The Magara road was widened and improved by communal effort, and its surface early in the dry season was of a high standard. Heavy storms in the short rains at the end of the year did much damage, and it is clear that drainage, which has yet hardly been tackled, will be a major problem. The heaviest vehicle to make the ascent up this road was a fully loaded 3-tonner.

Of Native Authority roads, the most work was done in Gidas, where volunteer labour greatly improved the new road to Riroda and Bonga.

23. Public Works

The Public Works Department completed in 1955 the £35,000, 94-bed, new hospital at Mbulu. It is an impressive group of buildings, and must be worth a good deal more than the whole of the rest of the station put together. They also erected the new District Office at Babati. A new Rest House at Oldeani is a valuable facility, while two Grade III quarters at Mbulu will help to relieve the housing shortage there.

The Native Authorities completed a building programme worth about £13,500. The most important building was a handsome new Court House for the Chief of Iraqw in place of the dilapidated hovel in which he used to work; this building was opened by the Provincial Commissioner. Four other Court Houses for Sub-Chiefs were built, and the most important of the other buildings were a school at Naisaka and the complete set of school, dispensary and produce market at Mangola in addition to the Court House there.

24. Population

Assuming an annual 2 per cent increase, it is probable that the African population of the District now numbers about 175,000. There are no significant changes among other races.

Charles Innes Meek

APPENDIX 3

Mbulu District Handing Over Notes, June, 1956 (prepared by C.I. Meek for his successor[1] as DC)

1. General

These Notes can be amplified in discussion during the week we shall have together, and are intended primarily as a guide to the topics worth discussing.

For a general picture of the District there are the Annual Reports; the Destocking Memorandum and Progress Reports, to which you might add a general account of the Destocking Campaign which I did for the Journal of African Affairs in October 1953, and the Colonial Development and Welfare Progress Reports.

Here are some staff matters for mention. The District Officers' Schedules will shew you how difficult it is to get a satisfactory division of safari issues. DO I combines Barabaig, which needs plenty of supervision, with Mbulumbulu and Karatu and Oldeani, with their complex problems. DO II has Gorowa and Mbugwe, which is quite enough. ADO has Iraqw, less the extreme North, which, now that there is a conciliar system to be nursed, is almost too much. In the past couple of years each officer has averaged ten days a month on tour, but even so it is all we can do to cover the ground – particularly in the clearings season.

You are unlucky in losing the Agricultural Officer so soon, since he has an extensive knowledge of the District, but I have managed to get his departure postponed to the end of July. On the other hand, you have in Austin[2] a large fund of experience to tap – he has been

219

17 years in this District altogether, nine of them in his present job. Unfortunately he intends to retire next year; I would therefore advise that he be used as much as possible during this dry season on the minor water works at which he excels, while we must hope to get hold of a Tsetse Officer to take his place in the clearings in the future (I was offered one a few months ago, but could not at that time house one).

2. *Native Authorities and Local Politics*

Iraqw
Of the District's four Chiefdoms, Iraqw is by far the most important, with two-thirds of the human population in the District and well over half the stock. In the Iraqw highlands you will be confronted with the most intransigent of our problems of land use. Under Chief Elias there are 19 Sub-Chiefdoms and, in addition, the Minor Settlement of Oldeani under its Headman. The whole Chiefdom can for most purposes be conveniently broken down into North, Central and South Iraqw. North Iraqw is the area north of the Aitcho escarpment. It is an expansion area. Settlers started to move into the southerly Endabash area some 35 years ago; as settlement spread northwards, Karatu was hived off as a separate Sub-Chiefdom in 1947, and Mbulumbulu acquired the same status only three years ago. The oldest inhabited areas make up Central Iraqw and include the 'cradle area' of Kainam. South Iraqw, which began to fill up in the early years of this century, is the main cattle area.

Until the last few months there has been no development of local government, in the modern sense of the term, in Iraqw. The emphasis has consistently been on the economic use of land, rather than politics, but nevertheless it has always been noteworthy how careful the Chief and Sub-Chiefs are to carry the people with them in new projects. In recent months, however, I have come to feel that the time was ripe for some more formal association of the people with the Native Authority, primarily in order to give more scope for educated youth than they can find at traditional meetings. A system of Councils in the Iraqw Sub-Chiefdoms, with a superior Tribal Council, has therefore been very fully explained to the people and welcomed with an enthusiasm which can in many cases be ascribed to lack of comprehension. Each

Sub-Chiefdom has a Council of Eight, half chosen by the people by acclamation and half by the Sub-Chief.

These bodies, in addition to any other meetings they may wish to have, are to meet monthly at a stated time and place (there is a list of these meetings up to the end of this year displayed in your office). This is to ensure that the people know when they may attend to listen to their own Council's deliberations, and also to enable Administrative Officers to attend as frequently as possible.

The Tribal Council, according to the proposals put to the people, is to be formed as follows:

1. DC, Chairman.
2. Chief of Iraqw.
3. Eight Sub-Chiefs (two from North, three from Central, three from South) nominated by the Chief in consultation with DC.
4. Nineteen Popular Representatives, one elected from each Sub-Chiefdom Council from among their own number.
5. Six nominees of the Chief in consultation with DC.

Sub-Chiefs were confined to eight, because a larger number would have made the Council unduly large. The six nominees make provision for representatives who may not get elected, such as teachers, Padres and others.

This is a very embryo system for you to shape. It may well be premature, but I have made it clear to the people that they must make it work, if they wish to claim to be consulted on policy (there has been no suggestion that the Councils are more than advisory). The first meetings of the Sub-Chiefdom Councils are only being held this month. All are being attended by District Officers, and they will certainly need careful nursing for some months if they are going to be of any use at all. The first reports of DOs I and II on the meetings they have attended are reasonably encouraging. The Tribal Council has yet to be chosen. It should be in being in time to replace the former meeting of Sub-Chiefs which was accustomed to consider the draft Estimates at the end of October or early November.

We will have time to discuss personalities. In Chief Elias you have a Chief of the highest character. The Sub-Chiefs are of variable calibre; they carry a great weight and influence with their people, and those who appear the most useless to a European eye are often surprisingly effective – Sub-Chief Amnaay is a case in point. Among the better ones, Stephano is a man of quality, but he also has business and large farming interests to consider, Leo is extremely effective, so is Simeon, despite his chequered past, and Amsi is a man of great ability. The Kainam Gause are weak, most particularly Hayuma, and Daniel, of Dongobesh, has recently been disappointing.

The main personal influence in Iraqw still remains Nade Bea, the chief rain-maker, whom we will meet together. The Chief is the first to recognise his predominant influence.

Gorowa

The small Gorowa tribe are closely allied to the Iraqw by blood and language. They are a very backward lot, despite the large infiltration of aliens along the Great North Road. They are firmly under the influence of the predominant Uo clan, of which the present head is Chief Amri. The Chief's duties as Member of Legislative Council have thrown more and more of the job of routine administration of the Chiefdom on to his able half brother Zuberi. The nepotic and autocratic character of local government in Gorowa makes desirable some system of popular representation there, and I have recently said publicly that I am glad to hear Chief Amri is considering this matter.

Mbugwe

The small Mbugwe tribe are our only Bantu. Chief Michael, like Chief Amri, once held a senior clerical post in the Native Treasury. He is quiet, but capable. There is a deep cleavage in Mbugwe between Mwada and Kaiti, each of which was until recent years a tiny separate Chiefdom. Michael was originally Chief at Kaiti, until he stepped down in favour of the older Mausa, when Mbugwe was amalgamated into a single Chiefdom. It was then that he came up to the Native Treasury at Mbulu, until he was chosen as sole Chief on Mausa's death. In recent years the Mbugwe have increasingly moved into the artificial alien settlement of Magugu (which was created by the settlement of labour from Kiru, when Kiru was evacuated owing to Sleeping Sickness), and this area, formerly owning only a nominal suzerainty to the Chief of Mbugwe, has been made definitely subject to him.

Barabaig

The Barabaig are nomad pastoralists and are noted for a long history of seemingly casual murder of members of other tribes of either sex and every age. The Barabaig Native Authority has been notoriously weak through the period of British administration. The institution of Chief has not shewn itself suited to the tribe's social structure, and, among other failings, successive Chiefs have shewn particularly strong partiality towards members of their own clan. In 1952 the Native Authority was reorganised, a Tribal Council of clan heads being set up, since sociological investigations had shewn the Barabaig clans to be the main repository of indigenous political authority. The insistence of the elders led to my retaining a Chief at the time, but my own view has been for some years that the Council itself should be the Native Authority, acting through the comparatively intelligent and educated Sub-Chiefs. It proved possible to bring this about at the end of last year, when serious troubles with the Wanyaturu led to the Barabaig being penalised to the tune of 500 head of cattle.

For the past six months the Barabaig have been in a better state of discipline than for many years past, and the Sub-Chiefs have been working well. There have been no murders and no major cattle thefts. It remains to be seen whether this condition will persist. In any case, I expect that you will in due course be faced by demands for the restoration of the Chief. Apart from this issue, the Councillors need to be much more active than they are at present. In particular, their Court work is lamentable. One necessary reform is to get the Chairman, Sarja, to move to Katesh, and I have just written to him accordingly. Sarja was Chief 20 years ago, but was then too young to handle his elders; in his maturity he is much your best prospect as Council Chairman.

TANU has branches on the periphery of Iraqw at Karatu and Dareda.

I mentioned that the Barabaig Council Court work was bad. This is also bad throughout Iraqw, and particularly at Endagikot. Chief Elias had two Deputies last year to help him run his very large Chiefdom; this year provision was made for a Magistrate as well as these two, or in substitution for one of them, the object being to free the Chief of Court work, and generally to improve the standard in Iraqw. However, a suitable candidate has not yet been found, nor has the Chief found a substitute for one of his Deputies whom he recently dismissed, so that matters are worse than ever. One of the results of bad Court work has been the appalling list of outstanding fines. Constant pressure in the past year has improved this, but we need to do better yet. We submit a monthly return of outstanding fines to the PC; the time has probably now come to write off a number of these as irrecoverable.

3. Natural Resources

A. Agriculture
You have two Natural Resources Committees, one for Above and one for Below the Rift. These replace the former Production Committee. They have at present a very indeterminate advisory status, but the two meetings of each Committee which have so far been held found them fulfilling the same invaluable 'sounding-board' function of the Production Committee, with the added advantage of strong African representation. I have always pictured things moving slowly from a conciliar system in the four Chiefdoms to a District Council, to which these Committees would become subject (see file 3/113 and footnote to f.31 therein for the miscarriage of our District Council). I hope on your arrival to fix dates for the next meetings, so that Cooper can be present! I think you would find it a great advantage to have his local knowledge available at your first sessions.

The season has been very dry indeed, a continuation of a dry cycle. The effect on grazing must be serious and the water-table will again be lowered, which may complicate operations in the clearings. Fortunately the distribution of rain was such that we should have enough food – even in the North where the people are worst hit.

North Iraqw contains all our would-be-progressive African farmers and most of our agricultural headaches. Mbulumbulu is an expansion area of great agricultural potential, as fine as anything the Northern Province can offer. Its past history will be relevant to anything you do there, and you may therefore wish to refer to a recent summary of the Agricultural Officer's in his own District Book. You should also read in the relevant confidential file the history of the short-term leases in the area. The fact that we now have Mbulumbulu clean and settled from top to bottom we owe primarily to the work of Ellis, both in private contracting for African farmers and in the operation of a share-cropping scheme with the Native Authority. The scheme is on the old Wheat Scheme lands in the North. It has been a bad bet for Ellis, after last year's disastrous rust in the wheat, but a profitable one for the NA. The contract, incidentally, is a gentlemen's agreement; you will find its terms in the relevant correspondence, but Ellis, who bears all risks, would never sign any documents.

The last of the Ellis lands revert to Native Authority use after this season's harvest. The 300 and more acres which reverted last year were divided into 10-acre plots for peasants, more than 400 people applying. We have had a plethora of advice as to how the latest lot should be divided. Factors in the balance are: (a) wheat is an uneconomic crop in this very rich land (Ellis's experience), and we should go for high-value cash crops, (b) coffee must be brought into the picture, (c) a whole block could be given up to coffee, but this presents most difficult problems of management, (d) 10 acres is too much for a peasant in this area (observation), (e) more people would mean more cattle, which the area will not stand, without which the Iraqw will not settle, (f) we have no African farmers who can handle large areas of this very valuable land.

Innumerable arguments and points of view have been thrust forward around these themes, and it merely remains to decide what to do. I have recently, in correspondence with the Assistant Director of Agriculture, come down in favour of 5-acre plots for smallholders (which the Native Authority will object to, as too small) and I have told the Agricultural Officer that the coffee plans and the very difficult problem of cattle holdings in an area where we could well dispense with cattle altogether should be fitted into that context. His decision has not been announced publicly, in case you have different ideas, but I do recommend adherence to it unless you wish to go over again much well-worn ground.

This may seem a long dissertation on 400 acres, but the principle of the best use of the land up there is of the highest importance. Ellis estimates that Mbulumbulu as a whole could produce an annual crop of 1000 tons of coffee. Regarding coffee, Mr Cooper can put you in the picture. He has trials going through the District. At the moment of writing he and DO I are investigating a report that the Mbulumbulu people are in fact averse to the amount of work involved in producing this crop.

There are three more points to mention about North Iraqw. One is that we have a six-mile electric fence to mitigate game damage there.

It has been a success and no doubt will come in useful elsewhere when the sisal hedge planted alongside it is established. The next point is that seven of our mechanised farmers up there have crop loans repayable on this year's harvest. They have been hard-hit by drought and there may be a case for an extension of time for one or two who tried to make good use of their money; but others, notably Ildefonsi and Ngaida, made no sort of effort at all after our strenuous efforts to help them and I hope they will be ruthlessly treated. The third point is that our one Co-operative is established at Karatu; I need not give you details, since Younie[3] is far more conversant with its affairs than I am.

The cultivation of swamps is an important subsidiary source of food in this District. The tendency of the local people to abandon dry-season swamp cultivation after good crops needs to be checked; in a large swamp like Hantlay, a season or two without cultivation leads to the complete ruin of the drainage system.

B. Veterinary

The control of stock numbers in Iraqw continues to be the dominant problem that the District faces. The 'voluntary' system which succeeded the three years of compulsory individual orders has not gone well this year and I have just felt compelled to re-introduce compulsion in Central Iraqw. It remains for you to see what reaction takes place in South Iraqw to the admonition which the people there have just had from me in *baraza*. Whatever you may decide, it will, I think, be of help to you that the machinery of compulsion, which has been in cold storage since the end of 1953, is now again working. It is unfortunate that no Administrative Officers now stationed here have experience of how things worked in practice in 1951–1953 but Mr Ali Lasseko is a mine of information. As far as Central Iraqw is concerned, there is nothing further to do this year but to watch the monthly sales figures and chase up Sub-Chiefs whose people are obviously falling behind, since the people have latitude until December to meet their quotas of sales. In January cattle not sold against quota will have to be branded by Veterinary Guards who are assigned to the various culling clerks; and then those who fail to sell branded beasts at the next market are due for prosecution. A small point – check with Ali Lasseko that the special brands are still at the Veterinary Office after the lapse of 2½ years.

Three other comments about destocking. I will give you orally an opinion on North Iraqw. The quotas for Central Iraqw on the chart in DO I's office must be revised to conform to the orders now issued, and I will do this before I go. The re-introduction of compulsion has necessitated the employment of an extra culling clerk, but I have not asked for supplementary expenditure, in case your decisions about South Iraqw necessitated further application.

I have always been keen on the ranching of immatures, which seems to me an excellent way of pointing the road for the economic use of stock. An imaginative scheme for securing alienated land at Essimingor for this purpose fell through last year. An area in North Iraqw proved too small for the purpose, and we have since had in mind an area in North Mbugwe. This has just received a tsetse survey, and the next step would seem to be an expert assessment of the possibility of putting in cheap water supplies.

Apart from the major grazing problems which are reflected in destocking policies, there are some special areas which need a mention. The highlands around Bashanet are taken up for miles by Pennisetum Schimperi, a coarse and barely edible wire-grass, which is a product of over-grazing. Closure and burning is the way to deal with this and we had great success with this on one experimental block. When this block was re-opened to controlled grazing, larger areas were closed instead of it. These areas are known to the Veterinary Officer, but I have not heard from him as to how things are going.

Certain Sub-Chiefs have been pushed very hard to keep closed to grazing particular eroded areas. These are the southern slopes of the Aitcho (Areray), the Waama ridge (Hatsinay and Mayumba) and an area of Hareabi (Hayuma) adjacent to and south of the Magara road. I recommend that they continue to be badgered about those areas, all of which are well known to Chief Elias.

The last of these special areas is Mbulumbulu, where it is most important that this fine agricultural land should not be ruined by cattle.

The rinderpest campaign is at present in full swing.

C. Water
Much the biggest scheme on hand is the North Iraqw pipelines extension. The people of Iraqw have agreed to pay a special levy of Shs. 10/– per head to meet the cost. Receipt books are now being

printed so that collection may start at once, although, with the present staff shortage in the Water Department, it does not seem likely that the work can be done until next year. No financial impost has ever been more fully agreed by the citizenry in general.

The next major scheme for mention is the Muchlur supply. This is a very large artificial lake, furrow-fed from the Yaida River, with the object of piping water into the Western Expansion Area. I suggest that Austin, whose creation this scheme is, should do as much as possible on the extension works before his departure. Incidentally, HE gave me a personal assurance that he would try officially to open this scheme for us, and you might be able to hold him to it.

Dams in North Iraqw are unsatisfactory, as you will see, presumably because of the nature of the soil. The big Setchet dam on the Iraqw–Barabaig border – this is a reconstruction of an old dam – is holding water satisfactorily. The new Ghalosabit dam in Barabaig is leaking badly, but may seal itself; it is to be hoped that it will do so, since a successful dam here should draw the Barabaig back from the Endesh waters, where there has been friction with the Wanyaturu in the past.

Here are some notes on other projects:

(a) Marera Forest Supply. See folio 214 and subsequent correspondence in file 24/6 for our dispute with the National Park. Apart from the dispute, Austin considers that water from this source can be led into the dry area between Marera Hill and Simba River. If that is so, this supply will be very well worthwhile piping.

(b) Gallapo Pipeline. The intake was destroyed by floods in December. The water people must get the repairs done by August, for there will be great difficulty in the Gallapo settlement otherwise. This is our only major demand on the maintenance and renewals fund since its inception. Our request for this work went in before Government made its new proposals about the fund and the cost of the work should therefore be met from the fund.

(c) There are possibilities of a major irrigation scheme at Mangola, and the water people have started surveys.

(d) It is important that the possibilities of water development in the Yaida should soon be surveyed, since our clearings programme should make it possible shortly to establish large herds down there. Two possibilities are the piping of the Endagulda supply and the large development of small *hafirs*, such as the successful one put in by Austin some years back.

(e) I have asked for survey of the possibilities of piping supplies from the Endabash River. Endabash Sub-Chiefdom needs many more water points and the Bassodowesh furrow scheme should go forward.

(f) There is a small scheme for improving a flume at Chemchem. This job must be done, since it is some years since the local people contributed money for the purpose. Austin has it in hand.

(g) We have had a furrow put in at Karatu by the Soil Conservation Service to fill the basin in front of the Mission. The Soil Conservation people must not raise their charges because they made the furrow 18 feet wide – our arrangements with them were made for a 6-foot cut.

(h) I asked Austin some time ago to list minor supplies in the District.

We are a long way behind with Water Court matters, there having been no hearings of recent applications. I have been trying to back-pedal as much as possible, pending the review that will be undertaken by Mr Kingdon's ad hoc committee. One result is that our Native Authority supplies are not secured by Permits; I do not think this matters much, save for the Permit which must be secured for an extension on the Karatu pipeline.

The whole water system Below Rift from Dohomo to the Dudumera swamp is bound to cause a lot of difficulty, since more and more new farms will be becoming dependent on it.

D. Tsetse

The clearing season is usually spread from July to September, with stragglers in October. The total liability of individuals is 30 days plus 15 days in their own villages for minor works (the 15 days are not enforced as a regular duty, but are used to carry out local works demanded by the local people). During the 30 days of the major programme the people are responsible for providing their own food. The NA responsibility is to mill the food, bag it, transport it and provide tools and wages for the small paid staff. The Sub-Chiefs, who now do the work of supervision formerly done by expensive Europeans, receive honoraria.

This year the campaign is already in full swing, since all three Barabaig gangs have been turned out in June, thus spreading the burden on our transport over a longer period. The programmes of work have of course to be worked out months ahead – see the working instructions to the Iraqw and Barabaig Sub-Chiefs. Mr Austin has vast experience of this work and is fully conversant with this year's plans. In broad outline, the intention is to establish ourselves firmly on the natural fly-free barrier of the Yaida Mbuga system, thereby achieving one of the great objects of the Development Scheme. This should be possible this year, unless water supplies in the Yaida dry out.

The concentration on the Yaida this year was only achieved at the price of a committal for next year. The proposals of these Sub-Chiefs who at present have to turn out their peoples to a place so remote from home as the Yaida is a good one – provided we are established on the Yaida, and, even if we do not get firmly established this year, the Southern Iraqw Gause's people should be adequate to complete the job in 1957. I would be glad to shew you next year's project, as desired by the Central Iraqw Gause, on the map.

Since we again failed to fill the silos after a poor season last year, food supplies for the clearings will not be easy. However, by my calculations there should be enough, even if you have a record turnout (we expect between one-third and one-half of the tax-payers). Please refer to a chart I have just drawn up; this shews available supplies and the mills to be used, and it should ensure that our own mill is used to capacity. I have been through these figures carefully with DO II, the District Accountant (DA) and the Forestry Officer (FO). Points to note are that the Barabaig have a good deal more cash to raise in July for food supplied to them, and that it will be urgent to hurry in the early harvest contributions for the silos at the beginning of August. It is most important to note that the ration per man per day is 2 lbs. If you get a bag and half, i.e. 300 lbs, being issued to 100 men, as happened at the start of the Barabaig clearings, all these arrangements will go by the board.

You should study the controversy about discriminative clearing et seq. leading up to the provincial team meeting at Mbulu in July last year, and finally by 3/6/5/VII/167 of 4/6/56 to the PTO.

E. Forestry
We need more consultation on forest policies than we have had recently.

A proposal to reserve the Rift Wall seems to me a doubtful proposition.

The Agricultural Officer and Senior Forester are due to put up proposals for a wattle scheme. See the most recent District Team minutes.

Firewood in Mbulu is a headache, and an expensive one. I thought we had solved the problem for the future with the plantations at Tango. With the recent dry cycle, these plantations have not done well, and there is talk of abandoning them – to be resisted, I suggest.

F. Alienated Land

There is much alienated land in the District and fresh alienations Below the Rift are increasing its proportion. The new alienations are designed primarily to eliminate the dangerous Sleeping Sickness bush and they have therefore been proceeding with the full support of the Native Authorities concerned. Close attention to the minutes of the Northern Province Land Use Committee (which are kept together in a Confidential file) is required to get a grasp of these various new schemes. I give some notes on them:

(a) Magara. These farms were given out last year. All the farmers have put in a splendid first year's development, except Prince Bernhard of the Netherlands, on whose land nothing has been done, and Mrs Kapu. Prince Bernhard's first year is up in August, and French, in the PC's office, was to take up the question of lack of development. The other farmers there have been hard hit after all their efforts by a very dry season. Almost as I write, I hear that Marinakis, who pioneered there by himself for 30 years, has died.

(b) Shauri Moyo. Three new units have just been allocated, so development has barely started.

(c) Maswere. Four new units have just been advertised.

(d) Kiru. Kiru was previously intensively farmed and was the centre of the Sleeping Sickness outbreak which led to total evacuation in 1943. A big block of new units, covering the best of the land, will shortly be advertised.

(e) Sangaiwe. These are really dry farms, although a couple of bore holes have been successful, and lie mainly to the east of the Great North Road. On their original advertisement there were no suitable applicants, and it is now proposed that they be re-advertised at a reduced rent – I should be surprised if good farmers are forthcoming for these areas. I would have liked to see unit 'F' go direct to M. Apokides as an extension to his Dudumera farm, but this proposal is now delayed by the question of whether water from the bore hole on unit 'F' should be shared with unit 'E'.

All these new alienations are governed by stringent special conditions designed to ensure early clearing of bush.

There is a proposal, originally made by Chief Amri for the re-alienation of Holland Estate, in order to push the bush back from Babati itself. This is held up, pending an enquiry into a local water source, in order to assuage the doubts of the Gorowa elders.

Oldeani divides into coffee lands and wheatlands. The coffee farmers are in good spirit, with a good crop behind them and another one to come. Not so for those who are dependent on wheat, mostly South Africans. With the disappearance of the GMR,[4] some of them are in for a bad time. The Riddlesbarger organisation now has six coffee farms up there, Sands having recently sold to him.

Personalities at Oldeani are interesting. Although our contacts are unfortunately less close than in the time of the Production Committee, one can still get a lot of co-operation from individuals, notably those who serve on the Natural Resources Committee.

4. Works

A. Roads

The main road programme is complete. With a succession of dry years, work has started earlier and earlier – this year and last we began on 1 May. Finance for roads I will mention to you. The DA should do as much paying as possible out on the spot, while for NA roads the Sub-Chiefs have been informed that they will get only so much per mile (we have suffered much in the past from inflated muster rolls produced months after the work is done, as the DA can tell you).

The Magara road is something on its own. We have dealt with it hitherto by using Hayuma's people on the top section instead of clearings, but this should obviously not continue longer than necessary. We sorely need to put in some main drainage and drifts, and I recommend that as much spare money as possible should be used from the Road Vote for this purpose.

Last year I had to use elsewhere some funds (£100) which Chief Amri had expected to get for the new Riroda–Gidas road. I promised him that I would ask you to try and restore the balance in the coming year.

We have got for nothing a long steel bridge for Massagaloda. It is an intricate piece of 'Meccano', which should give a lot of fun in erection.

The Dudumera road needs mention. We are authorised to spend on it funds allocated for the disused Endanahai road; these, and more, are at present going into a bridge which the Settlement Officer Babati is building, so the farmers (Matsis, in particular) have no ground for complaint.

B. Buildings

We can discuss building contracts. Most for the year have been allocated, but not those for the important Endagikot office buildings. It seems time we did a standard building by direct labour to compare costs with contract costs; the dispensary at Bashay is suggested.

Brown must take down a building at Basotu in which the bricks have been inadequately fired.

Many cattle market 'bomas' are in a shocking state, and major reconstruction will be needed next year.

5. Social Services

A. Health

The District is well covered with elaborate hospitals (Mbulu's cost £35,000). There is some question, as I discovered in conversation with the Assistant Director of Medical Services, about the extent of grant to be awarded to the Lutheran Hospital at Haidom. They deserve our fullest support, since they built in this remote expansion area on encouragement from the Boma, and they are doing an excellent job there.

There is constant complaint from the Native Authorities about the inadequacy of drug stocks at dispensaries.

As expected, with the new alienations Below Rift, we have had a recent flare-up there of Sleeping Sickness, and we can expect a good many more cases during the next year or two. Careful measures of precaution are under the full control of the Settlement Officer, Babati, who has very great experience.

B. Education

A District Education Committee meeting was due to be held in April, but was postponed when the new Five-Year Plan was subjected to further revision by Government. We have heard nothing further, nor have we had here the original plan, let alone the revised one; but a Committee meeting will be needed as soon as you have been put in the picture. Primary School fees are obtainable, with bullying. Middle School fees are the devil to get.

C. Welfare

Here we're a backward child, but beginning to crawl. A cinema projector and Land Rover is on order, jointly with Kondoa; and, in response to a number of demands, a District newspaper is due to be started, for which DO I is making arrangements. The latter project will need supplementary expenditure. The SSDO,[5] Arusha has promised us the help of an experienced African in getting the paper on its feet.

6. *Finance*

A. Government

There are no votes to cause concern. District Accountant keeps the vote-book for all works votes, and Cash Controller the others. 'Others' includes two votes secured on account of the Settlement Officer, Babati, one of which covers his Technical Allowance. He should be up in mid-June to sort out accounts before the end of the financial year. Note that Technical Allowance for Forestry Officer, Dongobesh, is shared between Government and Native Treasury votes.

Personal Tax, as a result of encouragement, has come in extremely well. The assessment machinery has worked satisfactorily. It must, of course, be tightened in years to come, in common with the Graduated Local Rates, which is much more closely under your observation as the result of the introduction of Personal Tax, the Register being the same.

In two and a half years we have had a dozen thefts of public moneys, both Government and Native Treasury. I doubt if any District has a worse record: heavy sentences, higher salaries and tighter security have all been equally ineffectual in stopping the rot. One recent consequence has been the dismissal of most of your tax clerks. Note that cement wells for tax boxes have still to be constructed at courthouses Below Rift.

This year revenue has been collected at Court Houses by Administrative Officers, saving the monthly waste of days of time by clerks coming in to Mbulu to pay in.

B. Native Treasury

Under charge of DO I, the books are well kept, but the Secretary and Treasurer badly needs a good assistant – advertisement has just yielded some promising applicants.

Please see my 11/1/9 of 12/4/56 for an assessment of the Native Treasury's financial strength in relation to the Five Year Education Plan. You will see that the Provincial Commissioner has subsequently requested a Five Year Plan forecasting all expenditure and means of meeting it. I have left this for you; the lines on which the Native Treasury at present uses its resources are set out in the current six-year development budget (due to expire in 1957), which you will find bound with the Estimates.

I have always kept an Estimates file one year ahead, and in the 1957 file you will find a number of suggestions. The most important is perhaps a house for Chief Elias more befitting to his dignity than his present hovel. I strongly recommend to you that the NA Finance Committee (names recorded in minute book of Endagikot *barazas*) should be allowed a first shot at next year's Estimates.

Revenue has come in exceedingly well this year, with the exception of school fees and uniforms, which require a 'blitz'. Outstanding fines need continual attention. Beer licences here are 10/– a drum, drinking time being nominally confined to a long weekend from Friday evening to Sunday night; 'customary' beer at 2/– for three *debes* gives a big loophole for evasion – but at least the NT gets a huge revenue, as the figures will shew you.

7. Minor Settlements

We have five: Mbulu, Babati, Oldeani, Magugu and Karatu. The two last are new. Oldeani is beyond despair. Mbulu and Babati have competent Authorities which have done a lot to improve conditions in both places.

Mbulu needs its boundaries re-defining, nothing south of the Endmaksin River being at present included – see my 22/5/940 of 4/6/56 to the Land Officer.

8. *Miscellaneous*

Firearms – the subject is on the agenda for the DC's Conference, and you may care to discuss it with me.

The Chief Surveyor keeps prodding us about a map of the District with details of NA establishments etc. Austin has this in hand, but has many other preoccupations.

NOTES

Introduction

1 Julius Kambarage Nyerere (1922–99), founder of the Tanganyika African National Union, Prime Minister of Tanzania 1961 and President 1962–85. His socialism was an exciting fusion of African, Christian and Fabian traditions.

2 John Iliffe, *A Modern History of Tanganyika*.

3 John Iliffe, *A Modern History of Tanganyika*, p.325.

4 E.K. Lumley, *Forgotten Mandate*.

5 John Beames, *Memoirs of a Bengal Civilian*.

6 Sir Richard Gordon Turnbull (1909–98), Chief Secretary, Kenya (1954–58), Governor, Tanganyika (1958–61), Governor, Aden (1964–67).

7 As the old rhyme has it, 'Beware, beware the Bight of the Benin, for few come out though many go in'.

8 Anthony Kirk-Greene, *Symbol of Authority*, p.248.

9 Kathryn Tidrick, *Empire and the English Character*.

10 'Colonial Rule' by John W. Cell in Brown and Louis' *The Oxford History of the British Empire*, vol. IV, p.233

11 Matthew 7:12

12 A.C.G. Hastings, *Nigerian Days*, p.82

13 Judith Listowel, *The Making of Tanganyika*, p.73.

14 The Groundnut Scheme was an initiative of the post-Second World War British Labour Government. In 1946, acting on the suggestion of Frank Samuel, Managing Director of the United Africa Company, a subsidiary of Unilever, the Minister of Food in London allocated land near Kongwa in central Tanganyika and substantial funds to the cultivation of groundnuts. The logistical difficulties of clearing the land were catastrophically

underestimated and the soil turned out to be unsuitable. The scheme was abandoned in 1952. It became a byword for colonial mismanagement.

15 Data from *History of East Africa*, edited by D.A. Low and Alison Smith, particularly the chapter on the Tanganyika economy by Cyril Ehrlich.

16 A.D. Roberts, *Cambridge History of Africa,* vol. VII, 1905–40, p.43.

17 See A.H.M Kirk-Greene's 'Thin White Line' in *African Affairs,* 1980 volume 79, pp.25–44.

18 Some have argued that the phrase should not be capitalised, on the basis that it is a concept rather than a theology. I have stuck to capitals for the sake of simplicity.

19 J.E. Flint, *Sir George Goldie and the Making of Nigeria*, p.262.

20 Clifford, minute addressed to Lt Governor of the Northern Provinces, 18 March 1922, reprinted in Kirk-Greene (ed.) *The Principles of Native Administration in Nigeria*, pp.174–86.

21 Nigeria Annual Report, 1902, p.26.

22 Margery Perham, *Lugard*, p.149.

23 Sir Donald Cameron, 'Native Administration in Tanganyika and Nigeria' in the *Journal of the Royal African Society,* October 1937.

24 See Lord Hailey's *Native Administration and Political Development*, p.235: 'It is probably true to say that in the area under notice there is as yet no native authority which is able to prepare its own estimates of revenue and expenditure. The budget is in practice prepared by the district officer.'

25 John Iliffe, *A Modern History of Tanganyika*, p.324.

26 This argument is made by Terence Ranger in the chapter entitled 'The Invention of Tradition in Colonial Africa', in *The Invention of Tradition*, eds Eric Hobsbawm and Terence Ranger, p.252. It has subsequently become the unexamined orthodoxy of Africanist history – see for instance John Reader, *Africa, A Biography of the Continent*, p.608 and Basil Davidson, *The Black Man's Burden*, pp.110–11.

27 Ibid., pp.211–62.

28 Ibid., p.262.

29 Ralph A. Austen, *North West Tanzania under German and British Rule*.

30 Lord Hailey, *Native Administration and Political Development in British Tropical Africa*, p. 3.
31 Judith Listowel, *The Making of Tanganyika*, pp. 320–21.
32 Kirilo Japhet and Earle Seaton, *The Meru Land Case*.
33 Ibid., p. 14.
34 For a contrary view, see Ralph A. Austen, *North West Tanzania under German and British Rule*, p. 254.
35 Draft report, 'Self-Reliant Rural Development in Tanzania', prepared by René Dumont, p. 18.
36 Alexander Pope, *Essay on Man*, III, lines 303–4.
37 E.K. Lumley, *Forgotten Mandate*, p. 13
38 These were my father's words. In reflective moments, he was prepared to acknowledge that, since nothing is perfect, it could have been more efficient and more just had it been less cheap.

Chapter 1

1 F.H. Page-Jones was at this time the Member for Local Government on the Executive Council in Dar es Salaam.
2 Nyerere would have been 35 at this time. He had set up TANU two and a half years earlier. The author was two years older.
3 Ivor Jennings, *The Approach to Self-Government*, Cambridge University Press, 1956.

Chapter 2

1 Sir Ralph Furse (1887–1973), who joined the Colonial Secretary's patronage staff in 1910 and remained under various designations until 1948. The dominating influence on recruitment and selection to the Colonial Service throughout this period.
2 Sir Mark Young was Governor of Tanganyika 1938–41. He left Tanganyika in July 1941 and arrived in Hong Kong in September. The Japanese invaded in December 1941.
3 Sir Wilfred Jackson was Governor 1941–45. He was previously Governor of British Guiana.
4 H.C. Stiebel was born in 1876 and was a veteran of the Boer War (1899–1902). His administrative career started in the Transvaal.

5 Kate Meyrick (1875–1933) was an Irish nightclub owner in London in the 1920s. She was the proprietor of the notorious '43 Club' at 43 Gerrard Street in Soho. She went to prison on five occasions, and was sentenced to 15 months in 1926 for bribing a police officer.

6 Cardinal Francis Spellman (1889–1967), prominent American prelate with well-known and sometimes controversial conservative views. An ally of Joseph Kennedy, he campaigned as Archbishop of Boston for the re-election of Franklin Roosevelt in 1936. Subsequently a supporter of Joseph McCarthy and the Vietnam War.

7 C.J.P Ionides (1901–69), like many of his kind, was a poacher turned game-keeper. Despite his Greek name, his upbringing and demeanour were impeccably British: after being expelled from Rugby, he went to Sandhurst and was commissioned in the South Wales Borderers, with whom he served in India. He was intrumental in developing the Selous Game Reserve in central Tanganyika. He was fond of snakes and kept them around himself and his house – hence the nickname. He had a well-earned reputation for capturing rare species on behalf of European zoos. Four species of snake are named after him.

8 Chief Thomas Lenana Marealle II OBE (1915–2007), Paramount Chief (Mangi Mkuu) of the Chagga and politician. Marealle was inaugurated as chief in January 1952. The government abolished the system of chieftainships in 1961, although Marealle, anticipating this, left his in 1960.

Chapter 3

1 Sir Henry Morton Stanley (1841–1904), explorer. This would have been his expedition, which set out in November 1874, to trace the route of the River Congo from its source at Lake Tanganyika to the Atlantic.

2 Liebig was a German chemist who invented a process for producing beef extract in 1840. A company was set up in London in 1865 under the name Liebig Extract of Meat Company to produce beef extract in Uruguay. The name Oxo was introduced in 1899. Liebig's became part of Vestey in 1924 and Unilever in 1984.

3 Abdullah Saidi Fundikira (1921–2007), Chief of the Nyamwezi and Minister of Water (1961) and Legal Affairs (1962). He contested the 1993 presidential elections, losing to Benjamin Mkapa.

4 Kidaha Makwaia (1922–2007). Succeeded his father as chief of Usiha in 1945 and elected paramount chief of Sukuma Federation 1949. Resigned as chief of Usiha in 1954 in favour of his younger brother, Hussein and took up post in Social Welfare Department in Dar es Salaam. Unofficial member of Governor's Executive Council 1953–59. Banished by Nyerere in 1961 after the abolition of the chiefs. Convert from Islam to Roman Catholicism.

5 A godown was a warehouse. The term is derived from the Malay word *gudong*, probably originally meaning a place where goods lie. The word was in common use in East Asia and India and like many such usages was transferred to East Africa.

6 John Thorburn Williamson 1907–58. After completing his studies in Canada, Williamson took a job with Loangwa Concessions, a De Beers subsidiary in Northern Rhodesia (now Zambia). He then moved on to work at the Mabuki diamond mine, which he purchased from the owners in 1936 when they had decided to shut it down. In 1940 he discovered the diamond-bearing kimberlite pipe at Mwadui. After his death from cancer in 1958, his siblings sold the mine to De Beers and the Tanganyika Government. It was nationalised by Nyerere in 1971, but failed to prosper and a majority stake was eventually sold back to De Beers in 1994.

7 Gavin Henderson, 2nd Baron Faringdon (1902–77), member of the set known as the 'Bright Young Things' in the 1920s. Joined Labour Party in the 1930s. Supported the Republican cause in the Spanish Civil War. A pacifist, he served in the Fire Service in the Second World War, and afterward sat on the executive committee of the Fabian Society until 1969.

8 His son, David Gower, inherited his father's excellent hand and eye co-ordination, without the handicap of poor sight, and became the most elegant cricketer of his generation.

9 Hamsa Mwapachu, 1918–62. An early nationalist associate of Nyerere's.

Chapter 4

1 Arthur Creech Jones (1891–1964), trade-union official and politician. A protegé of Ernest Bevin, he was elected to parliament in 1935 and served in the Colonial Office in the Labour Government of 1945–50.

Chapter 5

1 Walter Dalrymple Maitland Bell, 1880–1951. Served as a pilot in Tanganyika in World War I and subsequently in Europe, where he was awarded the Military Cross and bar. Wrote *Wanderings of an Elephant Hunter*, considered to be the classic of the sport. Karamojo is a district in Uganda.

Chapter 6

1 Sir Andrew Cohen (1909–68), Colonial Office official who became Governor of Uganda (1952–57) and Permanent Secretary at the Overseas Development Agency (1964–68).
2 Hans Cory (1888–1962), born Hans Koritschoner, came to Tanganyika before World War I. He fought with the German Army under von Lettow-Vorbeck during World War I and was wounded in the Southern Province. Between the wars he was a manager on various sisal estates in the south and on the coast. He became a temporary District Officer in the British Administration on the outbreak of World War II and in 1943 took up the post of government anthropologist. He was the original of Kandinsky, the sisal planter whom Hemingway meets at the beginning of his safari in *Green Hills of Africa*. Kandinsky inveighs against Hemingway's hunting of kudu, expresses his dislike of Rilke and has to listen to the author's sententious views on American literature. Koritschoner anglicised his name to Cory after the war.
3 A cess is a tax. The term has generally been superceded by 'rate'. Its use in Tanganyika probably derived from colonial India.

4 But see *Mountain Farmers* by Thomas Spear, p.200: 'Whilst the administration congratulated itself that the experiment was a splendid success in restoring legitimacy to "traditional" institutions, few Arusha considered the institutions either "traditional" or legitimate.' This claim misrepresents the Administration's actions to make them appear consistent with the banal and implausible conspiracy theory that the British 'invented' tribal traditions and then foisted them upon the tribes. Whether the processes introduced in this case were 'traditional' or not was entirely incidental. No sources are quoted for the assertion that they were not considered legitimate. Cant, is the word my father would have used, with careful enunciation.

Chapter 7

1 Groundnut Scheme – see Note 14, Introduction.
2 Louis Leakey (1903–72), paleoanthropoligist. With his wife and others, developed the thesis that early man's origins were in Africa, specifically in Olduvai.
3 Sir Theodore Ouseley Pike (1904–87) was Governor of British Somaliland 1954–59.
4 Sir Francis Edward Twining, Baron Twining (1899–1967), Governor of North Borneo (1946–49) and Governor of Tanganyika (1949–58). He was a member of the Twining tea family.
5 Sir William Battershill (1896–1959), Governor of Cyprus (1939–41) and Tanganyika (1945–49).

Chapter 8

1 In 1954 there was a District Officer I (DO I), R.W. Neath, later succeeded by Edward Younie, a DO II, A.C.W. Lee, and a DO III, Michael Dorey.
2 Tony Lee (DO II) remarks that when Peter Bell left, Nade Bea gave him a farewell party and had a 400-yard track dug from the road to his house in Kainam, so that the DOs and others who owned cars could drive there to join the party.

3 Mike Molohan, 'Molo' as he was known, a large and gentle man, played rugby for Ireland. Stubbings ('Stubbs') and Mickey Davies were both South African Rhodes Scholars. Fraser-Smith won a Military Cross in the war. They were of a type.

Chapter 9

1 Tony Lee recalls the Queen's Birthday Party in 1953 at Endagicot, attended by Donald Troup, as the PC. A parade and sports programme for children were on the agenda. The PC, DC and DOs, all in dress uniform and with their wives, sat in the shade of a hut awaiting the arrival of the children up the road from their school. Of a sudden, there came the sound of Irish pipes, and in due course Paddy Joly appeared, surrounded by hundreds of enchanted children.

2 Robin Johnston (1917–92), DFC and bar, commanded No 73 Hurricane Squadron in the Western Desert in 1942. His farm was bought in partnership with Sir Archibald McIndoe, the pioneer of plastic surgery, who had treated burns to Johnston's hands incurred in action.

Chapter 10

1 The Great North Road runs from Arusha to Dodoma. There is some hyperbole in the appellation.

2 It does survive, but is very rugged.

Chapter 11

1 Judith Listowel (1903–2003), journalist, author and campaigner. Daughter of a Hungarian diplomat, she was invited to write a history of Tanganyika in 1961, which was published as '*The Making of Tanganyika*' in 1965.

2 Sir John Fletcher-Cooke (1911–89) was promoted from Chief Secretary to Deputy Governor in 1960. Conservative MP for Southampton Test 1964–66.

3 Chama Cha Mapinduzi ('Party of the Revolution').
4 Rashidi Kawawa (1926–2009), Prime Minister of Tanganyika in 1962 and of Tanzania 1972–77.

Appendix 1

1 See Note 2, Chapter 3, above.
2 The East African currency in the colonial era was denominated in pounds, shillings and cents. The use of cents rather than pence reflected the region's beginnings as part of the Indian rupee zone. There were 100 cents to the shilling and 20 shillings to the pound, though in practice most transactions were conducted in shillings and cents. The fact that this figure is recorded in pounds, shillings and pence presumably reflects Liebig's accounting policies.

Appendix 2

1 That is, the Governor, Sir Edward Twining.
2 Member of Legislative Council.
3 GMR – presumably Grain Market Regulation, but I have not been able to find any other reference to these initials.
4 Dark heavy soils associated with valleys.

Appendix 3

1 This was to be J.S. Harris, MBE, MC.
2 Roger Austin, one of four Development Officers attached to the District Office.
3 Edward Younie was DO I at this stage.
4 GMR – See Note 3, Appendix 2, above.
5 SSDO – presumably Social Services District Office.

BIBLIOGRAPHY

Austen, Ralph A., *North West Tanzania under German and British Rule*, New Haven and London: Yale University Press, 1968. A well-researched expansion of a doctoral thesis.

Bates, Darrell, *A Gust of Plumes: A Biography of Lord Twining*, London: Hodder and Stoughton, 1972.

Brown, Judith M. and William Roger Louis (eds), *The Oxford History of the British Empire,* vol. IV, Oxford: Oxford University Press, 1999. Particularly, John W. Cell. 'Colonial Rule'.

Cameron, Sir Donald, *My Tanganyika Service and Some Nigeria,* London:George Allen and Unwin, 1939.

Davidson, Basil, *The Black Man's Burden*, London: James Currey, 1992.

Dobson, Kenneth Austin, *Mail Train*, London: Hodder & Stoughton, 1946. Dobson, who served as a DC in Tanganyika, wrote four novels based on his experiences. *Mail Train* is a crime mystery. Its setting on this railway line between Dar es Salaam and Mwanza, with each stop moving the plot onwards, is largely incidental, as is Egypt to Agatha Christie's *Death on the Nile*, which in some ways it resembles. The venues in the other novels, *The Inescapable Wilderness* (1956), *The District Commissioner* (1954) and *Colour Blind* (1955), though anonymised, are paradoxically more specifically Tanganyikan, as are the issues covered, which become increasingly political with each publication. All the novels feature DCs. They are depicted as figures of authority with an austere preoccupation with the welfare of their African charges. In the novel, *Colour Blind*, he has become irascible and ulcerated as he sees his authority draining away, but remains true to his calling.

Hailey, Lord, *Native Administration and Political Development in British Tropical Africa*, London: HMSO, 1942.

Hobsbawm, Eric and Ranger, Terence (eds), *The Invention of Tradition*, Cambridge: Cambridge University Press, 1983 Particularly Terence Ranger, 'The Invention of Tradition in Colonial Africa'. Provocative but unconvincing Marxian analysis.

Iliffe, John, *A Modern History of Tanganyika*, Cambridge: Cambridge University Press, 1979. Though one often has the impression that Iliffe would have preferred to write the story without reference to the colonial Administration, this is the most comprehensive, thorough and scholarly history of Tanzania.

Japhet, Kirilo and Earle Seaton, *The Meru Land Case*, Nairobi: East African Publishing House, 1967. Partisan, but clearly and succinctly written.

Kirk-Greene, A.H.M., *The Principles of Native Administration in Nigeria*, Oxford: Oxford University Press, 1965.

Kirk-Greene, Anthony, *Symbol of Authority*, London and New York: I.B.Tauris, 2006.

Listowel, Judith, *The Making of Tanganyika*, London: Chatto and Windus, 1965.

Low, D.A. and Smith, Alison (eds), *History of East Africa*, Oxford: Clarendon Press, 1976. Particularly Cyril Ehrlich 'The Tanganyika Economy'.

Lumley, E.K., *Forgotten Mandate*, London: C. Hurst & Company, 1976. A thoughtful, modest and interesting memoir of Tanganyika in the 1920s and 1930s.

Malcolm, D.W., *Sukumaland: An African People and their Country, a Study of Land Use in Tanganyika*, Oxford: Oxford University Press, 1953.

Parker, John and Richard Rathbone, *African History: A Very Short Introduction*, Oxford: Oxford University Press, 2007. Interesting and opinionated survey, a model of its kind.

Perham, Margery, *Lugard: The Years of Authority*, London: Collins, 1960.

Reader, John, *Africa, A Biography of the Continent*, London: Penguin Books, 1997.

Roberts, A.D. (ed.), *Cambridge History of Africa, vol. VII, 1905–40*, Cambridge: Cambridge University Press, 1986.

Spear, Thomas, *Mountain Farmers*, Berkeley, California: University of California Press, 1997.

Tidrick, Kathryn, *Empire and the English Character*, London: I.B.Tauris, 1990. A stimulating account of the imperial mindset.

GLOSSARY

Some frequently-used acronyms:
PC: Provincial Commissioner
DC: District Commissioner
DO: District Officer (I, II, etc)
NA: Native Authority
NT: Native Treasury
PWD: Public Works Department

The following are locally used words which occur in the text. They are mostly of Swahili origin.

askari: derived from the Arabic word for a soldier; by extension policeman or guard.

ayah: children's nurse or maid, derived from the Hindi aya, the Portuguese aia and ultimately the Latin avia, meaning grandmother

baraza: tribal meeting or assembly

bhang: a Hindi word for marijuana

Boma: fenced enclosure; by extension in East Africa, government office

bwana: respectful term of address, derived from the Arabic abuna meaning father. Bwana mkubwa means literally big bwana, but should be understood as suggesting particular respect. Bwana Shauri means bwana responsible for business.

debe: a tin, usually the size of a pail

fitina: quarrel, argument, trouble

hafir: a hollow dug in the ground to store water run-off

jambo: hello

jigger: a type of flea, which normally lives in the ground. The female burrows into the skins of humans or other animals in order to lay its eggs. After laying its eggs, the female expires and infection can easily ensue. Because the jigger lives in the ground, bare human feet are particularly vulnerable.

kanzu: a long, ankle-length tunic, usually white, worn by men in East Africa

kopje: an Afrikaans word for a small hill

kraal: an Afrikaans word for an enclosure

manyatta: a Masai word for an enclosure

memsahib: a term usually applied to a European woman in her role as domestic manager. Another term borrowed from the Raj, it is an elision of 'ma'am' and 'sahib'.

moran: a Masai age-grade, covering roughly the age from 12 to 25

moshi: locally distilled spirit, generally illegally

panga: a machete, normally used in the garden or fields

rondavel: an Afrikaans word for a round hut

Serikali: the Government

shamba: a field for growing crops

shauri: business, affair

sim-sim: sesame

sjambok: a hippopotamus-hide whip. Originally a Malay word referring to the wooden rod used for punishing slaves, its use was introduced by the

Malays to South Africa. Long and flexible, the sjambok's impact was notoriously painful.

tembe: an Iraqw house, windowless and usually flat-roofed, sometimes built into the side of a hill. Sheep and goats were corralled on the ground floor, the family on a reed floor above them.

INDEX

Alienated land 21, 91, 130,
  195, 213, 227, 231–2
Amri, Chief of the
  Mbugwe 191, 196,
  222, 232
Amri, Police Sub-Inspector,
  Shinyanga 61, 62
Arusha 12, 22, 46, 89–92,
  102, 110–11, 118, 121,
  123, 129–33, 135, 147,
  157–8
Arusha School 144
Austin, Roger,
  Development Officer
  132–3, 158, 219, 228,
  228–30, 236, 244n2
Authority
  and administration
    in Tanganyika 42,
    103, 123, 138,
    168
  of the Chiefs 20, 22,
    55–6, 139
  tradition of 2, 5–7
Azania, coastal steamer
  33, 36, 37

Bahi people 75
Baker's tropical outfitters 34

Banana
  as a staple 91
  cultivation of 90, 92
Barabaig people 19, 121,
  122, 129, 136–42,
  153–4, 157, 191–3,
  196–9, 206–7, 210,
  216, 219, 223, 228,
  229
  casual murders 122,
    139–42
  dispute with
    Wanyaturu
    136–9, 197,
    202, 208
  relationship with the
    Nandi in Kenya
    153
Baradau, dissident activist
  on Mt Meru 21–2,
  101–6
Battershill, Sir William,
  Governor 118,
  242n5
Beames, John 2
Bell, Peter, District
  Commissioner, Mbulu
  120, 123–4, 126, 161,
  242n2

Bell, William M. D.,
    elephant hunter 80,
    241n1
Boer farmers 108, 232
Bridge 35, 37, 51, 55, 122,
    159
Broadhead-Williams,
    Deric, prospector,
    hunting elephant with
    82–4
Burma, SS 34–5
Burton, Sir Richard,
    explorer, and naming of
    Tanganyika 1
Bush clearing
        in Mbulu 125–6,
            129, 132,
            137, 140–1,
            147, 157,
            192–3, 201,
            204, 206,
            209–12, 224,
            228–30, 232
        in Sukumaland
            53
Byatt, Sir Horace,
    Governor 13

Cameron, Sir Donald,
    Governor xvii, 8, 20,
    26, 56
        and Indirect Rule
            8, 13–16, 18,
            23
Cash Office 39
Cattle culling – *see under*
    Stock control
Chiefs, in the Legislative
    Council 8

ambiguous position
    20–3, 50, 53, 55–
    8, 100–7, 166
amongst the
    Barabaig 138–9,
    196, 210, 223
amongst the
    Gorowa 222
amongst the Iraqw
    195, 220–2, 227
amongst the
    Mbugwe 222
amongst the
    Sukuma 55–8,
    182, 184
amongst the
    Wa'arusha 94–
    100
amongst the
    Wameru 20–3,
    100–7
and education 164,
    182
and Indirect Rule
    14–20, 23, 57,
    72, 123, 126,
    129, 133, 175–9
remission of
    authority 56,
    77, 133, 177
Clarke, Jack, District
    Commissioner,
    Masailand 110, 114,
    119
Co-operatives 101, 179,
    182, 194, 202, 213,
    226
Coffee 11–12, 90–1, 99,
    101, 105, 121, 129–30,

146, 204–5, 216, 225, 232
Colonial Development and Welfare Acts 1940 and 1945 66, 120
Colonial Service 3–11, 26, 33–4, 70
    Africanisation 168–9
    continuity 120
    pay 10–11, 148
    structure and organisation 13–14, 120, 128–31
Communal self-help
    amongst the Sukuma 72, 190
    amongst the Wa'arusha 99
    arrangements governing in Mbulu 209–10, 229–30
    in Mbulu District 125, 158, 191, 193
Conscription 39, 42, 44
Corporal punishment 59, 61–3
Corruption and peculation 56–7, 197, 202
Cory, Hans, government anthropologist
    and the Wa'arusha 20, 89–99
    and the Wameru 22, 99–101, 104, 123, 241n2
    character 94

Creech Jones, Arthur, Secretary of State for the Colonies 77, 240n1

Dar es Salaam 1, 3, 9, 15, 29, 31, 33, 35–7, 42, 45, 51–2, 62, 64, 67–8, 86, 89, 99, 100, 104, 108, 126, 129, 136, 143, 157, 161, 163–6
Dar es Salaam school of history 2–3, 17–19, 26
Davies, Mickey, District Commissioner, Arusha 130, 242n3
Demobilisation after Second World War 70–2, 174
Diamonds, at Mwadui 52, 60–1, 63

East African Campaign (1914–18) 12
Ekman, Lale 113–14
Eldridge, Dan, miner 49–50
Elephant
    economics of 78
    fear 85–6
    gear 80
    hunting 78–86
    licensing 78
    tactics 79
Elias, Chief of the Iraqw 140, 158, 160, 195, 220–1, 223, 227, 235
Ellis, Jack, farmer in Mbulu 129, 194, 203, 224–5

'Fair Play' 5–7, 162
Family, health of 136, 143
    education of 143, 163
Famine, in Sukumaland in
    1944 53–4, 58–9, 176,
    199
Faringdon, Lord (Gavin
    Henderson) 62, 240n7
Findlay, Victor 54–5
Fletcher-Cooke, Sir John,
    Chief Secretary 164
Flood, Kenneth, and
    hunting elephant 81–2
Forestry 14, 38, 117, 122,
    183, 207–8, 230
Fraser-Smith, Pip, District
    Commissioner,
    Masailand 130, 24n3
Fundikira, Abdullah,
    Chief and politician 57,
    240n3
Fundikira, Saidi, Chief 20
    corruption 56–7
Furse, Sir Ralph, and
    recruitment to the
    Colonial Service 34

Gaitskell, Arthur, member
    of UN visiting Mission
    1954 131
Gillman, Harold ('Gilly')
    47, 68
Goldie, Sir George, and the
    evolution of Indirect
    Rule 14
Gorowa people 121, 126,
    156–8, 193, 196–9,
    204, 206, 212, 219,
    222, 232

Gower, Richard (Dick) 65,
    92–4, 108–9
Great North Road 30,
    121, 156, 158, 214,
    222
Groundnut Scheme 11, 86,
    99, 112, 121, 147,
    237n11

Hailey, Lord Malcolm,
    colonial administrator
    19
Halwenge, Edward, civil
    servant 73, 86
Hastings, A.C.G. 7
Health
        hospitals and clinics
        118
        in Mbulu District
        143, 201,
        214–15, 218,
        233
        in Shinyanga 180
        native medicine 73
Holmes, Sir Peter, oil
    executive 4
Hopkin, Shirley, District
    Commissioner 62–4,
    69
Hopkins, grandfather,
    Charles Innes 4
Hunter, Jane 146
Hunter, John coffee farmer,
    146–7

Iliffe, John, historian 2, 5
    tribalism and the
    'Invention of Tradition'
    17–19

Independence 1, 3, 7, 11, 22, 23, 45, 55, 57, 100, 161, 164–6, 169
Indians (East African Asians) 8, 9, 33, 42, 45, 52, 55, 60, 63, 65, 71, 90, 113, 129, 156, 210
   in the Cash Office 38
   and gifts 65
Indirect Rule
   in Tanganyika 14, 16–25, 37–8, 128
   origins 14–16
   see also under Chiefs
      Native Authorities, Native Courts, Native Treasuries
Ionides, C.J.P., hunter and conservationist 49, 239n7
Iraqw people 8, 121–2, 124–6, 129, 133, 140, 191–218 passim, 220–22, 224–36 passim
   and stock reduction 124–6
   Native Authority 220–2

Jackson, Sir Wilfred, Governor 36, 63, 239n3
Jennings, Sir Ivor 31

Johnston, Robin, coffee farmer 112, 147, 243n2
Joly, Paddy, farmer 146, 243n1

Kassum, servant 92–3, 154–5
Kawawa, Rashidi, Prime Minister 3, 172, 243n3
Kilimanjaro 1, 11, 21, 30, 50, 68, 90, 101, 109, 119, 130, 147

Land expansion,
   amongst the Wa'arusha 99
   in Mbulu District 157, 193–4, 209–12, 220, 224
Lasseko, Ali, clerk 166, 226
Le Treyes 149
Leakey, Louis, palaeoanthropologist 114, 242n2
Leave
   home (long) 29, 61, 71, 86–8, 148–52
   local 82, 109, 119, 147
   Nangi's furlough 65
   sick 68
Lee, Anthony, District Officer 242n1, 242n3, 243n1
Les Mougins 149
Liebig's, meat buyers 54, 174, 177, 181, 240n2

Lindi 33–50 passim 52, 55
Listowel, Judith, journalist and historian 164, 237n12
Lugard, Lord Frederick, colonial administrator and ideologue, and Indirect Rule 14–16
Lumley, E.K., District Commissioner and author 2–3, 26
Lyons, C.P., District Commissioner 49

Macfarlane, K.B., historian 5
Macleod, Iain, Colonial Secretary 169
Macmillan, Harold, statesman, 'Wind of Change' speech 30
Macpherson, Colin, District Commissioner 54–5, 58, 61–3, 65, 68
Macpherson, Violet 54, 59, 60, 65
Majebere, Chief 57, 177, 179–80
Maji-Maji Rebellion 6, 12, 48, 74
Makerere University 57–8, 66–7, 71, 165, 178
Makonde people 43
Makwaia, Chief 57
Makwaia, Kidaha, nationalist politician 58, 192, 240n5

Malcolm, Donald, District Commissioner 26, 69–70, 72, 85, 189
Malya 70, 71, 77, 177, 183, 184
Mandate System 12–13, 16–17, 42, 62, 131
Marealle, Thomas, Paramount Chief of the Chagga 50, 109, 239n8
Masai people 75–6, 90, 91, 96, 99, 111–12, 119, 122, 124, 126, 138, 178
    CIM's views on and approach to 111–14, 119
Maswa 26, 51, 53, 55, 57, 63–4, 69–77 passim, 173–190 passim
Mau-Mau Emergency 153–5, 167
Maynard, Nangi, missionary 65, 67
Mbugwe people 121, 157, 158, 196–9, 202, 204, 208, 212, 214, 222
Mbulu 8, 10, 19, 25, 30, 89, 120– 42 passim, 155, 157–62, 191–236 passim
Mbulu development plan 120–7
Mbulumbulu 194, 198, 202, 204, 208, 219–20, 224–5, 227
Meek, Charles (CIM) early life 3–4

education 4–5
marriage 88
mental outlook 5–10
posting to Dar es
    Salaam 29–33,
    164
recruitment to the
    Colonial Service
    33–4
relationship with
    Nyerere 167–72
remuneration 10–11
Meek, C.K., father 3–4,
    34, 44
Meek, Innes, son 110,
    143–4, 163
Meek, Kingsley, son 143,
    146–8
Meek, Nona, wife 88,
    92–3, 107, 109–10,
    112, 123, 131, 134–6,
    140, 143, 144, 146–7,
    150–5, 160–1
Meek, Sheena, daughter
    123, 143, 164
Meru, Mt 11, 20–1, 30,
    90, 97, 110
Meru District 6, 20–3, 91,
    94, 100–7
Meru Land Case 20–3,
    100–7
Meyrick, Kate nightclub
    operator 37, 239n5
Milner, Lord Alfred 1
Missions, in Maswa 182,
    215
    Pallotine Fathers,
        Norwegian
        Lutherans and

Augustana
    Lutherans in
    Mbulu 216–17
Möller, Matthis, doctor
    113
Molohan, Michael,
    Provincial
    Commissioner,
    Northern Province 130,
    135, 139, 140–1, 155,
    242n3
Monduli 111–14, 116
Moshi 89, 110, 111, 129,
    130, 156
Muggeridge, Malcolm,
    journalist 5
Mushuda, Chief 177
Mwanza xvii, 51, 55, 62–3,
    65–7, 70–2, 74, 183
Mwapachu, Hamsa,
    nationalist politician
    66, 240n9

Nade Bea, rainmaker 8,
    126, 222, 242n2
Nairobi 46, 87, 90, 114,
    147, 153–55, 167
Native Authorities 15, 17
    in Mbulu 128, 175,
        196–8, 201,
        203, 214, 215,
        218, 220–4,
        231
    in Southern
        Province 38, 43
    in Sukumaland 53,
        55
Native Courts 15–16, 20,
    39, 40–1

in Mbulu 124, 128, 199
in Sukumaland 179
Native medicine 73
Native Treasuries 15, 17, 20
    in Arusha 99, 101
    in Masailand 113–14
    in Mbulu 121–2, 133, 138, 160, 179, 181, 197–9, 203, 207, 213, 222, 234–5
    in Sukumaland 56, 71, 76, 179, 181
New Africa Hotel 36
Ngorongoro Crater 75, 112, 114, 119, 121, 181
Northern Province 19, 21, 23, 25, 30, 89, 108, 118, 120, 130, 155, 217, 224, 231
Norton, Micky, hunter 73–5
Nyalikungu 70, 71, 74, 179–80, 182–3
Nyerere, Julius Kambarage, statesman 2, 3, 7, 20, 23, 30–2, 45, 55, 58, 67, 164–172 passim, 237n1, 238n2
    character 31
    early life 164–5
    and nationalist politics 23, 31–2, 55, 58, 67, 165–67

    political philosophy 20, 23–4, 124, 171
    relationship with CIM 32, 45, 164, 167–72

Omari, cook 45, 50, 82, 92

Page-Jones, F.H., Permanent Secretary 29, 240n1
Peters, Dr Carl 12
Pike, Andrew, District Commissioner 36–7
Pike, Theodore, Provincial Commissioner 37, 115, 242n2
Pneumonic plague 135–6
Population
    Tanganyika 11, 70
    Sukumaland (1945) 184, 188
    Arusha (1948) 90
    Mbulu (1955) 25, 125, 218
Prisons and imprisonment 75, 77, 92, 104–5, 107, 116, 132, 134, 155–6, 167, 217

Railways xvii, 12, 26, 46, 51–2, 56, 58
    and the siting of Malya 70, 184
Ranger, Terence, historian 18

Reid, Alec, lawyer, and
   the Meru Land Case
   104–6
Rinderpest 74
   amongst the Masai
      91
   in Sukumaland
      180–1
   in Mbulu 207, 227
Roads xvii, 11, 25, 48, 69,
   113, 118
   maintenance 39–40,
      142
   in Sukumaland 181,
      190
   in Mbulu 217–18,
      232
   building 69–70, 72,
      122, 125, 218,
      232

Salt collection, Lake Eyasi
   76–7
Sante, Mangi, and the
   Meru Land Case 20–2,
   100–5
   character 100, 110
Sanya Corridor 21–3
Sarwatt, Herman Elias,
   Iraqw Chief and
   politician 160
Sears, Mason 131
Second World War 33–6,
   41, 43–6, 54, 70,
   171–5
Servants 44, 50, 154, 161
   Akonnae 160
   Kassum 92, 93,
      154–5
   Maria, ayah 145
   Omari, cook 45, 50,
      82, 92
   Phillipo 44–5
   Saiboku 114
Shaw, John, Deputy
   Provincial
   Commissioner 130
Shinyanga 20, 51–68
   passim, 183
Shirley, Canon John,
   headmaster 5–6
Singida 76, 122, 136–7,
   166, 178, 197, 201–2,
   211, 217
Sisal 39, 41–42, 52
   as Tanganyika's
      main export
      crop 11
   introduced by
      Germans 12
   in Arusha 90
   in Sukumaland 174,
      185, 190
Sleeping Sickness 121,
   130, 158, 192, 213–14,
   222, 231, 233
Somali people 59–60, 108,
   111
Sonjo people 115
South Africa 42, 62
   Nyerere and 170
Southern Province 33, 39,
   31–50 passim
Southworth, Frederick,
   and the Meru Land
   Case 100–5
Spellman, Cardinal Francis
   41

Stiebel, Cecil 14, 37–8, 42,
46, 239n4
Stock control
in Sukumaland 54,
202
in Mbulu 121–2,
124–6, 133,
161, 192–3,
219, 227
Stubbings, Basil 22, 130,
242n3
Sukuma people 11, 53–7,
166
character 30
Sukumaland Federation
183–4

Tabora 51, 56–7, 61–3, 72
Tabora School 58, 165
Tanganyika, naming 1
economy 11
early history 11–13
ujamaa 24
Tanganyika African
National Union
(TANU) 24, 30, 50, 58,
165–7, 172
foundation of 165
Twining's
opposition to
166
Tax 7, 19, 41, 156, 161
system of taxation
15, 17
progressive amongst
Wa'arusha 99
resistance to coffee
tax amongst
Wameru 101

as a test of good
administration
39, 40
collection amongst
the Masai 112
amongst the
Sukuma
179, 189
in Mbulu 198,
234
Tayari, coastal steamer 33,
51
Taylor, A.J.P., historian 5
Theeman, F.W., magistrate
105
Tie-ridging 175
Touring, as a tool of
administration 47–8,
95, 177, 192
Trash-bunding 127, 196,
204
Tribalism 17–19
Troup, Donald 22, 89,
92–4, 120, 123
Tsetse clearance 52–3, 72,
121, 125–6, 129–30,
132, 137, 140–1, 157,
193, 201, 204–6
organisation and
payment of
clearing gangs in
Mbulu 209–13,
229–30
Turnbull, Sir Richard,
Governor 3, 7, 167,
172
and Nyerere 167
and UK aid for
Tanganyika 169

Twining, Sir Edward,
    Governor 6, 8, 13
        character 118, 122–
            3, 138, 167
        and nationalist
    politics
            124, 167
        visit to Mbulu 139–
            42
        relationship with
            Nyerere 166

Ujamaa, philosophy of 24,
    171
Umoja, philosophy of 171
UN Visiting Mission 23,
    131, 165

Wa'arusha 20
    tribal restructuring
        91–100
Walden, Stanley, and the
    Meru Land Case 105–6
Wanyaturu 19, 122, 208,
    228
        dispute with the
            Barabaig 136–9,
            196–7, 202, 223
Wanyiramba people 178
Watataru 178
Water, provision of; in
    Sukumaland 72, 184

amongst the Masai
    119
in Mbulu 129, 140,
    194, 208–9
Webster, Geoffrey 56, 62,
    70
Wheat, cultivation 90,
    107, 158–9, 191, 194,
    201, 203–5, 225, 232;
    marketing 213
Wildlife, leopards 77, 134,
    144–6
    lions 116
    in Southern
        Province 48–9
    in Mbulu 146
    snakes 40, 44, 64,
        109, 144
Wilkins, C.B., District
    Commissioner 47
Williamson, Dr John, mine
    operator 60–3, 240n6
Wilson, Judge Mark 21–2

Young, Sir Mark,
    Governor 36, 239n2
Younie, Edward, District
    Officer 226, 242n1,
    244n3
Younie, Mary 144

Zanzibar 1, 7, 147–8, 161